Contents

Part 3. Korean TV Drama and Social Media

Part 4. Global Receptions of Hallyu 2.0

Hallyu 2.0

The Korean Wave in the Age of Social Media

Sangjoon Lee and Abé Mark Nornes, editors

UNIVERSITY OF MICHIGAN PRESS

Ann Arbor

Published in the United States of America by the
University of Michigan Press
Manufactured in the United States of America
⊗ Printed on acid-free paper

2018   2017   2016   2015   4   3   2   1

A CIP catalog record for this book is available from the British Library.

ISBN 978-0-472-07252-1 (hardcover : alk. paper)
ISBN 978-0-472-05252-3 (paperback : alk. paper)
ISBN 978-0-472-12089-5 (e-book)

This work was supported by the Academy of Korean Studies (KSPS) Grant funded by the Korean Government (MOE) (AKS-2011-BAA-2102).

Hallyu 2.0

CONTEMPORARY
K O R E A

SERIES EDITORS: NOJIN KWAK AND YOUNGJU RYU

Perspectives on Contemporary Korea is devoted to scholarship that advances the understanding of critical issues in contemporary Korean society, culture, politics, and economy. The series is sponsored by The Nam Center for Korean Studies at the University of Michigan.

Hallyu 2.0: The Korean Wave in the Age of Social Media
   Sangjoon Lee and Abé Mark Nornes, editors

Acknowledgments

This book was generated out of the academic conference of the same title, "Hallyu 2.0: The Korean Wave in the Age of Social Media," hosted by the Nam Center for Korean Studies at the University of Michigan, April 6, 2012. The Nam Center would like to express its sincere appreciation to the AKS (Academy of Korean Studies) in Korea for its generous support to make this academic event possible. This edited volume is part of the Nam Center's ongoing publication series Perspectives on Contemporary Korea. Special gratitude should go to Nojin Kwak, director of the Nam Center and series editor, series editor Youngju Ryu, and four faculty respondents at the conference: Aswin Punathambekar, Daniel Herbert, and Yeidy Rivero (all from the University of Michigan), as well as Nicholas A. Kaldis of Binghamton University. We thank the anonymous reviewers and participants in the conference for their wonderful comments, particularly five JYJ fans who drove hundreds of miles to attend this event. Special thanks to Jiyoung Lee, Do-Hee Morsman, and Adrienne Janney of the Nam Center; Yunah Sung and Sang-Eun Park of the University of Michigan Library; and Melody Herr and Christopher Dreyer of the University of Michigan Press, whose painstaking work has enormously contributed to the conference and its final outcome, this book.

Introduction

A Decade of Hallyu Scholarship:
Toward a New Direction in Hallyu 2.0

Sangjoon Lee

> I've only done this for 12 years, only for Korea, not for overseas at
> all . . . I didn't expect anything like this. So what can I say?
> Everything moves way too fast.
>
> —Psy, *New York Times*, October 11, 2012

On May 22, 2013, South Korean (hereafter Korean)[1]–born and
U.S.-educated Korean pop musician Psy (Park Jae-sang) had an interview
with MTV and said that he was wrapping up the promotional run for his
"Gentleman" single in order to work on his first U.S. album (Montgomery
2013). His first global-targeted single, "Gentleman" reached the fifth position on the Billboard singles chart, number one in Denmark, Finland,
Luxemburg, and Korea, and topped iTunes charts in over forty countries.
"Gentleman" was a follow-up to Psy's hugely successful "Gangnam Style,"
which stormed the world in the summer of 2012 (see Hu, this volume).
"Gentleman" was his first attempt to prove that he was not a "one-hit wonder" and that the seemingly unbreakable U.S. pop music market would
not make him a mere anecdote in U.S. pop music history, as Los del Rio,
Lou Bega, and Falco had already experienced.[2] The *Huffington Post*, just
before the release of "Gentleman," asked, "Will the Internet's favorite pony
dancer rise above one-hit-wonder designation? Will a new 'Gentleman'
themed dance craze sweep the globe?" (Anon. 2013). "Gentleman" exceeded any previous record by becoming the fastest music video to reach
300 million views on YouTube only three weeks after its initial release. By
December 2013, the music video had marked 598 million hits on YouTube,

becoming the most-viewed video of 2013 (Lewis 2013). "Gentleman" is still far short of the 1.9 billion views of "Gangnam Style" but did well enough to be recognized as one of the year's most successful pop singles.

No one, not even Psy himself, expected this wild success. Psy had been a stable pop musician in the Korean music industry since his debut single, "Bird" (Sae), came out in 2001. "Gangnam Style" was initially composed and produced for Korean fans, but it became a global sensation through YouTube and the social media world. Major U.S. media outlets like *Time* magazine, CNN, the *Wall Street Journal*, and the *Atlantic* covered how the comic and upbeat dance track took over the world. Y. C. Park, a music producer in New York, said that this is the first time a Korean song created real buzz. "It's always been the Korean media hyping up the success of Korean singers in the U.S. Honestly," he continued, "there was never any success, but (Psy) might serve as a turning point for K-pop to get good exposure to the masses" (Han 2012). What is most striking in the Psy phenomenon is that he has long been considered a "domestic" celebrity, and had never been promoted as an export commodity by Korean entertainment agencies (Cho 2012).

Indeed, since 2008 the Korean pop (hereafter K-pop) music industry has been pouring human and monetary capital into the U.S. popular music industry in order to gain access to the market. The female pop star BoA, who has been widely popular in Korea and Japan, made her U.S. debut in 2008 with the song "Eat You Up." However, the single flopped in that market (Jung 2011c). Se7en, the "king of K-pop" in Korea, also tested his luck in the U.S. market, releasing the English-language single "Girls," featuring Lil' Kim, in March 2009. Like BoA, he returned to Korea after "record low" sales of his single. Sun Jung, following BoA's and Se7en's dramatic failures in the United States, lamented that K-pop is still marginalized in the United States, despite the Korean media's continual reports of its global success stories. Jung writes, "It is still very rare to experience Korean popular culture on an everyday basis in any single city outside Asia" (123). But the situation is rapidly changing now, and by the time this volume is in print the whole K-pop industry may require a radically adjusted assessment. The turning point was generated not in the United States or Asia but in Paris, France—to everyone's surprise.

Five idol groups from the Korean entertainment agency S.M. Entertainment (hereafter S.M.)—Tong Bang Shin Ki (aka TVXQ), Girls' Generation (So Nyeo Shi Dae, aka SNSD), Super Junior, f(x), and SHINee—held their first concert in June 2011 at Le Zenith de Paris, and more than 14,000 fans from across Europe gathered to rave over K-pop. The first concert sold out in just fifteen minutes when online booking opened on April 26, and hundreds of French fans who failed to get tickets protested by performing a dance flash mob in front of the Louvre (Cha and Kim 2011). S.M. hurriedly scheduled two more concerts, responding to the explosive demand from the fans. Lee Teuk, the leader of Super Junior, an all-male idol band, said, "I think K-pop is gaining popularity thanks to S.M.'s global system, foreign composers and choreographers, and the singers' appearances. . . . It was also helped by social networking sites, such as YouTube" (Jung 2011c, 123). In February 2012, the Korean nine-girl pop group Girls' Generation made their official U.S. debut after astounding success in Japan, on the stage of CBS's *The Late Show with David Letterman*. Girls' Generation's U.S.-targeted single "The Boys," composed by American music artist Teddy Riley with a final touch of Snoop Dogg, was released simultaneously. Girls' Generation and its agency S.M. employed a new strategy this time, after their valuable "lessons" from Paris, by using social media such as YouTube, Facebook, and Twitter as new and powerful marketing tools.

As Noh Kwang-woo analyzed in his innovative study on the transnational circulation of Girls' Generation through YouTube, Korean entertainment agencies like S.M., JYP Entertainment (hereafter JYPE), YG Entertainment (hereafter YG), and Cube Entertainment (hereafter Cube) have become official YouTube users, being able to showcase their content directly to individual users through their YouTube channels. Since opening in March 2006, according to Noh, S.M.'s YouTube channel recorded more than 502 million visitors for music video views and more than 14.8 million discrete channel visits through August 5, 2011 (Noh 2011, 58).[3] But Girls' Generation, despite its enormous popularity in social media networks, failed to generate enough "hype" to penetrate the U.S. pop market—while "The Boys" sold more than 400,000 copies in Korea and reached the second spot on the Oricon Weekly Album Chart in Japan with sales of 100,000 copies. Why did Girls' Generation fail in North America? Perhaps, as Roald Maliangkay argues in this book, the most successful K-pop formula itself—"uniformity in physical beauty, styling, music, and performance"—was not attractive enough, or "culturally odorless" (Iwabuchi 2002), and the "chogukjeok (trans- or cross-national)" localization (Jung 2011c) of Girls' Generation did not work with the group's target audience in the U.S. consumer market. Kyung Hyun Kim aptly pointed out that "the tendency and thinking so far seems to have been that you have to erase Korean identity somehow to achieve success in the US or overseas but I think that's been proven wrong with

Psy's success" (Beavan 2012). Psy's unexpected craze in cyberspace (and subsequent "hype" in the material world), along with K-pop idol groups' popularity in Europe, suggests that the current global pop market landscape is changing dramatically. Music critic Solvej Schou writes, "You may not understand a single word of South Korean rapper Psy's club anthem 'Gangnam Style,' except for the only phrase in English, 'Hey, sexy lady!' but it doesn't matter. Fifty million views on YouTube, for the song's completely wacky, catchy, dance heavy video, need no translation. The tune, Ibiza-ready with a relentless synthy beat, is a worldwide hit" (Schou 2012). K-pop girl groups' uniformity, chogukjeok styles, and English-language songs—strategically planned, developed, and led by Korean entertainment agencies, most representatively S.M., JYPE, and YG—were not able to win the U.S. mainstream audiences' attention, but unexpectedly deterritorialized virtual communities in social media networks showed their grassroots power, and pushed Hallyu, the Korean Wave, into the new realm of what we call in this book *Hallyu 2.0*—a term explained in the latter part of this introduction.

Hallyu has evolved dramatically, as we briefly sketched using the case of Psy. Academic research and writing about Hallyu has also been flourishing since the early 2000s, in response to the stunning receptions of Korean TV dramas, films, and K-pop in Asia, Europe, and North America. Those who first noticed Hallyu as an academic subject were scholars working primarily in Asia (Chua 2004 and 2008; Lee 2004; Cho 2005; Lee 2005; Shim 2005 and 2006; Yin and Liew 2005; Jung 2006; Sung 2006; Chua and Iwabuchi 2008). Hong Kong University Press, in particular, has actively been introducing a series of edited volumes and monographs on the subject, including *East Asian Pop Culture: Analysing the Korean Wave* (Chua and Iwabuchi 2008), which is one of the first English-language works on the subject.[4] In Australia, *Complicated Currents: Media Flows, Soft Powers and East Asia,* edited by Daniel A. Black, Stephen Epstein, and Alison Tokita, was published in 2010, based on an international conference held at Monash University, and the volume explores transnational production and consumption of media products in East Asia, but paying particular attention to Hallyu. Do Kyun Kim and Min-Sun Kim edited a book in English for Seoul National University Press entitled *Hallyu: Influence of Korean Popular Culture in Asia and Beyond* (2011). Regarding the U.S. publishing market, Mark James Russell's *Pop Goes Korea: Behind the Revolution in Movies, Music, and Internet Culture* (2008) tells a story of the rapid growth and "wild success" of Korean popular culture by providing rich and vivid case studies of online gaming, films, music, TV dramas, and animations. There was, however, still no book-length study on the latter stage of Hallyu, "the fourth wave" (Jung, this volume), published in English at the time we were editing this book.[5]

Hallyu 2.0: The Korean Wave in the Age of Social Media seeks to comprehend and interpret the meaning of this new and powerful cultural industry in the digital era. Contributors to this book explore the ways in which Korean popular cultural products, focusing primarily on K-pop and TV dramas, have been circulated, disseminated, and consumed by audiences around the globe; how Korean popular cultural products are encountering new fans, markets, and consumers through social media networks like YouTube, Facebook, Twitter, and web-based video streaming services and torrent download sites; and how we should interpret, analyze, and forecast this unprecedented cultural phenomenon. The aim of this introduction is, as a first step, to trace the past decade of Hallyu scholarship produced around the globe, focusing primarily on English-speaking academia, from North America and the United Kingdom to the Asia-Pacific. This chapter will describe four distinct phases of Hallyu scholarship: (1) the initial stage when scholars sought to define Hallyu, why and to what extent Asians crave Korean popular cultural content, and the collective desire to utilize Hallyu as the nation's new engine of sustainable growth, (2) appropriating Hallyu as a sign of global shifts, from the cultural imperialism school's approach, to the Hollywoodization of the world, to the perspective of recentering globalization/reverse cultural imperialism in the new millennium, (3) Hallyu as a dynamic inter-Asian cultural flow and, finally, (4) situating Hallyu in the age of social media and embracing the notion of Hallyu 2.0. The following section begins with the initial scholarly responses on Hallyu in the early 2000s.

What Is Hallyu? And What Should Korea Do with It?

Jim Dator and Yongseok Seo (2004) begin their article, "Asia is awash in a wave of popular culture products gushing out of South Korea. Youth in China, Hong Kong, Taiwan, Singapore, and Japan, as well as Cambodia, Vietnam, the Philippines, Indonesia, and Malaysia, are agog at the sights and sounds of H.O.T., S.E.S., Shinhwa, god, and JTL" (31). Fans, scholars, entrepreneurs, and policymakers in Korea were altogether surprised, excited, and proud of the sudden explosion of Korean "low" cultures in adjacent countries, the Korean pop music craze in China in particular. Cho Yong-sik, a staff reporter of the *Korea Herald*, writes:

> Back in 1965, the Beatles were named "members of the most excellent order of the British Empire." Today, if Korea were to award the equivalent of British knighthood to a Korean celebrity, the first person on the list would be actor-cum-singer Ahn Jae-wook, who may have accomplished something that no politician, businessman nor diplomat could ever do for a nation. . . . Ahn now commands unrivaled popularity in China, having surpassed Leonardo DiCaprio as the most popular celebrity in a recent poll. (Cited in Cho 2005, 151)

Ahn Jae-wook and other "first wave" K-pop idol groups (Jung, this volume), such as Clon, H.O.T., and NRG, as well as Korean TV dramas—particularly *What Is Love* (Sarang i mwŏgillae, 1992) and *Star in My Heart* (Pyŏl ŭn nae kasŭm e, 1997)—and the films *My Sassy Girl* (Yŏpkijŏgin kŭnyŏ, 2001) and *My Tutor Friend* (Tonggap naegi kwaoe hagi, 2003) ignited the so-called Korean Wave, or Hallyu (Hanliu in Chinese romanization), in China, Taiwan, Hong Kong, and Singapore. The term *Hallyu* was first coined by Chinese media in 1998 to describe Chinese youths' sudden craze for Korean popular-culture products. Hallyu floated to the other side of Asia as well. After its initial airing in Japan in 2003, the soap opera *Winter Sonata* (Kyŏul yŏn'ga, 2002) drove Japanese audiences into something of a frenzy (Chung, this volume). The unexpected hype *Winter Sonata* ignited and the subsequent "Yon-sama (Bae Yong-joon; Pae Yong-jun) phenomenon" among Japanese middle-aged female audiences (Jung 2006; Kim 2006; Hanaki et al. 2007; Han 2008; Mori 2008; Han and Lee 2010; Tokita 2010; Lee and Ju 2011) and the critical and commercial success of Korean films—notably *Oldboy* (2003), *Memories of Murder* (Sarin ŭi ch'uŏk, 2003), and *Spring, Summer, Fall, Winter . . . and Spring* (Pom yŏrŭm kaŭl kyŏul kŭrigo pom, 2003)—in the global media market in the early 2000s (Shin 2005; Jin 2006; Klein 2008; Shim 2008; Shin 2008; Choi 2010; Park 2010; Yecies 2010) transformed the direction of the Korean media industry, government policy, and academic research altogether. Seoul, all of a sudden, became a "media capital" (Curtin 2003).

Scholars in Korea have begun to analyze the transnational appeal of Korean popular cultural products in Asia. The early phase of Hallyu scholarship defined it as a regional phenomenon and addressed almost identical questions, such as "What is Hallyu?," "Why are Asians consuming Korean pop songs and TV dramas?," and simply "Why now?" The notion of "geo-linguistic region" was among the first to be adapted to answer the queries. John Sinclair (1996) argued that "geo-linguistic region" referred to "all the countries throughout the world in which the same language is spoken" and, he argued, "Just as the United States dominates the English-speaking world, so there are other notable instances where the country with the largest number of speakers of a particular language in its domestic market is also the source of most audiovisual exports in their language" (42). The Korean language is, however, not widely spoken, and only ethnic Koreans can communicate with each other using it. The immensely popular Korean period-drama series *Jewel in the Palace* (Tae Changgŭm, 2003–4) was, hence, dubbed into Mandarin in Taiwan and Cantonese in Hong Kong. Hong Kong–based TVB (Television Broadcasts Limited), the largest distributor of Chinese-language television programs in the world, intervened to provide additional explanations in Cantonese voice-overs, which amounted to, Beng Huat Chua argued, "domesticating and localizing practices" (2011, 228–29).

"Cultural proximity," Joseph Straubhaar's term (1991), was considered more appropriate to decipher the phenomenon. Korea possessed, in some ways, a "cultural proximity," which is a comparative advantage factor based on cultural similarities with other Asian countries that go beyond language, including such elements as dress, nonverbal communication, humor, religion, music, and food. Myriad scholars have argued that traditional values and Confucian ethics—such as harmony, community, strong morality, and respect for family ties—attract cultural consumers in East Asia (Shin 2006a and 2006b; Hanaki et al. 2007; Jung 2009; Yun 2009). Hallyu in Japan is an appropriate example. Japanese middle-aged women, Yang Jonghoe writes, find in Korean dramas "their old-fashioned values such as respect for family and kinship networks, restrained expression of love, and pure love" (Yang 2012, 110). As Hallyu has swept to more remote corners of the world, however, the "Asianness" of Korean popular cultural products can no longer explain the unexpected enthusiasts of K-pop and television dramas in the world outside of Asia. Sociologist John Lie, in this regard, acutely discussed three factors that have brought K-pop to the world. First, K-pop filled a niche between the "urbanized and sexualized" American pop music and more local, national traditions of popular music in Asia and beyond. Second, the Korean state has backed the Korean Wave and K-pop. Lastly, K-pop has high production values (Lie 2012, 355–59). As Lie has pertinently argued, since the late 2000s, S.M., YG, JYPE, and other talent agencies have been manufactured collectively by artists and producers from global music industries,[6] and K-pop is no longer distinctively Korean or "something that can be universalized for the rest of Asia" (Oh and Park 2012, 392). K-pop has become a new "export product" that follows a pattern with Korea products that have broad appeal because of "the combination of reasonable price and dependable quality" (Lie 2012, 359; Choi 2013).

Korea, Hallyu, and the World

Hallyu has transformed Korea's perspectives on the world, from the West to East. This transformation occurred at the same time that the Asian market emerged as the nation's new engine of sustainable growth. Asia has not been regarded as the major market for Korea for many decades because of its nearly exclusive alliance with the West. Asia was just an invisible, dark region for Koreans, because the major target for products has been consumers in developed countries—that is, Western markets. However, like other Asian countries such as Japan and Taiwan, Korea turned its attention to the Asian marketplace during the late 1990s, after having ignored it since the 1960s. It was at this moment that the government embraced the "Globalization" slogan as a reaction to the economic globalization process, as Samuel S. Kim has illustrated in his innovative study *Korea's Globalization* (2000). In 2003, contrary to previous presidents' political slogans, "Globalization" (Kim Young-sam's Segyehwa) and inter-Korean issues (Kim Dae-jung's sunshine policy), the government of President Roh Moo-hyun (2003–8) proclaimed "an era of Northeast Asia," and Roh himself emphasized that Korea must participate actively in the new era (Shin 2006b). Roh's policy and current trends in the Asian film marketplace have affected the Korean film and media industries. Lee Myung-bak (2008–13), entrepreneur-cum-president, accentuated business effectiveness, neoliberalism, and an export-driven policy that have affected every sector of Korean society. Recent discourse on the Asian cultural market, on that account, suggests that Hallyu should cooperate with Korea's global corporations, IT businesses, and the government's foreign policies to penetrate Asian markets and exploit maximum profits to build a "Global Korea" (Kim et al. 2007; Kim, Long, and Robinson 2009; Ryoo 2009; Joo 2011; Lie 2012; Choi 2013; Nam 2013; Lee 2013). The culture industry has, Youna Kim (2006) states, "taken center-stage in Korea, with an increased recognition that the export of media and cultural products not only boosts the economy but also promotes the nation's image" (124). Kim Joo-sung, president of CJ Entertainment, the most influential media conglomerate in Korea, remarked:

The ultimate goal of the media business in CJ Entertainment is to produce and supply the best-quality contents in Asia, and grow to become "Asia's number one total entertainment group." We want to be recognized alongside the pre-existing industrial players like semiconductor, manufacturers, shipbuilding companies, and automobile manufacturers, as one of the "world's best Korean companies." (Korean Film Council 2007, 106)

In line with this, the Korean government established the Korea Foundation for International Cultural Exchange (KOFICE) in order to orchestrate all governmental and private endeavors in the making of Hallyu. According to official documents, KOFICE proclaims its aims and purposes:

Different countries around the world are cultivating their cultural industries competitively. They are in an intense competition to take cultural industries as the means to revive the nation's economy and to step onto the global stage. Korea, too, is focusing on the unlimited potential of its cultural industry and has recognized the cultural industry as a new growth engine. (KOFICE 2008, cited in Nam 2013, 221)

Academic-industry collaboration, based upon this logic, has been flourishing in Korea for several years. The Korean government has poured an enormous number of research grants, fellowships, and financial supports and incentives into selective research institutes and universities. According to Young-Hwa Choi (2013), new academic departments in the universities named "cultural industries," "culture and contents," "cinematic contents," "digital contents," and "digital culture and contents" have skyrocketed, from 932 in 2006 to 1,478 in 2010.[7] While those new or refurbished departments are churning out college-educated cultural workers who have been trained to produce "Hallyu contents," government-funded and nonprofit academic organizations have lured scholars in virtually all disciplines in Korea and even beyond.[8] "It is impossible to be critical," Choi lamented, "as almost all academic disciplines in Korea have received grants from the government for researching the strategies and creating cultural contents for sustainable development of Hallyu" (271). Hallyu discourse in Korea therefore soon migrated from the initial cultural/media studies approach to the realms of economics, business, science and technology, and tourism, which emphasize, Hyun Mee Kim (2005) points out, "the universal superiority of Korean culture or the economic effect of the phenomenon based on economism," with little study of "the actual processes behind this pop culture flow in each specific locale" (184). Kyung Hyun Kim (2011) also notes that most of the essays on Hallyu, even English-language ones, have placed "an excessive emphasis on data that range from numbers of foreign tourists to various annual figures from the entertainment industry" (4). Seung-Hye Sohn (2009), having analyzed more than 250 academic articles on Hallyu written in Korean, claims that academic discourse in Korea has rapidly transformed to explore the possible contributions Hallyu can make to boost the nation's economy.

Some scholars, however, have criticized the intervention of the government in the formation of Hallyu and its desire to promote Korea's new international identity through cultural products (Williamson 2011). The Korean government has become "a promoter of popular culture" (Lie 2012, 359), and therefore Hallyu should be considered a "cultural formation" rather than a popular "cultural trend" (Choi 2013). Hallyu as a "national campaign" or "corporate-state project" is, JungBong Choi argues in this book, "helmed by a handful of entrepreneurs, mainstream media, state bureaucrats, and professional consultants, mostly based in Korea" (45). Contrary to the collective desire to comprehend and utilize Hallyu as the nation's new engine of growth, predominant among scholars in Korea, the pages that follow shift the regional focus and discuss three interlocking, but not necessarily chronological, phases of Hallyu discourses in English-speaking academia.

Globalization, Hybridity, and Hallyu

Globalization and the postcolonial notion of hybridity were among the first theoretical frames actively adapted to discourses on Hallyu in English-speaking academia. Having departed from the initial explanations and analyses of Hallyu generated in Korea, largely based on neoliberal thinking and cultural nationalism, the first wave of Hallyu scholarship in English embraced the notions of globalization, hybridity, and regional/transnational/transcultural media flows of Korean cultural products, notably film, television drama, and popular music, in and beyond Asia.

The 1990s' phenomenal buzzword, "globalization," is often understood as "time-space compression" (Harvey 1990) or "complex connectivity" (Tomlinson 1999) that has accelerated the cross-border movement of capital, commodities, and people, and as a result brought the world closer than ever before. It is, more often than not, perceived as an economic experience encircling such trends as economic liberalization, deregulation, and the heightened mobility of capital, commodities, services, and labor around the world. In the field of cinema, media, and communication studies, globalization is, based on a political-economy approach, often a synonym for media-imperialism, that is, the Disneyization (Wasko 2001; Bryman 2004) or Hollywoodization of the world (Guback 1969; Schiller 1976; Mattelart 1979; Tomlinson 1991; Miller et al. 2005). The media imperialism school's basic thesis is that, following Herbert Schiller's classic definition, "under the aegis of world system," there is only "a one-directional flow of information from core to periphery and it represents the reality of power" (Schiller 1976, 5–6). This notion of media imperialism has been criticized for its rather simplified view that the globalization process involves a cultural homogenization that is destroying the autonomy of indigenous cultures. It is, however, still a widely circulating concept, especially for countries where the Hollywood image industry dominates the local market.

Accordingly, for 1990s' Korean society, globalization was perceived as another name for American cultural imperialism. The wave of globalization during this period pressured Korean government to open the door of its film market to foreign products (Yecies 2007), and it initially faced strong resistance within the domestic industry. Hyangjin Lee's *Contemporary Korean Cinema* (2001), arguably the first English-language book on Korean cinema, is representative in this regard. At the time she was writing, Lee could not be aware of the Korean media's global outreach on the cusp of the new millennium, and viewed the nation's cinema as prey to Hollywood's global domination, that is, its ever-expanding capitalist mode of accumulation. The opening up of the Korean market to foreign film distribution companies in 1987, Lee argued, "worsened the already shrinking Korean film industry," Her hope lay in the young filmmakers of the 1980s, who had been armed with historical consciousness and initiated the Korean national film movement (Lee 2001, 57). Kyung Hyun Kim has an almost identical concern: "The Korean film marketplace was effectively 'liberalized' without consulting filmmakers themselves, and the national cinema now had to fight a battle to protect its backyard, with the home team advantage removed" (Kim and James 2001, 34).

Interestingly enough, within a decade, scholarship on Korean cinema and media in Anglophone academia has been thoroughly transformed. Arriving after film scholars like Kim and Lee, the first wave of Hallyu critics were writing after the *Winter Sonata* phenomenon in Japan in 2004, and the "new" Korean cinema and media had successfully defended itself from the influx of Hollywood capital, and even achieved a renaissance. Jeeyoung Shin states: "South Korean cinema has undergone remarkable growth over the past decade. By substantially improving technical and aesthetic qualities, and by responding to the sensibilities of contemporary Koreans, recent Korean films have distinguished themselves from their predecessors" (Shin 2005, 51). Various Hallyu scholars holding distinctly new perspectives are now arguing that globalization, in the end, benefited Korean media, as the industry is now celebrating its global recognition and enjoying multiple penetrations in adjacent markets and beyond. Doobo Shim argues that the current commercial success of Korean media is "an outgrowth of Korea's struggle for cultural continuity when confronted by the threat of global cultural domination" (Shim 2005, 31). That is, Korean media industries emulated and appropriated the American media system during the 1990s and early 2000s to survive with the mantra "learning from Hollywood" (32), and, in that process, as Eun-Young Jung notes, "cultural hybridization has occurred as local cultural agents and actors interact and negotiate with global forms, using them as resources through which Koreans construct their own cultural spaces" (Jung 2009, 38). In other words, neoliberal policy in the end helped to build up Korean cinema and media's global competitiveness.

Therefore, if we accept this collective assertion, Hallyu is a vehicle for dismantling scholarship on critical globalization studies, in collaboration with the reverse cultural imperialism school, reorienting/recentering globalization practitioners, and cultural pluralism theoreticians who are arguing that the predominant center-periphery perspective cannot explain global media relations today and that a new epoch of cultural pluralism has now arrived (Straubhaar 1991; Chadha and Kavoori 2000; Park and Curran 2000; Iwabuchi 2002; Jin 2006; Curtin 2007). The Hallyu phenomenon, in this logic, should be seen as a way to counter the threat of the Western-dominated media market.

Hallyu as Dynamic Inter-Asian Cultural Flow

Inspired by Hae-joang Cho (2005), Korea-based cultural critic Keehyeung Lee suggests that the Hallyu phenomenon be situated "in the larger context of transnational cultural formations in the making," and advocates furthering "inter-regional cultural understanding and dialogues" (Lee 2005, 6). He understands Hallyu as an opportunity for building toward cultural regionalization (19). Lee and Cho, along with Shim (2005) and

Jung (2009), are indebted to Koichi Iwabuchi and Beng Huat Chua, two prominent cultural critics who have analyzed transnational cultural flow in Asia. Singapore-based sociologist Chua has published a series of studies on East Asian popular cultural flow since 2004, when he first introduced his seminal concept of "East Asian popular culture" in an essay entitled "Conceptualizing an East Asian Popular Culture." He has since revised the essay continuously. In his most recent update, Chua writes:

> At least since the 1980s, regionally produced pop culture products have criss-crossed the national borders of East Asian countries and constitute a significant part of the routine consumer culture of the regional population. Side by side with American pop culture, in every major urban center in East Asia—Hong Kong, Tokyo, Seoul, Singapore, Shanghai, and Taipei—there are dense flows of pop culture products from the same centers into one another, although the directions and volumes of flows vary unevenly among them . . . this thick and intensifying traffic between transnational locations—the economics of this cultural industry, the boundary crossing of products, the criss-crossing of artists not only geographically but across different media, and the multiple media and modes of consumption of audiences in different locations—lends substance to and warrants the concept of "East Asian Popular Culture" as an object of analysis. (Chua 2011, 224)

Partly inspired by Arjun Appadurai (1990), whose five "scapes"— ethnoscape, mediascape, technoscape, financescape, and ideoscape—refer to the progressively more frequent movement from one location to another of people, media, information, images, ideologies, technology, financial information, and world views, Chua argues that along with the obvious existence of American popular culture's influences throughout the regions there are dense flows of cultural products from every major urban center in East Asia. Hence, recent Asian cultural productions are dealing with a new Asian generation that enjoys popular culture from other Asian countries. Iwabuchi's argument (2004) is, from this point of view, a highly appropriate one. He states: "What has become more prominent is the emergence of popular Asianism and Asian dialogues whose main feature is not Asian values or traditional culture but capitalist consumer/popular culture," and he rejects the idea that the "impact of West-dominated cultural globalization homogenizes Asian cultures, or indeed that Asia can simply replicate Western modernities" (Iwabuchi 2004, 2).

Having focused on the significant popularities of the Japanese "trendy drama" that was ignited by 1992's *Tokyo Love Story* in Taiwan, Singapore, and Korea, Iwabuchi's earlier work (2002) claims that Japanese soap operas that were popular in Taiwan around 2000 had a different status from Western popular culture, like the Hollywood movies that dominated the Taiwanese market back in the postwar period. He points out that Taiwanese audiences accepted Japanese popular culture as a part of Asian culture because it had had a similar experience of modernization. After the *Winter Sonata* craze in Japan—along with *Jewel in the Palace*, *Full House* (P'ul hausŭ, 2004) and *The 1st Shop of Coffee Prince* (K'ŏp'i P'ŭrinsŭ 1-hojŏm, 2007) in China, Hong Kong, Taiwan, and Singapore in the mid-2000s— Korean television dramas have rapidly replaced Japanese and Hong Kong products and become part of the daily programming of many free-to-air and satellite television stations in East Asia and, thus, "part of the routine viewing habits of their respective audiences" (Chua and Iwabuchi 2008, 2). Iwabuchi, Chua, and other scholars of the inter-Asian cultural product flow have, accordingly, slowly but steadily migrated to the study of Hallyu.

A new group of researchers in Korea, namely the "culturalists" (Lee 2005), emerged in this circumstance, tracing and resituating the emergence of Hallyu as a "complex trans-border cultural phenomenon and formation in the era of poly-centered cultural production" (15). Accordingly, empirically based research has been published in recent years, with subjects as varied as Korean TV dramas and pop music in Taiwan (Kim 2005; Sung 2006), analysis of Korean "trendy drama" and its Japanese counterpart (Lee 2004), Korean American youth's reception of Korean TV dramas and pop culture (Park 2004), and the Chinese new generation's consumption of Korean popular culture (Yin and Liew 2005; Pease 2006 and 2009; Maliangkay 2010; Maliangkay and Song 2014). This wave of cultural studies scholars has shown that inter-Asian cultural consumption has brought about new kinds of cross-border relationships, mutual understanding and self-reflexivity about people's own society and culture. But, once again, scholarship on Hallyu transformed again around the late 2000s as Hallyu entered its new and latest wave: K-pop and social media.

Hallyu 2.0: The Korean Wave in the Age of Social Media

By the late 2000s Hallyu discourse in English-speaking academia had significantly weakened. Scholars in the field of Asian studies, communications, and cultural studies claimed that Hallyu, or the Korean Wave, had

already been significantly studied and written about, and even suggested
that Hallyu is "all but dead" (Oh and Park 2012, 366). The new Hallyu
movement, surprisingly enough, came with a catchphrase: "sorry sorry
sorry sorry" from an international hit song "Sorry Sorry" by Super Junior
in 2009. As Jung suggests in this book, "While the earlier phase of Hallyu
(from the late 1990s to mid-2000s) was driven mainly by numerous television drama hits throughout Asia and among overseas Asian communities,
the latest Hallyu development has been led by a relatively small sector of
Korean pop music known as [idol] bands, which have been attracting a
broader range of fans around the world" (74). The development of socio-
technological innovations, epitomized by social media networking services and video sharing sites provided platforms to disseminate K-pop
products around the world at an unprecedented pace.

K-pop idol bands such as Big Bang, 2AM, 2PM, 2NE1, Girls' Generation, SHINee, JYJ, Super Junior, and Wonder Girls, with the accelerating
engines of scientifically planned/managed entertainment agencies like
S.M., JYPE, YG, and Cube, rapidly established their status in the global
entertainment industry by adopting new digital technologies and utilizing
social media spaces. Young-min Kim, chief executive of S.M., said:

> Five years ago, if we wanted to launch and promote an artist, we had
> to follow a traditional path and work with traditional media like
> TV, but these days, with the rise of Internet media like YouTube,
> even before our talent leaves Korea, a lot of fans have a chance to
> watch them. (Ramstad 2011)

Fans all around world also participate in fandom activities through social
media, as Jung's essay in this volume explains, using examples like K-pop
flash mob contests, cover-dance contests, and music festivals all over the
world, including New York, Chicago, Milan, London, Paris, Mexico City,
and Dubai. The current wave formation of Hallyu is "an intriguing example of how both the industry and the consumers successfully transform
themselves into equally important players in the global game of social networking" (Jung, this volume, 85). The era of Hallyu 2.0 began at this juncture. The term *Hallyu 2.0* first appeared in August 2010. NHK, FUJI TV,
and Japanese newspapers named "the second invasion of Hallyu" after the
showcase of Girls' Generation at Ariake Coliseum in Tokyo. Korean media
have competitively analyzed, appropriated, and glorified the success of K-
pop musicians and their new status as global pop stars ever since then.
According to *MK Business News*:

The first Hallyu generation began with the representative drama, *Winter Sonata*. However, since the end of 2009, the Hallyu wave has expanded to music, musicals, and theater. . . . The first wave was led by male stars, but the concept has expanded to now include female stars as well. The fanbase has also expanded to include all age groups as opposed to the previous fanbase of women in their 30's and 40's. . . . The Hallyu wave was previously focused on just East Asia, but has now reached out into the world such as Uzbekistan, Turkey, Egypt, and Romania. (Huh 2010)

While Hallyu 1.0 is a one-way flow of Korean pop culture from artist to fans in Asia and was ignited by the *Winter Sonata* phenomenon in Japan and the popularity of male pop starts in China (Jung 2011b; Jung and Hirata 2012), Hallyu 2.0 came with digital technologies. Dal Yong Jin, in this volume, defines Hallyu 2.0 as "the combination of social media, their techniques and practices, and the uses and affordances they provide, and this new stage has been made possible because Korea has advanced its digital technologies" (54). Consuming patterns and demographic changes in fandom, from middle-aged consumers of Korean dramas in Japan to teens and twenties in the virtual world as the core group, are indeed two distinctive points distinguishing 2.0 from Hallyu 1.0. Hallyu 2.0, however, should not be defined as simply an upgraded version or replacement, nor should it contribute to the government's new "institutional campaign." Instead Hallyu 2.0 is an unparalleled cultural phenomenon and, as a scholarly endeavor, should scrutinize the ways in which Korean popular-cultural products are embracing new fans, markets, and consumers, and should interpret, analyze, and forecast the novel phase of Hallyu in the age of social media and participatory media cultures. Our volume, however, does not claim to be comprehensive. In particular, film, online gaming and gambling, and fashion and lifestyle remain underexplored compared to our extensive coverage of K-pop and TV dramas. The limitation this book has is reflected in the broader field of Hallyu studies. We hope that forthcoming articles, monographs, and edited volumes fill the void and enrich this ever-growing field of Hallyu 2.0.

Themes and Essays

The chapters in this book are arranged into four thematically linked parts. Essays in the first part of the book explore new perspectives on Hallyu 2.0

by setting the agendas, theorizing the concept, problematizing the role of the state and the multifaceted meanings of consuming and disseminating Korean popular cultural products. JungBong Choi defines Hallyu as the phenomenal success of Korean cultures in overseas market, then discusses two manifestations of Hallyu: as a transnational cultural phenomenon and as a national-institutional campaign. Concerning Hallyu as a transnational cultural phenomenon, Choi looks into the "productive" role played by consumers (audiences, fans, users, and so on) vis-à-vis that of content producers based in Korea. He draws on various cases that demonstrate how the growing creative control of fans, enthusiasts, and users correlates with the pervasive use of social media. Choi then discusses the other Hallyu, the national-institutional campaign. As this introduction has already discussed, Hallyu has been strategically produced and reproduced, as it is strongly supported by diverse government organizations, large corporations, mainstream media, state bureaucrats, professional consultants, and the academic world, mostly based in Korea. Choi boldly argues that "Hallyu is less a unified phenomenon than a meeting of two distinct waves: one propelled by people outside Korea, the other by powerful institutions in Korea with a nationwide consensus. One is a labor of individual passion, while the other arises principally through collective, social desire. One seems innocuous, the other inexorable" (50). Dal Yong Jin's chapter, on the other hand, provides an innovative perspective that asks why we need to emphasize Hallyu 2.0 in the context of creative industries, particularly intellectual property (IP) rights. By mapping out the issues of IP rights in conjunction with the rapid growth of social network services and smartphones, Jin discusses whether Korea has developed its strength in the global market in the context of the Hallyu 2.0 phenomenon. He raises the question of why IP rights should be a major consideration in order to shift the emphasis primarily from the flow of cultural products to the inclusion of the significance of platforms and intellectual property. Jin claims that we need to extend our scope to new areas, not only cultural flows, but also institutional and historical issues in order to fully grasp the new Korean Wave—Hallyu 2.0.

Essays in the second part bring the readers into the realm of K-pop. Each essay situates K-pop in a new academic arena—historicizing wave(s) of K-pop, collective fan movements against powerful and tyrannical entertainment agencies, and the packaging of K-pop idol groups. Doobo Shim (2010) cautiously notes that "the glory days of the Korean drama may have passed." He nevertheless points out that "audiences gradually search for sources of entertainment other than television dramas" (130).

As most of our contributors express, K-pop is currently the most important driving force in Hallyu 2.0. Eun-Young Jung's chapter serves as the guide post for mapping and historicizing this global phenomenon. She impeccably surveys multiple waves of K-pop, from the pre-social media explosion era of the late 1990s and early 2000s to current Hallyu K-pop (her term), and explores how the K-pop music industry, K-pop idols, and those idols' transnational fans have successfully deployed social media and accelerated the transnational K-pop presence, placing it under a bright spotlight in the contemporary transnational popular culture scene. Roald Maliangkay and Seung-Ah Lee analyze the heart of the K-pop system: Korean boy and girl bands and their manufacturers—entertainment agencies like S.M., YG, and JYPE. Roald Maliangkay provides a fresh perspective on the formation of Korean all-girl groups, which have proven to be the most successful K-pop formula: summed up as uniformity in physical beauty, styling, music, and performance. Maliangkay analyzes how all-girl acts have been packaged over the years in order to target specific audiences and meet their expectations, and delineates how bands manage to compete in an arguably conformist environment. In his conclusion, Maliangkay states, "I expect that as K-pop further develops, a greater number of female idols will seek ownership of their work and by doing so actually resist the hegemony, much like the boy band JYJ has done in recent years" (this volume, 104). Seung-Ah Lee's chapter begins right at this point. As a veteran practitioner and a noted fan of JYJ (Jaejoong, Yoochun, and Junsu) who has already written numerous essays on the subject in Korea, Lee, with an insider's perspective, discusses the all-male idol group JYJ, and unveils the hidden, ugly face of entertainment agency S.M., a powerful industrial machine that maintains complete control over the products it manufactures—the dancing and singing teenage boys and girls who are carefully marketed as "idol groups." Myriad scholars have admitted that K-pop has high production valued and praised Korea's unique system of producing idol bands, but the dark side of the system has rarely been studied. Lee's highly informative chapter will give the readers a new perspective on the K-pop industry. Throughout this vividly written chronology of JYJ and fan's trajectories, Lee views JYJ fandom as an emerging social movement, paying particular attention to the way JYJ fandom troubles a clear distinction between mainstream popular culture and counterculture.

The third group of essays, which focus on Korean TV drama and social media, takes a broader view of the cultural-textual-industrial geography of Hallyu, focusing on the interactive nature of Korean television drama production, the textual and metatextual spaces of Hallyu, and the history of consumption and distribution of Korean TV dramas in the United States. Youjeong Oh's chapter takes the reader deep inside the Hallyu factory: Korea's prime-time television drama production scenes. Having conducted in-depth ethnographic research on DC Inside, one of the biggest online communities in Korea, and the creative personnel in Korean TV drama production, Oh examines the live production system, which is a unique norm in the Korean drama industry, and the rise of social media that has fostered the practices of discursive consumption of Korean TV dramas. Under the live production system in Korea, two episodes are produced weekly for the following week's broadcasting, which entails interesting twists; while last-minute production imposes an immense load on those who create the programs, and thus rests on labor exploitation, it also allows room for audience participation in the making of dramas. Therefore viewers of Korean TV dramas actively share the experiences of drama watching, discuss stories and characters, and suggest hoped-for plots and endings. Unlike the U.S. media industry, fans' responses actually affect the production of TV dramas. Oh's innovative study reveals that, because of the practices of live production, "Korean drama producers actually change ongoing narratives in response to viewer ratings and reactions to previous episodes" (this volume, 134).

Michelle Cho examines the recent cycle of Korean TV dramas about the mass media, culture industries, celebrity construction, pop idols, and publicity. In other words, metatextuality has become a fixture in Korean popular culture, particularly films and TV dramas such as *Rough Cut* (Yŏnghwa nŭn yŏnghwa ta, 2008), *200 Pounds Beauty* (Minyŏ nŭn koerowŏ, 2006), *Worlds Within* (Kŭdŭl i sanŭn sesang, aka *The World That They Live In*, 2008), *You're Beautiful* (Minam isineyo, 2009), *Dream High* (Tŭrim hai, 2011), and *The King of Dramas* (Tŭrama ŭi chewang, 2012). Having analyzed two recent Korean TV dramas, *Oh! My Lady* (O! Mai leidi , 2010) and *The Greatest Love* (Ch'oego ŭi sarang, 2011) that dramatize Hallyu idol celebrity culture, Cho carefully investigates social media's disciplinary power and regimes of self-representation and the ways in which two the TV dramas just mentioned incorporate fan dynamics and the demands on the star as a commodified body into their narratives. Cho argues that "Korean TV drama's current obsession with metatextuality suggests that media consumption remains a dynamic and contested arena for the construction of models of public participation and social relations, rather than a monolithic apparatus for shaping consumer behavior" (this volume, 169). While Oh and Cho delineate the domestic and virtual realm of Korean TV production and consumption, Sangjoon Lee invites us to the U.S. media industry. Lee traces the history of Korean television dramas' distribution, circulation, and consumption in the United States, from Korean-language television stations and video rental stores exclusively for Korean diasporas, to YouTube, Hulu, and the first legitimate video-streaming website DramaFever. Lee argues that before the new millennium Korean television dramas had only been distributed, circulated, and consumed by Korean immigrants (mostly first-generation) and students studying abroad (yuhaksaeng) until Hallyu arrived at America's two coasts with the help of digital technologies. In the second half of the chapter, Lee examines DramaFever, Viki, Crunchyroll, and many other legitimate or illegitimate video-streaming websites that have actively been distributing Korean TV dramas in the United States.

The final set of essays begin with Hye Seung Chung. Instead of accounting for the economic and cultural impact of the so-called "Yon-sama craze" in Japan, which generated an estimated USD 3 billion profit, Chung pays critical attention to a patriarchal, xenophobic backlash against the Korean Wave in Japan. By meticulously analyzing TV Tokyo's *Nerima Daikon Brothers*, an adult-themed musical anime program aired in early 2006, Chung explores the darker flip-side of the Yon-sama phenomenon in Japan, which otherwise improved images of Korea and, by extension, Zainichi Koreans among the Japanese populace. Concluding with the show's reception in the United States through YouTube, Hulu, and Netflix, Chung writes that *Nerima Daikon Brothers'* "potential to disseminate distorted images of monstrous Koreans to a new generation of YouTube users worldwide suggests that a major critical intervention is needed to guide informed consumption of this and other cyber popular culture texts suffused with regressive racial content" (this volume, 208). Irina Lyan and Alon Levkowitz bring us to the global reception of Korean popular cultural products. Their chapter is based on data they acquired through electronic survey deployment, content analysis, and interviews. As discussed earlier in this introduction, the notion of cultural proximity does not explain the global phenomenon of Hallyu. Traditional values and Confucian ethics have been cited to explain the cultural consumers of Korean popular cultural products in East Asia. However, as Lyan and Levkowitz argue, these explanations cannot elucidate the Israeli case, "where Korean culture is perceived as exotic, distant, and different" (this volume, 215). The main argument of their essay is that the audiences for Korean culture in Israel are not just passive recipients in a one-way process, but rather cultural agents that shape and construct "Koreanness" in adjustment to the local environment. Finally, Brian Hu examines the Psy phenomenon. In this boldly titled chapter, "RIP Gangnam Style," Hu proclaims that "Gangnam Style" happened. Past tense. Many contributors in this volume discuss, to some extent, what has been called the "Psy phenomenon," but Hu's chapter surveys the length and breadth of the phenomenon without losing critical perspectives. While Hallyu as a national-institutional campaign (Choi, this volume) has celebrated Psy's huge success in the United States and its impact on the nation's economy, the U.S. mainstream media have repeatedly declared the death (or near-death) of "Gangnam Style." Why? In the U.S. cultural industry, Hu argues, Psy is another example of what Sue Collins has called the "dispensable celebrity"—like Lou Bega, Falco, and Los del Rio earlier. Hu sharply observes that the American entertainment media industry has a history of making Asians invisible in the mainstream media, and in the hierarchies of the celebrity world "real celebrity" rules the system, while a "dispensable celebrity" like Psy is marginalized when juxtaposed with "real race" American celebrities. Even Asian American critics who suspect that Psy's mainstream popularity stems from a racial stereotype of Asian masculinity consider Psy to be "not just one in a revolving door of dispensable celebrities, but also the latest in the revolving door of stereotypical Asians" (this volume, 238). However, Hu suggests we reconsider the "death" of "Gangnam style." Delineating a parody wedding video of two Asian Americans living in San Francisco, Hu shows that bride, groom, and their friends, in their parody video celebrate the moment by showing vivacity and true friendship instead of stereotypical representations of Asian Americans. "The fleetingness of 'Gangnam Style,'" Hu writes, "gave many of those who mimicked Psy's original video a vernacular with which to memorialize the present—to celebrate it, laugh at it, and then let it go so as to clear the way for the future" (240–41).

NOTES

1. Because the chapters in this volume explore a cultural phenomenon pertaining to the country known formally as the Republic of Korea (also known as South Korea), within this volume the term "Korea" refers to this nation.

2. Lou Bega, an Italian/Ugandan artist from Germany, released an international hit single, "Mambo No. 5," (1999) which reached number one in the United States, although no single was issued. Both Nena and Falco are German-language pop artists whose singles "99 Luftballoons" (1984) and "Rock Me Amadeus" (1986) marked the second place and topped the Billboard Hot 100 chart respectively. Falco became the first German-speaking artist ever to top the U.S. pop chart. Los del Rio is probably the case most similar to the Psy phenomenon. This Spanish music duo shook the world with one of the

hottest dance crazes of the 1990s, "Macarena" (1994). Kyu Sakamoto's "Sukiyaki" (1963) is still the only Asian pop song ever to top the Billboard chart.

    3. It reached 1.4 billion visitors as of February 2014.

    4. See Iwabuchi 2004; Iwabuchi, Muecke, and Thomas 2004; Berry, Liscutin, and Mackintosh 2009; Chua 2012; and Jung 2011a.

    5. Now, however, see Kim and Choe 2014, Kim 2014, and Choi and Maliangkay 2014.

    6. Seung-Ah Lee shows a dark side of the Korean entertainment agencies by analyzing S.M. Entertainment and JYJ fandom. See her chapter in this volume.

    7. Those new or reshaped departments, many of them previously called "communication and culture" or "broadcast and media," attract young high school graduates by advertising that "students are equipped with both the practical and creative skills necessary to work and flourish in this field and a full understanding of humanity as well as culture content subjects are included in the completed degree program." From the web page of Hanyang University's Department of Culture and Contents. Accessed at http://www.hanyang.ac.kr/user/structureDirectEng.action?structureSeq=395.

    8. As an example, on March 11, 2013, the World Association for Hallyu Studies (WAHS), housed at Korea University, one of the most prestigious universities in Korea, was inaugurated. The association is dedicated "to advancing Hallyu Studies as a multidisciplinary body of knowledge and profession serving the public good." According to publicity material, members of WAHS will explore such diverse academic disciplines as humanities and social sciences, medical science, Hallyu policy and management, sports science, entertainment business, tourism, textile/fashion, beauty, and food, and will collaborate with its twelve regional offices in the United States (eastern and western offices), Canada, Argentina, Europe, Middle East (Israel), Oceania, China, Indonesia, Malaysia, and Japan.

WORKS CITED

Anon. 2013. "Psy 'Gentleman' Video: Will the 'Gangnam Style' Star Hit Viral Gold with His Follow-Up Song?" *Huffington Post,* April 12.

Appadurai, Arjun. 1990. "Disjuncture and Difference in the Global Economy." *Public Culture* 2 (2): 1–24.

Beavan, David. 2012. "Despite the Record-Shattering Success of 'Gangnam Style,' the most Fascinating Pop Phenomenon of the Year Sputtered in Its Attempt to Dazzle the US." *Spin Magazine,* December 12.

Berry, Chris, Nicola Liscutin, and Jonathan D. Mackintosh, eds. 2009. *Cultural Studies and Cultural Industries in Northeast Asia: What a Difference a Region Makes.* Hong Kong: Hong Kong University Press.

Black, Daniel A., Stephen Epstein, and Alison Tokita, eds. 2010. *Complicated Currents: Media Flows, Soft Power and East Asia.* Melbourne: Monash University ePress.

Bryman, Alan. 2004. *The Disneyization of Society.* London: Sage.

Cha, Hyunhee, and Seongmook Kim. 2011. "A Case Study on Korean Wave: Focused on K-POP Concert by Korean Idol Group in Paris, June 2011." In *Proceedings of Springer Briefs in Computer Science,* 153–62.

Chadha, Kalyani, and Anandam Kavoori. 2000. "Media Imperialism Revisited: Some Findings from the Asian Case." *Media, Culture and Society* 22 (4): 415–32.

Cho, Hae-Joang. 2005. "Reading the 'Korean Wave' as a Sign of Global Shift." *Korea Journal* 45 (4): 147–82.

Cho, Wu-Suk. 2012. "Riding the Korean Wave from 'Gangnam Style' to Global Recognition." *Global Asia* 7 (3): 35–39.

Choi, Jinhee. 2010. *The South Korean Film Renaissance: Local Hitmakers, Global Provocateurs.* Middletown, CT: Wesleyan University Press.

Choi, Young-Hwa. 2013. "The Korean Wave Policy as a Corporate-State Project of the Lee Government: The Analysis of Structures and Strategies Based on the Strategic-Relational Approach." *Economy and Society* 97: 252–85.

Chua, Beng Huat. 2004. "Conceptualizing an East Asian Popular Culture." *Inter-Asia Cultural Studies* 5 (2): 200–221.

Chua, Beng Huat. 2008. "Structure of Identification and Distancing in Watching East Asian Television Drama." In *East Asian Pop Culture: Analysing the Korean Wave*, ed. Beng Huat Chua and Koichi Iwabuchi, 73–89. Hong Kong: Hong Kong University Press.

Chua, Beng Huat. 2011. "East Asian Pop Culture." In *Genre in Asian Film and Television*, ed. Felicia Chan, Angelina Karpovich, and Xin Zhang, 222–45. New York: Palgrave Macmillan.

Chua, Beng Huat. 2012. *Structure, Audience and Soft Power in East Asian Pop Culture.* Hong Kong: Hong Kong University Press.

Curtin, Michael. 2003. "Media Capital: Toward the Study of Spatial Flows." *International Journal of Cultural Studies* 6 (2): 202–28.

Curtin, Michael. 2007. *Playing to the World's Biggest Audience: The Globalization of Chinese Film and TV.* Berkeley: University of California Press.

Dator, Jim, and Yongseok Seo. 2004. "Korea as the Wave of a Future: The Emerging Dream Society of Icons and Aesthetic Experience." *Journal of Futures Studies* 9 (1): 31–44.

Guback, Thomas H. 1969. *The International Film Industry.* Bloomington: Indiana University Press.

Han, Benjanin Min. 2008. "Reliving *Winter Sonata*: Memory, Nostalgia, and Identity." *Post Script* 27 (3): 25-36.

Han, Hee-Joo, and Jae-Sub Lee. 2010. "A Study on the KBS TV Drama *Winter Sonata* and Its Impact on Korea's *Hallyu* Tourism Development." *Journal of Travel and Tourism Marketing* 24 (2–3): 115–26.

Han, Jane. 2012. "Americans Dance to 'Gangnam Style.'" *Korea Times*, August 12.

Hanaki, Toru, Arvind Singhal, Min Wha Han, Do Kyun Kim, and Ketan Chitnis. 2007. "Hanryu Sweeps East Asia: How *Winter Sonata* Is Gripping Japan." *International Communication Gazette* 69 (3): 281–94.

Harvey, David. 1990. *The Condition of Postmodernity: An Enquiry into the Origins of Cultural Change.* Cambridge, MA: Blackwell.

Huh, Yeon. 2010. "*Hallyu* 2.0 Has Begun." *MK Business News*, September 24.

Iwabuchi, Koichi. 2002. *Recentering Globalization: Popular Culture and Japanese Transnationalism.* Durham: Duke University Press.

Iwabuchi, Koichi, ed. 2004. *Feeling Asian Modernity: Transnational Consumption of Japanese TV Dramas.* Hong Kong: Hong Kong University Press.

Iwabuchi, Koichi. 2008. "When the Korean Wave Meets Resident Koreans in Japan: Intersections of the Transnational, the Postcolonial and the Multicultural." In *East

Asian Pop Culture: Analyzing the Korean Wave, ed. Chua Beng Huat and Koichi Iwabuchi, 243–78. Hong Kong: Hong Kong University Press.

Iwabuchi, Koichi, Stephen Muecke, and Mandy Thomas, eds. 2004. *Rogue Flows: Trans-Asian Cultural Traffic*. Hong Kong: Hong Kong University Press.

Jin, Dal Yong. 2006. "Cultural Politics in Korea's Contemporary Films under Neoliberal Globalization." *Media, Culture and Society* 28 (1): 5–23.

Joo, Jeongsuk. 2011. "Transnationalization of Korean Popular Culture and the Rise of 'Pop Nationalism' in Korea." *Journal of Popular Culture* 44 (3): 489–504.

Jung, Eun-Young. 2009. "Transnational Korea: A Critical Assessment of the Korean Wave in Asia and the United States." *Southeast Review of Asian Studies* 31: 69–80.

Jung, Sun. 2006. "Bae Yong-Joon, Hybrid Masculinity and the Counter-coeval Desire of Japanese Female Fans." *Participations* 3 (2). Accessed at http://www.participations. org/volume%203/issue%202%20-%20special/3_02_jung.htm.

Jung, Sun. 2011a. *Korean Masculinities and Transcultural Consumption: Yonsama, Rain, Oldboy, K-Pop Idols*. Hong Kong: Hong Kong University Press.

Jung, Sun. 2011b. "K-Pop, Indonesian Fandom, and Social Media." *Transformative Works and Cultures* 8. Accessed at http://journal.transformativeworks.org/index.php/twc/ article/view/289/219.

Jung, Sun. 2011c. "K-Pop Beyond Asia: Performing Trans-Nationality, Trans-Industriality, and Trans-Textuality." Conference paper, Korean Society for Journalism and Communication Studies.

Jung, Sun, and Yukie Hirata. 2012. "Conflicting Desire: K-Pop Idol Girl Group Flows in Japan in the Era of Web 2.0." *Electronic Journal of Contemporary Japanese Studies* 12 (2). Accessed at http://japanesestudies.org.uk/ejcjs/vol12/iss2/jung.html.

Kim, Do Kyun, and Min-Sun Kim, eds. 2011. *Hallyu: Influence of Korean Popular Culture in Asia and Beyond*. Seoul: Seoul National University Press.

Kim, Hyun Mee. 2005. "Korean TV Dramas in Taiwan: With an Emphasis on the Localization Process." *Korea Journal* 45 (4): 183–205.

Kim, Kyung Hyun. 2004. *The Remasculinization of Korean Cinema*. Durham: Duke University Press.

Kim, Kyung Hyun. 2011. *Virtual Hallyu: Korean Cinema of the Global Era*. Durham: Duke University Press.

Kim, Kyung Hyun, and Youngmin Choe, eds. 2014. *The Korean Popular Culture Reader*. Durham: Duke University Press, 2014.

Kim, Kyung Hyun, and David E. James, eds. 2001. *Im Kwon-Taek: The Making of a Korean National Cinema*. Detroit: Wayne State University Press.

Kim, Samuel S., ed. 2000. *Korea's Globalization*. Cambridge: Cambridge University Press.

Kim, Samuel S., Jerome Agrusa, Heesung Lee, and Kaye Chon. 2007. "Effects of Korean Television Dramas on the Flow of Japanese Tourists." *Tourism Management* 28 (5): 1340–53.

Kim, Sangkyun, Phillip Long, and Mike Robinson. 2009. "Small Screen, Big Tourism: The Role of Popular Korean Television Dramas in South Korean Tourism." *Tourism Geographies: An International Journal of Tourism Space, Place and Environment* 11 (3): 308–33.

Kim, Youna. 2006. "The Rising East Asian 'Wave': Korean Media Go Global." In *Media on the Move: Global Flow and Counter-Flow*, ed. Daya Kishan Thussu, 121–35. New York: Routledge.

Kim, Youna. 2014. *The Korean Wave: Korean Media Go Global.* New York: Routledge.

Kim, Youn-jung. 2002. "Korean Pop Culture: Craze *Hallyu* Sweeps through Asia." *Koreana* 22 (4).Klein, Christina. 2008. "Why American Studies Needs to Think about Korean Cinema, or, Transnational Genres in the Films of Bong Joon-ho." *American Quarterly* 60 (4): 871–98.

Korean Film Council. 2007. "Kim Joo-sung." *Who's Who in Korean Film Industry*, 105–9. Seoul: Korean Film Council.

Lee, Dong-Hoo. 2004. "Cultural Contact with Japanese TV Dramas: Modes of Reception and Narrative Transparency." In *Feeling Asian Modernities: Transnational Consumption of Japanese TV Dramas*, ed. Koichi Iwabuchi, 251–74. Hong Kong: Hong Kong University Press.

Lee, Hyangjin. 2001. *Contemporary Korean Cinema: Identity, Culture and Politics.* Manchester: Manchester University Press.

Lee, Keehyeung. 2005. "Assessing and Situating 'the Korean Wave' (*Hallyu*) through a Cultural Studies Lens." *Asian Communication Research* 9: 5–22.

Lee, Moonhaeng. 2013. "Star Management of Talent Agencies and Social Media in Korea." In *Handbook of Social Media Management*, ed. M. Friedrichsen and W. Muhl-Benninghaus, 549–64. Berlin: Springer-Verlag.

Lee, Soobum, and Hyejung Ju. 2011. "The Meaning of Korean Dramas in Japanese Fandom: Re-emerging Sentiment of 'Asianness.'" In *Hallyu: Influence of Korean Popular Culture in Asia and Beyond*, ed. Do Kyun Kim and Min-Sun Kim, 273–304. Seoul: Seoul National University Press.

Lewis, Randy. 2013. "Psy's 'Gentleman' Is YouTube's Most-Viewed Video of 2013." *Los Angeles Times*, December 11.

Lie, John. 2012. "What Is the K in K-Pop? South Korean Popular Music, the Culture Industry, and National Identity." *Korea Observer* 43 (3): 339–63.

Maliangkay, Roald. 2010. "Keep Your Enemies Closer: Protecting Korea's Pop Culture in China." *Korean Histories* 2 (1): 34–44.

Maliangkay, Roald, and Geng Song. 2014. "A Sound Wave of Effeminacy: K-pop and the Male Beauty Ideal in China." In *K-Pop—The International Rise of the Korean Pop Music Industry*, ed. JungBong Choi and Roald Maliangkay, 164–77. London: Routledge.

Mattelart, Armand. 1979. *Multinational Corporations and the Control of Culture: the Ideological Apparatus of Imperialism.* Cambridge: Harvard University Press.

Miller, Toby, Nitin Govil, John MuMurria, Richard Maxwell, and Ting Wang. 2005. *Global Hollywood 2.* London: British Film Institute Press.

Montgomery, James. 2013. "Psy's Looking to Release an Album Just in Time for 'Summer Season.'" *MTV*, May 22.

Mori, Yoshitaka. 2008. "*Winter Sonata* and Cultural Practices of Active Fans in Japan: Considering Middle-Aged Women as Cultural Agents." In *East Asian Pop Culture: Analyzing the Korean Wave*, ed. Beng Huat Chua and Koichi Iwabuchi, 127–41. Hong Kong: Hong Kong University Press

Nam, Siho. 2013. "The Cultural Political Economy of the Korean Wave in East Asia: Implications for Cultural Globalization Theories." *Asian Perspective* 37: 209–31.

Netburn, Deborah. 2012. "Giddy Up! S. Korean Rapper Psy's 'Gangnam Style' is Unstoppable." *Los Angeles Times*, August 4.

Noh, Kwang Woo. 2011. "A Study on the Transnational Circulation of K-Pop through YouTube: The Case of Girls' Generation's Online Fandom." Conference paper, Korean Society for Journalism and Communication Studies.

Oh, Ingyu, and Gil-Sung Park. 2012. "From B2C to B2B: Selling Korean Pop Music in the Age of New Social Media." *Korea Observer* 43 (4): 365–97.

Park, Jane Chi Hyun. 2010. "Remaking the Korean Romcom: A Case Study of *Yeopgijeogin geunyeo* and *My Sassy Girl.*" In *Complicated Currents: Media Flows, Soft Power and East Asia.* Accessed at http://books.publishing.monash.edu/apps/bookworm/view/Complicated+Currents/122/xhtml/chapter13.html.

Park, Jung-Sun. 2004. "Korean American Youths' Consumption of Korean and Japanese TV Dramas and Its Implication." In *Feeling Asian Modernities: Transnational Consumption of Japanese TV Dramas*, ed. Koichi Iwabuchi, 275–300. Hong Kong: Hong Kong University Press.

Park, Myung-Jin, and James Curran, eds. 2000. *De-Westernizing Media Studies.* New York: Routledge.

Pease, Rowan. 2006. "Internet, Fandom, and K-Wave in China." In *Korean Pop Music: Riding the Wave*, ed. Keith Howard, 176–89. Kent, UK: Global Oriental.

Pease, Rowan. 2009. "Korean Pop Music in China: Nationalism, Authenticity, and Gender." In *Cultural Studies and Cultural Industries in Northeast Asia: What a Difference a Region Makes*, ed. Chris Berry, Nicola Liscutin, and Jonathan D. Mackintosh, 151–68. Hong Kong: Hong Kong University Press.

Ramstad, Evan. 2011. "YouTube Helps South Korean Band Branch Out." *Wall Street Journal*, January 14.

Russell, Mark J. 2008. *Pop Goes Korea: Behind the Revolution in Movies, Music, and Internet Culture.* Berkeley, CA: Stone Bridge Press.

Ryoo, Woongjae. 2009. "Globalization, or the Logic of Cultural Hybridization: The Case of the Korean Wave." *Asian Journal of Communication* 19 (2): 137–51.

Schiller, Herbert I. 1976. *Communication and Cultural Domination.* New York: International Arts and Sciences Press.

Schou, Solvej. 2012. "'Hey, Sexy Lady!' Korean Rapper Psy Has a Viral Moment with 'Gangnam Style.'" *Entertainment Weekly*, August 23.

Sekoff, Hallie. 2012. "PSY's 'Gangnam Style': K-Pop Star's Viral Comeback Is Impossible to Resist (Video)." *Huffington Post*, August 1.

Shim, Doobo. 2005. "Globalization and Cinema Regionalization in East Asia." *Korea Journal* 45 (4): 233–60.

Shim, Doobo. 2006. "Hybridity and the Rise of Korean Popular Culture in Asia." *Media, Culture and Society* 28 (1): 25–44.

Shim, Doobo. 2008. "The Growth of Korean Cultural Industries and the Korean Wave." In *East Asian Pop Culture: Analysing the Korean Wave*, ed. Beng Huat Chua and Koichi Iwabuchi, 15–31. Hong Kong: Hong Kong University Press.

Shim, Doobo. 2010. "Whither the Korean Media?" In *Pop Culture Formations across East Asia*, ed. Soobo Shim, Ariel Heryanto, and Ubonrat Siriyuvasak, 115–34. Seoul: Ji-moondang.

Shin, Chi-yun. 2008. "Art of Branding: Tartan 'Asian Extreme' Films." *Jump Cut* 50. Accessed at http://www.ejumpcut.org/archive/jc50.2008/TartanDist/text.html.

Shin, Hochang, and Hyungshin Roh. 2011. "*Hallyu* as a Strategic Marketing Key in the Korean Media Content Industry." In *Hallyu: Influence of Korean Popular Culture in Asia and Beyond*, ed. Do Kyun Kim and Min-Sun Kim, 339–430. Seoul: Seoul National University Press.

Shin, Jeeyoung. 2005. "Globalization and New Korean Cinema." In *New Korean Cinema*, ed. Julian Stringer and Shin Chi-yun, 51–62. New York: New York University Press.

Shin, Kyeong-mi (Sin, Kyŏng-mi). 2006a. "Hallyu yŏlp'ung ŭn Asia kongtong munhwa ch'angch'ul ŭi kiwŏdŭ: Ilbon ŭi Hallyu" (The Hot Korean Wave Is the Key Word to the Creation of Asian Common Culture: Korean Wave in Japan). In *Tong Asia ŭi Hallyu* (Korean Wave in East Asia), ed. Yoon-Whan Shin and Han-Woo Lee, 221–61. Seoul: ChŏnyewŏnShin.

Shin, Yoon-Whan (Sin, Yun-hwan). 2006b. "Tong Asia ŭi Hallyu rŭl ponŭn nun: tamnon kwa silch'e" (A View of the Korean Wave in East Asia: Discourses and Reality). In *Tong Asia ŭi Hallyu* (Korean Wave in East Asia), ed. Yoon-Whan Shin and Han-Woo Lee, 221–61. Seoul: Chŏnyewŏn.

Sinclair, John. 1996. "Culture and Trade: Some Theoretical and Practical Considerations." In *Mass Media and Free Trade: NAFTA and the Cultural Industries*, ed. Emilie G. McAnany and Kenton T. Vilkinson, 30–62. Austin: University of Texas Press.

Sohn, Seung-hye (Son, Sŭng-hye). 2009. "Haksul nonmun ŭi met'a punsŏk ŭl t'onghae pon Hallyu 10-yŏn" (Ten Years of Hallyu, the "Korean Wave": What We Have Learned about It). *Ŏllon kwa sahoe* (Media and Society) 17 (4): 122–53.

Straubhaar, Joseph D. 1991. "Beyond Media Imperialism: Assymetrical Interdependence and Cultural Proximity." *Critical Studies in Mass Communication* 8 (1): 39–59.

Sung, Sang-yeon. 2006. "The Hanliu Phenomenon in Taiwan: TV Dramas and Teenage Pop." In Korean Pop Music: Riding the Wave, ed. Keith Howard, 168–75. Kent, UK: Global Oriental.

Tokita, Alison. 2010. "*Winter Sonata* and the Politics of Memory." In *Complicated Currents: Media Flows, Soft Power and East Asia*. Melbourne: Monash University ePress. Accessed at http://books.publishing.monash.edu/apps/bookworm/view/Complicated+Currents/122/xhtml/chapter3.html.

Tomlinson, John. 1991. *Cultural Imperialism: A Critical Introduction*. London: Continuum.

Tomlinson, John. 1999. *Globalization and Culture*. Chicago: University of Chicago Press.

Wasko, Janet. 2001. *Understanding Disney: The Manufacture of Fantasy*. Cambridge: Polity Press.

Williamson, Lucy. 2011. "The Dark Side of South Korean Pop Music." BBC News Asia-Pacific, June 14. Accessed at http://www.bbc.co.uk/news/world-asia-pacific-13760064.

Yang, Jonghoe. 2012. "The Korean Wave (*Hallyu*) in East Asia: A Comparison of Chinese, Japanese, and Taiwanese Audiences Who Watch Korean TV Dramas." *Development and Society* 41 (1): 103–47.

Yecies, Brian. 2007. "Parleying Culture against Trade: Hollywood's Affairs with Korea's Screen Quotas." *Korea Observer* 38 (1): 1–32.

Yecies, Brian. 2010. "Inroads for Cultural Traffic: Breeding Korea's Cinematiger." In *Complicated Currents: Media Flows, Soft Power and East Asia*. Accessed at http://books.publishing.monash.edu/apps/bookworm/view/Complicated+Currents/122/xhtml/chapter10.html.

Yin, Kelly Fu Su, and Kai Khiun Liew. 2005. "Hallyu in Singapore: Korean Cosmopolitanism or the Consumption of Chineseness?" *Korea Journal* 45 (4): 206–32.

Yun, Gyong-woo (Yun, Kyŏng-u). 2009. "Chungguk ŭi Hallyu suyong yangsang: sŏnt'aekchŏk suyong,chŏhang, kŭrigo pyŏnyong mit chubyŏnhwa" (The Korean Wave in China: Selective Reception, Resistance, Transformation, and Marginalization). *Chung-So yŏn'gu* (Studies on China and Russia) 120: 199–238.

PART 1.

New Agendas

1

Hallyu versus Hallyu-hwa

Cultural Phenomenon versus Institutional Campaign

JungBong Choi

The Fuzziness of Hallyu Boundaries

Are the meaning and boundaries of Hallyu transparent? At first glance, little seems terribly opaque. Common descriptions of Hallyu tend to merge on the soaring popularity of Korean television dramas, films, music, as well as some idols and beauty products in foreign countries. Contrary to this descriptive clarity, however, few can confidently pinpoint the logic by which one determines what counts as Hallyu or what does not.[1] For example, is every Korean TV drama a legitimate part of Hallyu or only those commanding a measure of commercial success in markets abroad? Similarly, is every Korean music genre a part of Hallyu or only the particular types known as K-pop? What about films, cartoons, and video games with a resounding domestic success yet lukewarm international reception?

If *Hallyu* is not an indiscriminating term referencing "whatever" in Korean popular culture, the next question one has to raise in applying the term is "Who makes the decision and by what standard?" In fact, the answer is quite antidramatic; much of it depends on the response of overseas fans, regardless of the situation in Korea. After all, *Hallyu* is meant to signify the tidal wave of Korean popular cultures generated outside Korea. However, this does not offer a satisfactory answer to the conundrum of Hallyu's fuzzy boundary. Let us zoom out and take a macroscopic view. Suppose that Hallyu is defined as a transnationally expanding current wherein cultural products of/from Korea *by and large* are fervently sought after. One must ask, then, whether or not the Korean-language boom in Southeast Asia can be considered a part of the phenomenon, and, by the same token, whether or not the rising popularity of the Samsung Galaxy S-class smartphones has a place in it.

The question being tackled here is "What specific cultural forms/genres/categories does Hallyu encompass?" No doubt that popular culture is the mainstay. But few can say if it is confined to the entertainment sector only, or rather freely roves across other zones of culture, broadly construed. A moving target as it is, Hallyu has evolved since the late 1990s, tirelessly traversing other cultural domains such as food, language, fashion, tourism, beauty products, and the like. Following this pattern of expansion, there hardly is any justification for excluding the large market share of Choco Pie in Russia, Nongshim Cup Noodles in China, NCSOFT's *Guild Wars 2* in the United States, or LG plasma television sets in the Middle East from the roster of Hallyu.

Since Hallyu bestrides various sections of culture—popular, public, anthropological, and quotidian—let us be equally "broad-minded," and take a liberal stance toward it. Even then we are faced with another set of befuddling questions: Are we certain that Hallyu is a "cultural" matter? Has Hallyu not moved beyond the purview of culture into the neighborhood of diplomacy and export industry? And, more fundamentally, can Hallyu—and the concept of culture itself as well—be severed from what is considered "nonculture," such as technology, education, business, and politics? My stance is simple. It would be a flagrant mistake to nail Hallyu down to a "cultural" matter in its narrowest sense. The plastic and networked nature of Hallyu defies any certitude regarding the border between culture in general and economy or politics, let alone the one between popular cultures and daily routines.

It is not my goal to rehash the century-long debate about the notion of culture, running from Matthew Arnold and Frank Raymond Leavis through Bronislaw Malinowski and Raymond Williams all the way down to Andreas Huyssen and James Clifford.[2] My aim is first to question the assumed intelligibility of Hallyu and its reach, and second to annotate the differing desires of two major forces underlying the mobility of its boundary. Curiously enough, discussions on Hallyu so far have barely illuminated the inexactitude of Hallyu's boundaries, and how its alterability correlates with the question of governance over the substance of it. My position is that the volatility of Hallyu's edge—although same can be said of any cultural matters in today's transnational mishmash—testifies to the unceasing negotiation among the affective and cultural stakeholders over the curious surge of popular cultures from the periphery. Hence, I consider the fluidity a clue indispensable for the identification of two principal players in charge of re/shaping Hallyu's substance and boundary. In what follows, I shall discuss what I call the duplex governance system, or simply, biformity in Hallyu that materializes in two different manifestations: as a transnational cultural phenomenon and as a national-institutional campaign. Let me stress that my study does not focus on the production and reception of Korean popular cultures in the domestic setting, because, again, I define Hallyu as the phenomenal success of Korean cultures in **overseas** markets.[3]

Classifying Hallyu Modules

Let me begin with a brief discussion on the stratified configuration of Hallyu. There is an abundance of journalistic and industrial reports that survey the multilayered edifice of Hallyu. It appears that a concentric circle model cataloging various components of Hallyu is a common approach shared by many Hallyu pundits in Korea.[4]

In figure 1, the smaller the size of a circle, the greater its impact on generating spinoffs and broadening the diameter of Hallyu. But not only is this a simplistic model but also void of any discernible account for the intercircular relationship. A more structured anatomy of Hallyu that takes into account its evolving mechanism would look more or less like this table 1.

One can add more elaborate breakdowns in accordance with specific modes of development in different geocultural areas and with demographic groups. A potential drawback of this technical classification is, however, its inability to identify the impetus that causes the multipronged propagation of Hallyu, which may also breed a false impression that Hallyu is a self-governing organism immune from human/institutional interventions. Hence, this clean-cut chart is in need of hermeneutic enrichments with analytic and interpretive strength in grasping the erratic kinesis of Hallyu boundaries. For this reason, an ethnographic study offering firsthand, detailed accounts by Hallyu fans would be of great help. In fact, a number of respondents to the online survey on Hallyu and K-pop I conducted suggest how "leaky" and open-ended the boundary of Hallyu is and how intricately braided the circuitry of culture is with other membranes of society.[5] The following is a statement from a female K-pop fan in Indonesia.

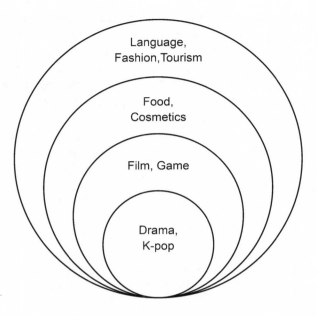

Fig. 1. Stratification of Hallyu

TABLE 1. Concentric Model of Hallyu

Category	Content
Essential content	Television dramas, K-pop, and other media products
Semiessential content	Films, videogames, performing arts, and foods
Para-Hallyu products/services	Tourism, cosmetic products, plastic surgery, fashion items, and language service
Distributive channels	Broadcast/satellite/cable televisions, overseas cultural/educational institutions, diasporic community/media, social-network media, and the Internet
Short-/long-term effects	Sales improvement in content industries/retail business, positive impacts on national image/branding, and higher competitiveness in international trade and public diplomacy

I got to know K-pop before knowing other Korean popular cultures. For a lot of people, K-pop and Korean dramas is [sic] the entryway to knowing other Korean popular cultures. It open [sic] up the opportunity for people to broaden their knowledge about Korea. To understand K-pop and dramas better, I've studied Korean language for three years and continue to be an active speaker. I participated in various Korean culture activities where I interacted with native Koreans and learned of their culture. I once learned how to make rice cake soup for the lunar new year's day celebration, also how to properly do the new year's greetings. I've had bibimbop, ddokbokki, bulgogi, champpong, kimbap, and many more. I learned how to play various traditional Korean games, yet I've forgotten their names. It has definitely made me seriously consider continuing my graduate studies there. I have heard that they have exceptional education quality and the local culture seems very interesting to explore. K-pop idols promote good, clean looks and this has drawn me to their cosmetic products. BB creams are becoming really popular lately, but I love The Face Shop products because the makeup and treatment products they provide don't create bad effects for the skin.

Obviously, the elasticity of Hallyu has a lot to do with both the structured-ness of human interest and the multidimensional nature of culture that inextricably crisscrosses other provinces of everyday life. Based on this tale, one can possibly construct a flow chart that illustrates how the boundary of Hallyu shifts: for example, listening to K-pop → watching Korean drama → joining online fan clubs for Korean popular cultures in general → trying Korean food → learning Korean language → purchasing Korean cosmetic/electronic goods → studying abroad in Korea → making Korean friends → picking up cultural idioms and local, traditional customs → launching personal blogs on Korea → working for Korea-related institutions of various sorts.

Though seldom unidirectional or mono-patterned as delineated in figure 2, the hypothetical arc that unfolds from media products via culinary, linguistic, and educational experiences to socioeconomic engagements is not quite fictitious. In fact, similar narratives are found among the answers provided by other respondents, albeit with some variations. Here are some more.

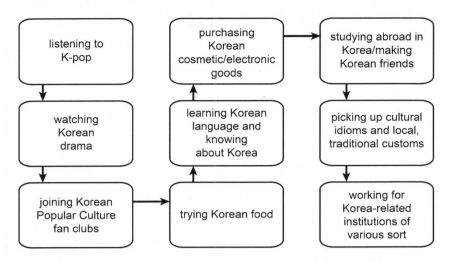

Fig. 2. Hypothetical flow of action

To me K-pop is more than just music; K-pop is like adapting to a new lifestyle. . . . When taking interest in K-pop you automatically set aside some of your prejudice and you're willing to try something new. I could almost say it's a fact that your daily routine will change dramatically once you become really into K-pop (there's so much to see and catch up with and so on). (A female fan from the United States)

K-pop and dramas have definitely motivated me to learn Korean. I've studied Korean actively for around four months. Ever since I began listening to K-pop I've been interested in the language (when hearing the same words being repeated in different songs and TV shows, it's easy to form a basic vocabulary). I believe I appreciate K-pop more than before now that I actually can read, write, and understand what is being said and not having to entirely rely on translations provided by the fans. (A male fan from Malaysia)

Before I got interested in Korean dramas I did not have any idea about the way of thinking or acting in Korea. I belonged to the group of people who only knew that the country's capital is Seoul and that Samsung is Korean. By getting to know Korean dramas I've learned so much about the cultural differences between Korea and Western countries, which I really appreciate! Nowadays I tend to compare a

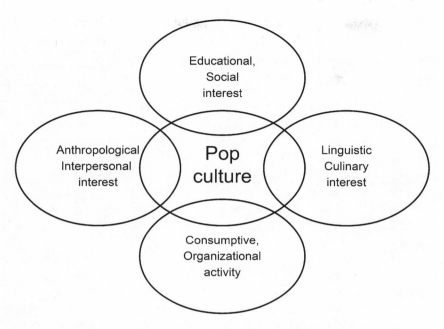

Fig. 3. Interlocking structure of Hallyu models

lot of thing I encounter with the Korean equivalents to see what new knowledge I can find. (A female fan from Germany)

Again, what these statements point up is that culture, like a rhizome, consists of countless connective tissues extending across theoretically divided sections of human life and interests. It may not devour other social instances like religion, education, economy, sports, or politics; but none of the latter is free from the permeation of and some degree of fusion with the former. The same holds true for Hallyu, perhaps more so than others. As illustrated below, the core of Hallyu infiltrates other contiguous zones. And it is through this movement that the boundaries and constituencies of Hallyu get redefined (figure 3).

What Causes the Border Porosity in Hallyu

Here let me briefly touch on three domestic conditions that keep the boundaries of Hallyu protean to an unusual degree, namely, the despecialization of the culture industry, the synchronization of social and cultural changes, and the near-ubiquity of digital technologies. First, the peculiar formation of cultural landscapes in Korea is a keystone for the polygonal yet overlaying pattern of Hallyu. Popular cultures in Korea grow out of the airtight interdependence among various sectors of the creative industry, which endows multitalented celebrities with untrammeled mobility across diverse genres—film, dramas, talk shows, popular music, musicals, comedy shows, advertisements, home shopping, and the like. This in turn encourages what might be called intermedia or intergenre pollination, a practice enforced by three powerful broadcasters in their desperate effort to streamline the nation's finite human/creative resources.

For Hallyu fans, the media/genre "incest" would mean a boon, since their beloved idols would sing, talk, act, run, or even sell products in a variety of programs/genres/media, presenting different looks and personae. Cruising along the path of the intermedia/intergenre nexus, Hallyu fans are prone to widen their interest in and exposure to the greater topography of Korean culture. Conversely, the perimeter of Hallyu gets broadened in proportion with the breadth of the cultural knowledge Hallyu fans accumulates. Just as Hallyu is a platform to thrust people's interest in Korean popular culture into other socio-anthropological matters of the nation, random curiosities about Korean society can reversely funnel into Hallyu. It must be noted that the intermedia/intergenre kinship is not just endemic to the industry; it resembles the unique social formation of such small nations as Korea, which usually exhibit a higher degree of societal density. In this respect, it is not surprising that variegated modules of Hallyu are closely adjoined and imbricated, like fish scales.

Second is the synchronization of the social and the cultural. One can hardly deny that the country's formidable leap forward in economic globalization and social democratization forms the backbone of the robust growth in its cultural faculty. It has enriched and diversified the cultural foundation of the formerly secluded society by prompting brisk flows of people, capital, knowledge, goods, and language on an increasingly global scale. The dizzying transformation and its staggering speed, however, have left the nation with plenty of side effects: political unrests, social hysteria, institutional violence, and, above all, dramatic/traumatic human stories—priceless raw materials from the standpoint of artistic and cultural productions. In a way, the appeal of Korean television dramas is comparable to the rise of melodramas following the calamitous experience of French Revolution. They commonly exhibit sentimentalism in mood, convolutedness in plot, excess in style, and illogical jumps in narrative, traits also found in the U.S. soap operas and Latin American telenovelas. It can be argued that Korean television shows, films, and music are an oblique narration of, and a roundabout testimony to, the stunning yet tumultuous transformation the nation has undergone. On the proscenium called Hallyu, hence, there unfolds a wealth of intriguing plays about the nation's unique path to modernization and strife to confront turbulent social changes before the curious eyes of its cultural neighbors.

Another indispensable factor is the national preoccupation with digital technologies, which have become part and parcel of the unruly expansion of Hallyu. For younger generations, digital technologies/media are akin to what Erving Goffman (1961) calls a "total institution": they embody virtually anything and everything, ranging from identity, fashion statements, and socialization to learning tools and friendship, not to mention a wide window on the world of popular cultures. By merging digital media, Hallyu is fast becoming an all-encompassing technological regime that affords the user synesthetic experiences along myriad functions the media can perform: work/play, read/watch, make/spend, create/copy, study/space out, talk/listen, buy/sell, socialize / bunker in, and so on. The boundary of Hallyu could have been far narrower and simpler than it now is, were it not for the versatility of social media and digital technologies Korea manages to retain its competitive edge.

The Biformity of Hallyu: Content Production and Cultural Production

All cultural boundaries or categories involve a degree of imprecision. Hence, the trouble in perceiving the outer margin of Hallyu relative to the ease in identifying its core may not seem particularly unusual. Take national cinema for example. One would readily agree that the nucleus of contemporary Korean national cinema entails such figures as Im Kwon-taek, Park Chan-wook, Kim Ki-duk, Hong Sang-soo, Lee Chang-dong, and arguably Bong Joon-ho. But can diasporic films also lay claim to a seat in the chamber of national cinema? This would be a contentious issue, because the farther one moves away from the center of a cultural category, the trickier it becomes to decide. Indeed, defining the edge of cultural boundary is always a politically hazardous task.

Yet the instance of Hallyu differs from the case of profiling a national cinema. First and foremost, Hallyu is not necessarily defined in terms of an ethnonational paradigm in the way national cinema is—for example,

Chinese, Taiwanese, or Australian cinemas. Second, while national cinema only designates the locus of "origin" in cinematic production, the term *Hallyu* designates both the origin of content and the site at which it has gained currency to the degree meriting a "cultural wave" label. Let us remind ourselves, again, that *Hallyu* (Korean Wave) denotes not Korean popular culture per se, but the high tide of Korean culture in non-Korean territories. For Koreans residing in Korea, the "Korean Wave" label would be gratuitous, for it simply is "domestic" popular cultures, no matter how hybridized they are.[6]

Here, the *elsewhere-ness* intrinsic to Hallyu cannot be overemphasized. For it foregrounds the question of governance in the Hallyu phenomenon and, more directly, the significance of non-Korean nationals as one of the main engines of Hallyu.[7] Put differently, not only does Hallyu imply two geographic sites—Korea and elsewhere—but it also alludes to two autonomous agencies in content production on the one hand and cultural production on the other. The former is primarily responsible for the production of Hallyu *content*, while the latter is for the production of the Hallyu phenomenon.

Of course, the wave cannot wake by itself without content provision from the creative industries in Korea. But this does not disprove that fans outside Korea are the bona fide "producer" of the Hallyu phenomenon. The elsewhere-ness or exteriority, ironically speaking, is central to the axis of Hallyu governance, an axis formed where content production merges with cultural production.[8] In other words, the web of governance in the Hallyu phenomenon is woven along the interaction between content production mainly by the creative industry in Korea and cultural production by the overseas fans of Korean cultural products.[9]

Content production vis-à-vis cultural production, as well as two agencies involved in the respective areas, can be grasped in terms of cultural *formulation* and cultural *formation*. As a cultural formulation, Hallyu is in the realm of engineering, a synthetic arrangement of cultural flows administered by the syndicate of Korean state officials, electronics conglomerates, and the media industry. As a cultural formation, on the other hand, the substance and boundary of Hallyu is an expression of the aggregate desire and practice of fans—or users and "consumers"[10]—dispersed athwart multiple localities, who mold intricate feed-forward/feedback loops with the former, the "official" steersmen of Hallyu. The biformity of Hallyu, like Janus, has one head with two faces, united but not uniform. This makes the Hallyu phenomenon a crosscurrent moving along the interaction between cultural formulation and cultural formation. The following two sections will explicate the biformity of Hallyu in some more details.

Hallyu as a Cultural Phenomenon/Process

Seeing Hallyu as a cultural phenomenon/process means acknowledging the significance of cultural production independently of content production. At the same time, it means duly crediting the people whose actions shape the long cultural processes subsequent to the initial production of Hallyu content. The reason why I state what appears to be axiomatic is to underscore the "ownership" issue of Hallyu. Bluntly put, Korea is not in possession of Hallyu. By denying the exclusive ownership of Korea over Hallyu, I do not wish to catapult it into the obscure, universalizing discourse of nation-less hybridity. The Korean creative industry irrefutably remains the linchpin in the protean architecture of Hallyu. Nonetheless, Hallyu as a transnational cultural phenomenon is profoundly dependent on the cultural masonry carried out by a legion of underrecognized "craftsmen," namely, overseas fans.

Nothing is inherently wrong with Koreans taking pride in Hallyu, of course. Yet the belief that the origin and ownership of Hallyu are in the hands of Korea/ns is an egregiously false assumption. The tacit yet pervasive misconception proliferated by mainstream media, state officials, and even some entrepreneurs in Korea conspires with two interrelated, problematical stances. The first is an overemphasis on the productive force of cultural content, that is, writers, composers, directors, singers, actors/actresses, management companies, stars, and so on. The second is a disseminationist view on the cultural phenomenon, whereby Hallyu is perceived as a linear propagation from the productive core to the consumptive periphery—in this case, from Korea to the world. The proprietary consciousness of Hallyu exhibited by various social groups in Korea is simultaneously a root cause for and a corollary of these two questionable ideas. As a matter of fact, the dispersed ownership of Hallyu held by countless overseas "shareholders" does affect in various fashions the vector, volume, and velocity of the transnational cultural phenomenon in different stages.

Remedying the proprietary consciousness over what is essentially a "transnational common" is not an easy task. But understanding the dispersed nature of agency in cultural phenomena would certainly help. Generally speaking, there are different types of creative agencies in cultural phenomena, agencies exercised by content makers, financiers, distributors/brokers, policymakers, and the fans. Note here that the very term fan, together with other cognate concepts like user, consumer, and audience, falls far short of representing the magnitude held by the people involved in the labor of cultural nourishment and refinement. These are deficient concepts, if not outright misnomers, unable to capture the roles and functions of those so labeled in the area of cultural participation. While deserving the designations of "cultural curators," they are misconceived to be complacent shoppers at the receiving end. Contrary to the ancillary role pictured from the standpoint of market and content production, they are in fact protagonists in the theater of semantic and socio-anthropological constructions of Hallyu. Movers and shakers of the transnational cultural affairs, they do indeed curate, manage, and catalyze the formation of the Hallyu phenomenon.

The life of Hallyu as a cultural process/phenomenon does not begin or end with the supply of content as such. Instead, it is animated by affective and communicative actions taken by overseas fans who also are in close contact with domestic fans through various channels. Therefore, the fan is a vital force *interior* to the workings of Hallyu as a cultural process, though *exterior* to the productive site of Hallyu content, both geographically and physically. Conversely speaking, the fan's exteriority to content production is integral to the semantic and sociocultural practice of Hallyu as a cultural phenomenon/process. In spite of the lack in organizational hubs, these agents shape interactive circuits through fan-club sites, YouTube, Twitter, concerts, and conventions, among other forms of interaction.

The swift establishment of so-called social media in particular affords distinct ecosystems for cultural interactions, endowing the myriad of cultural craftsmen with heightened capacity to redesign the productive and distributive patterns for what was initially offered to them. A Polish respondent to the online survey I conducted said,

> Through Twitter and Facebook we get closer to the idols and can see how they are in real life. Nowadays a lot of K-pop idols have Twitter accounts. Besides, it's a very good way to communicate with fans from other countries. I think Twitter and Facebook give fans closer contact with idols and other fans than TV or Radio does.

She sees the social media as an empowering tool that enhances the communicative accessibility to stars and the collectivity among fans scattered across different places. Another respondent from the United Arab Emirates (UAE) confirms the solidarity-fostering function of social media:

Through Twitter and Facebook I could meet with other K-pop fans around the world. . . . TV and radio are more limited and they don't connect us with other people or help share photos, info, and thoughts. Even though there are many radio shows that accept phone calls, they are still limited in time, but Facebook and Twitter are all time around [*sic*].

Indeed, the Hallyu *culture* has been shaped and altered by fans themselves, who shoulder the role not just of information provider/mediator/distributor but also of cultural designer/administrator. The fan from UAE indicated,

UAElovesKorea is a forum founded by my friend and her sisters. Through the forum I could share any news related to Korean cultural events here in UAE. Also in my previous college, Abu Dhabi Women's College, there is a fan club that is just about anything related to Korea, and similar ones are at Zayed University and Al Ain University. So we have lots of clubs that are active in sharing Korean cultures, for which I volunteer here in UAE.

Online fan clubs are arguably by far the most powerful pacesetters of Hallyu and K-pop fandoms. The ones that stand head and shoulders above the rest are Soompi and allkpop, multimedia online fansites, into which a nonstop flurry of information, gossips, reviews, rumors, comments, and videos are streamed. They run their own newsrooms, galleries, forums, shops, and even music charts. "It's definitely allkpop," says the Polish respondent, "where I can find a lot of information about my favorite artists." The immediacy and unmediated-ness of this site by means of English language, crowdsourcing, and a poly-media system epitomize the type of creative spurs and interventions fans give to Hallyu flows. "What is more," she continues, "it's the best source of news about Korean music, dramas, etc. It's in English so it's easy for me to understand. Moreover, I think allkpop has verified information because it has so many different sources and informed fans. There are other sites I frequently use: sup3rjunior and dbsknights."

There is no question that content production is a prerequisite for the cultural production of Hallyu. But the Hallyu phenomena fashioned by the cultural catalysts do "produce" another form of "content" integral to the next stage production of Hallyu content. This reciprocation/confluence between content production and cultural production does counter the above-mentioned linear, disseminationist framework whereby cultural productions are speciously construed derivative of the "original" content production. It is nearly impossible to grasp Hallyu without proper understanding of the reasons why Hallyu contents are hailed by the overseas fan, how these products are handled and reprocessed—as opposed to received and consumed—and how the act of caring and engaging these products is generative of the cultural climates under which the next stage production of Hallyu content is envisioned and conditioned, if not determined. Hence, the myopic and monistic view of production, products, and producers has to be renegotiated, or better yet, replaced with a multifocal perspective on Hallyu as a fluid cultural ecology in which nominal distinctions across producers, distributors, and users of Hallyu content dissolve into a larger system of *creative cultural participation*.

Hallyu as a Campaign/Policy Initiative

Understanding Hallyu as a polycentric process of creative cultural participation is critical. However, there are some limits in viewing Hallyu as a transnational cultural phenomenon only. After all, Hallyu is neither just cultural in its valence nor determined solely by international fans. I argue that Hallyu has to be seen also as a national-institutional campaign with clear ambitions reaching beyond the cultural domain. Should the word campaign sound too strong, one might instead use the term *policy initiative* without necessarily toning down the purported meaning of Hallyu as a planned, concerted effort for the whole of Korea's national interest.

To regard Hallyu as Korea's national policy initiative is to emphasize the following aspects. First, Hallyu is not an organic manifestation of rational market exchange in a cultural economy, nor is it an upshot of the fortuitous crossing of cultural supply and demand. It might have been so at the incipient phase, but lately some new dynamics are set in full motion. Second, while being a cultural outgrowth, certain aspects of Hallyu can be seen as a bureaucratic program operated from the stage of preproduction through the stage of marketing. Due to the exponential growth in value and gross revenue, a good portion of Hallyu has become a government-steered undertaking commissioned to the creative industry but intensely arbitrated by numerous state bureaus that once were extraneous to Hallyu. Third, Hallyu means much more than an "export industry" for Korea; it is the fulcrum with which national accumulation of "symbolic capital" in Bourdieuian[11] sense is leveraged, the tool with which the nation's stature can be boosted in the race for global prestige and what Antonio Gramsci calls "hegemony."[12]

Hallyu as a national campaign is helmed by a handful of entrepreneurs, mainstream media, state bureaucrats, and professional consultants, mostly based in Korea. The quorum administers the allocation of human/material resources to magnetize cultural, economic, and diplomatic returns. For such Korean chaebol as Samsung, LG, Amorepacific, Orion, and to a lesser extent, Hyundai, Hallyu is an unprecedented windfall. Nearly every commercial advertisement they produce features Hallyu stars in an obvious effort to impress their products in the expanding register of Hallyu as well as in the mind of Hallyu fans. Consumer-electronics giants, Samsung and LG in particular, avidly interpolate their mobile devices into the affect economy of Hallyu by fanning mythic narratives that their commodities intrinsically champion the "spirit" of Hallyu and the lifestyles global youths root for. The boundary of Hallyu gets altered through this act of forging a long product-association chain, whereby images and motifs of existing Hallyu are speciously concatenated with hot commodities such as cellular phones and 3D televisions.

On the other hand, the intervention of the mainstream media is most pronounced in the construction of discursive environments conducive to the unconditional national support for the global expansion of Hallyu. Notwithstanding genres—news, editorials, investigative reports, documentary programs, or talks shows—they feed the whole nation with a daily diet containing bombastic sagas of global Hallyu. The oversaturation of epic narratives about Hallyu paralyzes or forestalls any critical, oppositional voices, as exemplified by the recent case of Psy's "Gangnam Style." In fact, Psy's eccentric music video unambiguously transgresses the stylistic norms of K-pop and even lampoons the unstoppable progression of vulgar materialism in contemporary Korea, as epitomized by the lifestyle of the Gangnam area of Seoul.

Despite the critical undertone of the music video, mainstream media have crafted a cult status out of Psy by dwelling exclusively on the number of YouTube hits (over 1.9 billion as of February 17, 2014) and the song's phenomenal performance in the U.S. Billboard charts (see Brian Hu's chapter in this volume). Overwhelmed by the nationwide adulation pumped up by media, Psy has ceased to be a symbol of unruly subculture; instead, he has meekly capitulated to the new identity media industries have conferred on him, the heroic icon of globalizing K-pop and funky ambassador of Hallyu.

As the Psy occult indicates, the whole nation is about to plunge into euphoric hypnosis through the captivating spell of Hallyu. And the mainstream media acts like a wicked shaman amassing its cultural and political clout amidt the nation's narcotic state of mind. Ominously enough, the near-stoppage of counterdiscourses, not to mention self-criticism, bodes well for the surge of aggressive cultural nationalism in Korea that has already hitched a ride on the K-pop juggernaut. The high-flown tone of domestic media concerning Hallyu sounds strikingly redolent of the fascist propaganda that brutalizes reason, self-reflexivity, and doubt.

The corporate and media maneuvers cannot be divorced from state-initiated campaigns. Since the Kim Dae-jung administration entered office in 1998, the Korean government has seldom loosened its grip on the creative industry. Not surprisingly, the government has poured an obscene quantity of money for R & D (research and development) and PR (public relations) in addition to enacting business-favorable laws and direct financial support.[13] Take Korean food, for example, an item recently designated by the government to spearhead what it calls the "third phase" of Hallyu. The Lee Myung-bak government (2008–13) instituted the Korean Cuisine Globalization Committee in May 2009. The chairperson was then-incumbent First Lady Kim Yoon-ok. The committee engaged thirty-six "experts" including Yu In-chon (minister of culture, sports and tourism), Chang Tae-pyong (minister of food, agriculture, forestry and fisheries), as well as the chief executives of various food companies in Korea. Hallyu star Bae Yong-joon, who runs a number of Korean restaurants in Tokyo, was also appointed a committee member.

In her inaugural speech, the First Lady of Korea pronounced that "The globalization of hansik (Korean food) will not only help expand Hallyu but also help enhance Korea's global reputation" (Na 2009). Even U.S. ambassador Kathleen Stephens was involved in publicizing the campaign. She writes on the official website promoting tourism for Korea:

> I was pleased to be invited to a conference on April 7 dedicated to the globalization of Korean food. Korean Cuisine to the World 2009 highlighted a globalization plan for Korean cuisine and was hosted by the Presidential Commission for Future and Vision and the Ministry for Food, Agriculture, Forestry and Fisheries. Food experts from around the world and many government officials were in attendance, including First Lady Kim Yoon-ok. The announced goal is to establish Korean food as a major global cuisine.[14] (Stephens 2012).

Even before the launch of the committee, the government had unveiled an ambitious plan to make Korean food one of the five most popular ethnic foods in the world, and earmarked 50 billion won to open Korean cooking classes at world-renowned culinary schools. No news has been heard about the magnificent plan ever since. Notwithstanding, the committee announced an equally extravagant plan to increase the number of Korean restaurants overseas to 40,000 by 2017 and promote "the uniqueness and healthy nature" of the food. Under the auspices of the committee, numerous events have been organized, books published, and media spotlights given to the multi-billion-dollar endeavor. In August 2010, for example, the committee established the grandiosely named "United Food Globalization Committee" in Los Angeles to further promote Korean cuisine and culture in the United States. In August 2011, the Korean Culture Service (part of the Ministry of Foreign Affairs and Trade) and Korean Cuisine Globalization Committee jointly organized a food exhibition in Central Park in New York to showcase the most popular Korean dishes and demonstrate how they are made.

Interestingly, this event featured a booth for visitors to try on *hanbok* (traditional Korean outfits) and a K-pop contest wherein contestants competed for free round-trip tickets to Korea. Since the late 1990s, South Korean governments have remained pioneers on the cultural front, relentlessly blazing trails for Hallyu by laying new building blocks, such as Korean food and traditional costume, onto the solid ground of K-pop and dramas. Hallyu in this respect needs to be seen as a state-financed marketing stunt, not just a self-governing cultural occurrence. Much as an unstructured outbreak of cultural fever, it is also an expensive state initiative, albeit with no promise of success.

A revealing example is the amusement park HallyuWorld, yet another illustration of the administrative maneuver to reconfigure existing forms of the Hallyu phenomenon. This project was initially named Hallyuwood, a composite term mixing Hallyu with Hollywood, by the government of Gyeonggi Province, Korea, in 2008. In simple terms, HallyuWorld mimics the models provided by Universal Studio Tour or Disneyland, which consolidate theme parks, hotels, broadcasting and media facilities, commercial services, sports complexes, and waterside parks into a total entertainment space based on Hallyu contents. It is a colossal project with the professed aim of building "a world-class cluster of cultural and tourist infrastructure and a center of mass culture in East Asia."[15] The following recapitulates some of the objectives and expected results of HallyuWorld listed on its official website.[16]

- Nurture HallyuWorld as an outpost to lead the industrialization and globalization of Hallyu culture.
- Attract tourist and cultural facilities to promote consumption and distribution of Hallyu content.

- Develop HallyuWorld as a mecca of entertainment, combining tourism, culture, content, and IT.
- Create an industrial base to foster venture businesses in cultural content.
- Create jobs and train cultural specialists.
- Strengthen cultural capacities in the northwest Seoul metropolitan area and invigorate the local economy.

As shown, the innocence of Hallyu as a cultural affair is muddied, if not dead on arrival. A good portion of Hallyu is mortgaged to the administrative, economic, and political imperatives asserted by Korean corporations, media, and government. Yet lamenting the "adulteration" is pointless, for the clustering of cultural, economic, and political agendas is the fate of any transnational culture today. This, of course, does not mean that Hallyu as a cultural phenomenon will succumb to Hallyu as an institutional campaign. No success is guaranteed for the state-corporate-media intervention in redefining or expanding the boundary of Hallyu. In the end, the new Hallyu materials they put forward are only secondary and parasitic to the existing content hailed by transnational fans.

Therefore, one must be cautious not to overstate their power in charting the future course of Hallyu, while at the same time careful not to underplay the significance of Hallyu as an institutional campaign. In an odd sort of way, the state and other powerful institutions' attempt to arrogate Hallyu vindicates the significance of popular cultures in general and Hallyu in particular for academic research. No longer does it seem feasible for highbrow intelligentsias to disparage Hallyu as vacuous entertainment and a circus of infantile regression. It is a bizarrely "carnivalesque" site in the Bakhtinian sense (Bakhtin 1984), at which state power, corporate drive, and nationalist ideology "rub elbows" with popular youth culture, commodity cosmopolitanism, and social media.

The Inscrutable Zeal of Hallyu-hwa

In the paragraphs above I have made an analytic distinction between content production and cultural production in Hallyu. I did so in order to highlight the distinct agencies responsible for different attributes of the cultural phenomenon. Generally, they go hand in hand to keep Hallyu in motion. Another important distinction I made was the one between Hallyu as a cultural phenomenon/process and Hallyu as an institutional campaign. In the first instance, it refers to the warm reception and active use of Korean cultural goods in foreign markets, which owes itself to the creative participation of international fans in shaping the meaning and value of said artifacts. The second instance defines Hallyu as a conscious and concerted undertaking to expand its current scope by political and economic forces not directly involved in the Hallyu phenomenon. The first case is decidedly transnational in nature, whereas the second is unambiguously a national/ist project jointly run by the Korean government, Korea-based media/culture industries, and some corporate giants.

For both cases, my point was that Hallyu is not a natural but a "man-made" phenomenon. Identifying subjects at work is critical to understanding the ir/regularity and il/logic of Hallyu's shifting boundary. This is not to say that the agents are almighty, or what they try to achieve is guaranteed to succeed. To the contrary, much of the governmental initiative to add fuel to the current momentum of Hallyu has ended with less than mediocre results. Despite this uncertainty, the systematic and institutional effort to steer the direction of Hallyu begs thorough, critical examinations.

Hallyu, when seen as a national-institutional campaign, can be reconceptualized as what I would call *Hallyu-hwa*. Here, "hwa" is equivalent to "-ize" in English, denotative of "to cause to be" or "to become." One of the main properties of Hallyu-hwa is to envelop what was initially extrinsic to Hallyu, thereby expanding the latter's boundaries and repertoires. Through Hallyu-hwa, fields/objects bearing no direct relevance to media-based popular cultures—for example, tourism, cosmetic products, local traditional artifacts, medical services, or educational programs—are hemmed in by the "conscripting agent" Hallyu. Hallyu-hwa intensifies because Hallyu has proved to be something of a supercapital in the international marketplace of cultural esteem, the value of which is recognized also in the provinces of diplomacy, economy, and politics. Hence, *Hallyu-hwa* refers to a conscious and concerted effort to set preceding models of Hallyu (mostly media-based popular cultures) as a national template, after which other sectors of Korea are re/modeled to gain higher visibility in the global race for cultural prestige.

Thus construed, Hallyu-hwa is essentially a "political" movement fueled by the ever-growing influence of Korean popular cultures, mediated by the ethos of neoliberal globalization, and yet compelled by the nation's profound will to power. That is, with the notion of Hallyu-hwa, one can situate Hallyu within the nation's two-decade-long struggle to cast off the stigmatic tag of an "underdeveloped" society and to secure the prestigious membership of "developed"/"advanced" society. In this regard, Hallyu-hwa is as much a national project as a state-run program. It is so because a good majority of Korean nationals (i.e., the people) are emotionally invested and/or materially implicated in one way or another, even though it is carried out mainly by the government hand in hand with big corporations and mainstream/public media.

Though hard to substantiate, Hallyu is a godsend to realize the nation's intense desire to break away from the wretched trajectories of modern history. Hallyu is taken, deep in the national psyche of Korea, as a holy vehicle to exit the long, dark tunnel of postcolonial and Cold War adversities fraught with war, underdevelopment, tyranny, corruption, international obscurity, and indignity; a vehicle motored by the nation's determination to sprint to the stage of wealth, autonomy, and pride. Hallyu-hwa is a crystallization of the people's collective yearning in the form of state-initiated, media- and corporate-supported policy campaigns passionately espoused by the great majority of the nation. Entrenched in the trope of Hallyu-hwa, therefore, is the undertone of retribution, sublimation, and redemption.

As the title of this article suggests, I have talked about a crosscurrent in Hallyu. Both analytically and organizationally, Hallyu is less a unified phenomenon than a meeting of two distinct waves: one propelled by people outside Korea, the other by powerful institutions in Korea with a nationwide consensus. One is a labor of individual passion, while the other arises principally through collective, social desire. One seems innocuous, the other inexorable. Frankly speaking, the second Hallyu, or what I call *Hallyu-hwa*, is a contentious enterprise: politically questionable, economically untenable, and culturally unpolished. In addition, I find it hard to support the way in which Hallyu-hwa is executed: crude bureaucratic approaches, explicitly mercantile mind-sets, and all. Nevertheless, I cannot help being sympathetic to the inscrutable zeal behind it, the historical gravity and political solemnity it carries. And I would like to ask if I am alone having this ineffable ambivalence.

NOTES

1. The answer to this question might hinge on deciding what exactly *Hallyu* refers to.

2. It is no secret that the concept of culture is a notoriously treacherous terrain often lacking assuring signposts. The interminable debate with regard to the fuzzy foundation of culture led Tony Bennett (1980) to a profound skepticism toward any attempt to de-

fine it. He calls it a "melting pot of confused and contradictory meanings capable of misdirecting inquiry up any number of theoretical blind alleys" (18).

3. By no means is this to dismiss the fact that "domestic" and "overseas" production/receptions are closely knit into "transnational" dynamics.

4. For detailed information, see strategic reports on Hallyu in Webzine, published by Korea Foundation for International Culture Exchange (KOFICE). http://webzine.kofice.or.kr/eng.html.

5. The survey was conducted from February 22–29, 2012, on the website of the KBS World. Over 1,400 respondents from 84 countries participated in the study.

6. For some, the interior/exterior or national/foreign divide may appear incongruous with the unambiguously transnational nature of Hallyu. However, the analytic breakdown is a precondition for specifying particular modes of transnational interlocking in Hallyu.

7. It compels a redistribution of attention in Hallyu study, which is currently overapportioned to *content production* by the Korean culture industry. Of necessity for a due balance is beefing up ethnographic and cultural studies centering on *cultural production* by a multitude of Hallyu devotees across different localities.

8. The two areas of creative cultural process (production and use/participation) may not be united organizationally but integrated communicatively through various methods/channels including marketing, sales performance, media coverage, fan activities, and so forth.

9. Some may insist on the term *transnational* in lieu of overseas in order to stress the confluence of domestic and overseas fans, which results in the creation of border-crossing alignments. But given the ex-territoriality of Hallyu, international or overseas would be a better choice.

10. Again, I use the term *consumers* only to refute its flawed connotation as ones completely severed from the process of production, which I shall elaborate later.

11. Craig Calhoun (2002) talks about symbolic capital in reference to Pierre Bourdieu's earlier discussion of social capital (474).

12. I prefer Gramscian hegemony to Joseph Nye's "soft power" (2004), which tends to dilute the political implications of cultural leadership in the contemporary mode of globalization coupled with cognitive capitalism.

13. For example, the Ministry of Culture, Sports, and Tourism has consistently subsidized colleges dedicated to research on creative/culture industries and has created massive tax breaks and lavish underwritings for content-producing businesses such as computer graphics, digital games, animations, character industry, etc.

14. "Globalizing Korean Cuisine" by Kathleen Stephens, accessed on August 21, 2012. http://english.visitkorea.or.kr/myeyes.kto?cmd=view&md=enu&lang_se=ENG&bbs_ sn =1590130.

15. HallyuWorld website, accessed on Sept 14, 2012, http://eng.e-hallyu.com/eng/introduction/work.asp.

16. HallyuWorld website.

WORKS CITED

Bakhtin, Mikhail. 1984. *Rabelais and His World*. Trans. Helene Iswolsky. Bloomington: Indiana University Press.

Bennett, Tony. 1980. "Popular Culture: A Teaching Object." *Screen Education* 34: 17–30.

Calhoun, Craig, ed. 2002. *Dictionary of the Social Sciences*. New York: Oxford University Press.

Goffman, Erving. 1961. *Asylums: Essays on the Social Situation of Mental Patients and Other Inmates*. New York: Anchor Books.

Na, Jeong-ju. 2009. "Steering Committee Launched to Globalize Korean Food." *Korea Times*, May 4. Accessed on September 14, 2012, http://www.koreatimes.co.kr/www/news/special/2009/08/178_44334.html.

Nye, Joseph S. 2004. *Soft Power: The Means to Success in World Politics*. New York: Perseus Books, 2004.

2

New Perspectives on the Creative Industries in the Hallyu 2.0 Era

Global-Local Dialectics in Intellectual Properties

Dal Yong Jin

Since the mid-1990s, Hallyu has become a global sensation. Several Asian countries, including Japan, China, Taiwan, and Vietnam, have absorbed Korean popular culture, and several Korean cultural genres have become major cultural activities in these countries. Korea has also recently started to penetrate European and North American countries with popular music and online gaming. Hallyu has been unique because it indicates the unusual growth of local creative industries in the midst of neoliberal globalization (Kim 2011; Kim and Kim 2011; Lee 2009). Once peripheral and small, the Korean creative industries have developed their own local cultural products and services, and Korea's creative industries have been among the most successful contributors to its own national economy compared to other nations.

In recent years, Hallyu has experienced a significant transformation with the growth of digital technologies, in particular, social media, such as YouTube, social network sites (SNSs), and smartphones (Goldsmith, Lee, and Yates 2011). These digital technologies, as new driving engines of Hallyu, have initiated and supported the popularity of Korean popular culture in many countries. Unlike Hallyu 1.0, which emphasized the export of local cultural goods to East Asia, the growth of digital/social media in Hallyu 2.0 has uniquely influenced the Korean creative industries, because new media outlets, such as YouTube, SNSs, and various digital media have become significant parts of the new Korean Wave (Kim 2008; VITALSIGN 2010).

Hallyu 1.0, which was the initial stage of the Korean Wave, relied on several male actors and the fanbase of Asian women in their thirties and forties. After the latter part of 2006, Hallyu 2.0 has exhibited some significant characteristics differentiating itself from Hallyu 1.0. The new Korean Wave has emphasized the convergence of creative content, in particular K-pop, online gaming, and new technologies. Hallyu 2.0 has also included female stars and expanded to include all age groups beyond Asia. This means that Hallyu 2.0 is a combination of social media, their techniques and practices, and the uses and affordances they provide, and this new stage has been made possible because Korea has advanced its digital technologies. As JungBong Choi in this book aptly puts it:

> The swift establishment of so-called social media in particular affords distinct ecosystems for cultural interactions, endowing the myriad of cultural craftsmen with heightened capacity to redesign the productive and distributive patterns for what was initially offered to them. . . . the social media [work] as an empowering tool that enhances the communicative accessibility to stars and the collectivity among fans scattered across different places. (42)

In fact, online gaming and K-pop have become the two most significant cultural genres in the Korean creative industries and have initiated the growth of Hallyu 2.0, since K-pop fans and online game users heavily access these social media to enjoy local popular culture.

The growth of digital/social media has also changed the nature of Hallyu because the new Korean Wave needs to emphasize the importance of several services, such as intellectual property (IP) rights and the exportation of virtual goods. *Hallyu* denotes not Korean popular culture per se, but the high tide of Korean culture in non-Korea territory (Choi, this volume). This means that it is also worth stressing that as cultural export, K-pop and online gaming in the social media era have high production values (Lie 2012). This is because IP is much more significant than the cultural goods themselves in terms of capital accumulation and national economy (Klein 2000).

In a Hallyu research tradition, little attention has been made in capturing international flows of copyrights and measuring the trade balance of countries in IP rights (UNCTAD 2008, 101). Hallyu 2.0 should not only be about flows of cultural goods but also about IP rights based on the growth of digital/social media, because Hallyu 2.0 heavily relies on platforms, such as SNSs and YouTube, that are major resources of IP rights in the

creative industries. Of course, this does not mean that we need to champion an industry-led perspective on the propagation of local popular culture. The current popularity of Korean cultural products has relied on social media as the distributors of relatively less-popularized local cultural
genres. Local creative industries in addition to many fans of Korean popular culture are benefiting from the dissemination of local cultural genres
on social media, because these corporations are able to distribute their
cultural products due to the social media frenzy of their products, while
continuously organizing cultural events throughout the world.

Therefore, I am not intending to provide any legal or policy measures
to protect IP rights, nor any practical arguments on behalf of the creative
industries. Instead, I aim to discuss the normative reasons why Hallyu
research needs to contemplate the role of IP rights alongside cultural flow
as a major consideration in the context of creative industries. I first discuss
whether the nascent growth of social media has resulted in the popularity
of Korean culture, including K-pop and online gaming, in other parts of
the world. By mapping these relationships out, I investigate whether or
not Korea has developed its IP strength in the global market. I articulate
whether social media-driven consumption and cultural production flows
are contributing to our current debates on the power dynamics of creative
industries in Asia and across the globe. I believe that this discussion will
shed light on Hallyu 2.0 theory, which focuses on social media alongside
Korean popular culture.

From Cultural Industries to Creative Industries in the Hallyu 2.0 Era

The notion of cultural industries originally started in the nineteenth century when the commercialization of cultural production began (Hesmondhalgh and Pratt 2005, 2). Later, cultural industries were very much
bound up with the rise of mass culture—a phenomenon that troubled
many twentieth-century intellectuals. Reacting against what they saw as
the misleadingly democratic connotations of the term *mass culture*, Max
Horkheimer and Theodor Adorno (1969) developed the idea of the culture industries as part of their critique of the false legacies of the Enlightenment. The term was intended to draw critical attention to the commodification of art. For Horkheimer and Adorno, art could act as a form of
critique of the rest of life, and could provide a utopian vision of how a
better life might be possible. However, in Horkheimer and Adorno's view,

culture had almost entirely lost this capacity to act as utopian critique because it had become commodified, a thing to be bought and sold (Hesmondhalgh 2007, 16).

The term *cultural industries* helps us see how artistic practice has moved closer to the center of economic action in many countries across much of the world. Cultural industry companies can no longer be seen as secondary to the real economy (Hesmondhalgh 2007). As the United Nations Educational, Scientific, and Cultural Organization defined it, "A cultural industry is held to exist when cultural goods and services are produced, reproduced, stored or distributed on industrial and commercial lines, that is to say on a large scale and in accordance with a strategy based on economic considerations rather than any concerns for cultural development" (UNESCO 2005, 21). Several media scholars have advanced a more contemporary concept of cultural industries in conjunction with information communication technologies (ICTs). Herbert Schiller (1989) especially provided the fundamental basis for the contemporary definition of the cultural industries. Since policies toward the cultural industries can no longer be separated from ICTs in their various forms, and policy is formulated within a wider information society perspective, *cultural industries* now must include publishing, the press, film, radio, television, recording, advertising, sports, and most recently, the many components that now make up the information industry.

Since the mid-1990s, the concept of the cultural industries has shifted with the growth of digital technologies and IP rights toward "creative industries." In 1994 Australia sought to chart a cultural policy combining the arts with new communications technologies, transposing the notion of cultural industries into creative industries. The notion of creative industries subsequently gained much wider acceptance following its adoption by the UK government, which set up its Creative Industries Task Force in 1997 (Flew 2012; Huang 2011; British Council 2010). The UK government defined creative industries as "those activities originating in individual creativity, skill and talent and which have a potential for wealth and job creation through the generation and exploitation of intellectual property" (British Council 2010, 8). These activities included not just the traditional art forms, but service businesses such as advertising, manufacturing processes that feed into cultural production, and the retail of creative goods (British Council 2010, 6–7; Cunningham 2009). Nicholas Garnham emphasizes the concept of information or knowledge economy. He points out that "in current debates over digitalization and the impact of the Web, the industries can be understood and assessed in the context of a wider debate about the impact of ICTs and digitalization" (Garnham 2005, 20).

UNESCO (2005, 10) has recently emphasized the importance of copyright-based industries driven by technological development, because the transformation of cultural industries occurred in parallel with developments in copyright protection. This has become increasingly important in the last twenty years in relation to nonartistic areas of intellectual creation, for example, software development, hardware design, and information management. Not surprisingly, the World Intellectual Property Organization (WIPO) points out that creative industries are involved directly and indirectly in the commercial exploitation of IP-based goods and services, that is, mainly cultural, information, and entertainment goods (WIPO 2003). Unlike the term *cultural industries*, which has its origins in the ideological critique of art and culture under industrial capitalism and has associations with the neo-Marxist theories, creative industries have developed in tandem with the growth of digital technologies and convergence (Cunningham 2005).

In the twenty-first century, the Korean government has emphasized the importance of cultural content for the national economy. With some tweaks, the Lee Myung-bak government (2008–2013) had shifted its focus to (commodified) creativity in conjunction with content since 2008. Korean policymakers have used the term *creative contents industry* instead of *creative industry* since 2009.[1] Using the United Kingdom's creative industry as a model, the Lee government included the content industry as a new driving engine for the national economy (Kim 2008). Since IP rights are some of the most significant parts within the notion of the creative contents industry, the government focuses on IP rights as a primary characteristic of the new Korean Wave, which makes the role of IP rights crucial in Hallyu 2.0.

The Korean Wave Shifts toward Hallyu 2.0

The discourse of the new Korean Wave emphasizes the crucial convergence of social media and local popular culture, including K-pop and online gaming (Goldsmith, Lee, and Yates 2011; Lee 2009). Korea has made innovations in SNSs (e.g., Cyworld) and smartphones (e.g., Samsung's Galaxy III and IV), as well as online gaming (e.g., Lineage [I] and II and Aion). Western-based social media and smartphones have also taken pivotal roles in spreading K-pop and other cultural genres, because fans in many countries enjoy these products through social media (meaning a group of Internet-based applications that build on the ideological and technological foundations of Web 2.0, which allows the creation and exchange of user-generated content) (Kaplan and Haenlein 2010, 61).

To begin with, the Korean cultural firms had developed many of their cultural products and expanded the exportation of these products to East and Southeast Asia in the Hallyu 1.0 era. They first penetrated the Chinese cultural market with television dramas, including *What Is Love* (Sarang i mwŏgillae, 1992), which was popular in several Asian countries. The Korean cultural products boom in Asia has been further bolstered by the advance of Korean films. Starting in the late 1990s, Korea began to export films to East Asia, such as *Silmido* (2003) and *Tae Guk Gi: The Brotherhood of War* (T'aegŭkki hwinallimyŏ, 2004). Among these, *Shiri* (1999), which was Korea's first Hollywood style blockbuster movie, was successful throughout the rest of Asia. It reached the top of the box office in Hong Kong in 1999 and attracted 1.2 million viewers in Japan (Chun 2004). When *My Sassy Girl* (Yŏpkijŏgin kŭnyŏ, 2001) was released throughout East Asia, it became a mega blockbuster hit in many countries, including China, Japan, and Taiwan. In the midst of the growing popularity of Korean films, several domestic films received international film awards, including *Oldboy's* (Oldŭ boi, 2003) Grand Prix at the Cannes Film Festival in 2004.

As table 2 shows, the Korean broadcasting industries have increased their exports from only $13.1 million in 2000 to $151 million in 2007, and to $228 million in 2010 (Ministry of Culture and Tourism 2002; 2006; 2011). Television dramas have become some of the most significant cultural products initiating and driving Hallyu. Unlike the broadcasting sector, the Korean film industry has experienced a sharp decline since 2006, partially due to the reduction of the screen quota as part of its free trade agreement (FTA) with the United States. The export of Korean films increased from $7.0 million in 2000 to $76 million in 2005; however, it fell to $13.5 million in 2010 (Ministry of Culture and Tourism 2006; 2011). This means that Hallyu, which was driven by the broadcasting and movie industries, has been troubled and shifting.

Since late 2007 or early 2008, Korean creative industries have witnessed a few new engines of growth with digital technologies and social media. With the rapid advancement of broadband services, online gaming has become a burgeoning new cultural sector with global revenues rivaling those of film and music (Jin 2011). Korea exported $102 million worth of games in 2000; in 2010, the country exported as much as $1.6 billion worth of games. During the period 2000–2010, exports increased 15.7 times (table 2). The Korean online game industry has rapidly gained status as an empire in the gaming sector and is one of the most significant exported cultural products of Korea.

Most of all, K-pop has become one of the most distinct cultural genres in the Hallyu 2.0 era. While K-pop was the part of the early growth in Hallyu, Korea did not achieve impressive popularity in the global music markets until recent years. However, K-pop has become a driver of Hallyu 2.0 as Korea exported $80.9 million worth of music in 2010, a 159 percent increase from 2009. What's more, in 2011 the music industry exported $177 million, a 112 percent increase from the previous year (Ministry of Culture, Sports, and Tourism 2012). Psy's "Gangnam Style" was a YouTube sensation and became popular around the world in 2012, as Brian Hu correctly observes in the final chapter of this book. Online gaming and K-pop have been the two most significant cultural sectors in the Korean creative industries.

While there are several elements impacting the growth of Hallyu 2.0, one of the most significant aspects has been the rapid growth of social media. This is because K-pop fans are heavily involved with social media in their enjoyment of K-pop and games. From user-generated content websites to peer-to-peer networks, these channels play a central role in global cultural circulation. With youth consumer groups as central figures, SNSs have become the fastest-growing platforms to circulate global

TABLE 2. Exports of Cultural Products in the Twenty-First Century (millions of dollars)

	2000	2001	2002	2003	2004	2005	2006	2007	2008	2009	2010
Broadcasting	13.1	18.9	28.8	42.1	70.3	122	134	151	171	170	228
Movie	7.0	11.2	14.9	31	58.3	76	24.5	24.4	21	14.1	13.5
Animation	65.0	85.0	83.8	75.7	61.8	78.4	66.8	72.7	80.5	89.6	96.8
Music	8.3	9.1	4.5	13.3	34.2	22.3	16.6	13.8	16.4	31.2	83.2
Game	102	130	141	182	388	585	672	781	1,094	1,241	1,606
Character			86	116	117	164	189	203	228	237	276
Manga				4.1	1.9	3.3	3.9	3.9	4.1	4.2	8.1
Publication	49.1	62.6	139	150	182	191	184	213	260	251	357
Total	244.5	316.8	498	614	914	1,242	1,291	1,463	1,875	2,037	2,668

Source: Ministry of Culture, Sports, and Tourism (2012, 201); Ministry of Culture and Tourism (2011, 2006, 2002), Cultural Industry Whitepaper.

Note: Until 2002, the publication category included manga, which was separated in 2003. Until 2001, there were no reliable data on the character market, and the first official data about the character industry, published in 2001, did not include global trade (Do 2002).

cultural products (Jung 2011). The cultural markets have rapidly shifted—from virtual goods-driven to access-oriented watching markets—because global consumers watch and play cultural genres through social media instead of buying cultural goods. In the era of volatile changes in global creative industries driven by technological innovation and globalization dynamics, understanding the role of social media and its impact on cultural accumulation is crucial.

In fact, one of the major drivers for the growth and development of the Korean creative industries and Hallyu 2.0 is certainly technological advancement (UNCTAD 2008). The innovation and convergence of multimedia and telecommunication technologies has led to the integration of the means by which creative content is produced, distributed, and consumed. Digital technology has brought about enormous growth in the range of media, such as increased television services through cable and the Internet, which further increases the demand for media content (Rosnan and Ismail 2010, 34). Korea has harnessed the potential of developing creative content with new technologies in video games, animation, and K-pop. The scale of current K-pop expansion was simply unimaginable during the periods prior to the current period of social-media explosion. The Korean Wave has long conquered Asia, but before the proliferation of global social networks, attempts by K-pop stars to break into Western markets, including the United States, had largely failed. But now YouTube, Facebook, and Twitter make it easier for K-pop musicians to reach a wider audience in the West, and those fans are turning to the same social networking tools to proclaim their devotion (Choe and Russell 2012, cited in Jung, this volume).

Regardless of the fact that Korea has enjoyed its recent popularity of cultural products in many parts of the world, the new Korean Wave has not emphasized the significance of IP rights yet. As Garnham argues (2005), the motive behind using the term *creative industries* had primarily to do with the promotion of industries based on the exploitation of IP. That does not mean that the Korean government and cultural industries corporations have to garner profits through tight IP regulations. What we need to understand is what the current status of IP rights is in the context of global flows in the creative industries and why IP is to be analyzed in the Hallyu 2.0 era. Needless to say, many scholars and media emphasize the importance of global fandom of local popular culture; however, it is also vital to understand the ways in which cultural industries corporations gain monetary profits. Again, it is not necessary to champion an industry-led monetization process. Instead, the primary discussion in the next section is to provide the normative reasons why we consider IP rights as part of Hallyu, given that *Hallyu* is a comprehensive term encompassing several fields, including fashion, food, language, and digital media, in addition to cultural products.

Intellectual Property Rights in the Hallyu 2.0 Era

The recent growth of the Korean creative industries relies on accessibility, which means that fans in many countries access the Internet, in particular, social media, to enjoy local popular culture. Due to the strong growth of Korea's cultural products in many countries, Korea has been entitled to gain much profit through both the sales of these cultural products and IP rights in cultural flows. Since some Western countries, including Japan, have reliable legal measures, the Korean creative industries can make profits through the fair legal systems actualized in these countries. For example, the recent growth of K-pop in Japan and Europe has made them newly profitable markets for the Korean music industry because they have a relatively fair IP rights tradition. The reality is not the same because rampant IP infringements in many Asian countries, including China and Taiwan, because there are less dependable legal systems for Hallyu 2.0 (Korea Creative Contents Agency 2011). We cannot deny that the convergence of social media and K-pop has greatly developed the current boom of Korean popular music in many countries. However, it does not guarantee that Korean creative industries can benefit from increasing popularity, due to illegal piracy. Although the popularity of K-pop is growing through YouTube and SNSs, the revenue from IP rights is not increasing; therefore, Korean cultural industries corporations have relied on their revenues from the sales of cultural goods, unlike several Western countries that also utilize IP rights.

More specifically, great numbers of people in several Asian countries have illegally downloaded Korean popular music, so the major revenue source in these countries is through events (Korea Creative Contents Agency 2011). In fact, a 2005 study showed that about 80 percent of cultural firms in Korea experienced the infringement of IP in many countries, particularly in China, Hong Kong, and elsewhere in Southeast Asia (Ministry of Culture and Tourism 2006). In Indonesia, there were 189 retail shops selling Korean cultural products in 2008; however, only 6 shops (3.2 percent) sold qualifying cultural products. In Malaysia, among 107 retail shops, about 40 percent sold only bootlegs (Ministry of Culture and

Tourism 2011, 211). In another survey conducted in 2008, the infringement of IP in Chinese telecommunications corporations delivering Korean popular culture escalated to 83 percent. In 2010, among thirty-two major portals in China, the infringement rate of IP of 7,801 Korean dramas was 32.5 percent, and it was 78 percent for cinema. During the same period, Thailand had fifty-one Internet sites delivering Korean content and they provided about 62,000 popular Korean songs; however, almost all of them were bootlegs (Ministry of Culture and Tourism 2011).

In the social media era, the music industry has experienced the dual role of digital technologies. On one hand, K-pop has achieved a recent global stardom, if not fully, at least tangibly. Music companies license a range of services, offering not only ownership of tracks and albums, but also ubiquitous access to comprehensive music libraries. The range of consumer choice for digitally accessing music grew significantly in 2010 (IFPI 2012). Music subscription numbers in many countries are advancing steadily; new social network and recommendation functions have been added to existing offerings; a new generation of smartphones and applications has made more services available across different devices and has helped boost the popularity of music downloads in key markets; new commercial partnerships are emerging between record companies, ISPs, and mobile operators; and new services have emerged that enable consumers to access music from digital lockers or through devices in the living room, such as TVs (IFPI 2012). In other words, social media and music fans are driving the digital music revolution. Consumers worldwide are embracing social media, using new programs like YouTube and Facebook and changing the way they access entertainment.

On the other hand, the music industry has been hard hit because of IP infringements, both domestically and globally. Digital piracy is the single most important factor holding back further development of the legitimate music business. Illegal file-sharing on peer-to-peer (P2P) networks remains rife, and alternative forms of illegal distribution such as cyberlockers, illegal streaming services, and forums are also a growing problem. The overall impact of digital piracy has been to contribute substantially to the dramatic erosion in industry revenues in recent years. Despite a surge from 2004 to 2010 by more than 1,000 percent in the digital music market—to an estimated value of US$4.6 billion—global recorded music revenues declined by 31 percent over the same period. These two figures powerfully illustrate how, in the face of piracy, even the most progressive strategy of licensing hundreds of digital music services has been unable to prevent a steady decline in the overall legitimate music market, and that decline will continue unless further action is taken (IFPI 2012). For this economic reason, several countries and international agencies, including WIPO, have tried to protect IP through international laws. Despite these international conventions regarding IP, the nature of protection policies differs from country to country; therefore, the protection measures are still limited (Ki, Chang, and Kang 2006).

In the context of the Korean creative industries, it is important to understand that the Hallyu 2.0 era is, again, different because of the changing patterns of access to cultural genres. IP rights become significant in the digital/social media era, and Hallyu has supposedly benefited from these new developments. However, IP profits have recorded huge net losses, and these losses have grown significantly. In 2000, Korea earned $688 million through IP rights, while paying $3.2 billion, so the net loss was $2.55 billion. In 2010, the net loss in the IP sector grew to $5.9 billion, which was one of the biggest in international trade (table 3). Although it is not clear how much of these losses come from cultural and information technologies areas, they certainly explain the huge gap between IP receipts and payments.

Having acknowledged that Hallyu 2.0 includes not only cultural products but also digital and/or social media technologies, it is crucial to understand the IP rights issues in conjunction with the IT sector more broadly construed. In the new Korean Wave era, IP rights in the creative industries are major resources for capital accumulation. While contributing to cultural identity and the enhancement of social values, creative industries are also generating wealth, creating jobs, and promoting trade (UNCTAD 2008). IP rights should be the most significant area to be measured in Hallyu 2.0 because of their importance in both protecting creative works and enhancing the national economy. As the Korea Creative Contents Agency (KCCA) points out (2011, 3), one of the most significant policy measures to advance Hallyu 2.0 further is cooperation between the government and cultural corporations to protect intellectual property. In that sense, the government must initiate intergovernmental collaboration

TABLE 3. Trends in Intellectual Property Trade (millions of dollars)

	2000	2001	2002	2003	2004	2005	2006	2007	2008	2009	2010
IP net losses	2,553	2,129	2,167	2,269	2,585	2,652	2,605	3,399	3,274	3,989	5,887
IP receipts	688	924	835	1,311	1,861	1,908	2,046	1,735	2,382	3,199	3,145
IP payments	3,221	3,053	3,002	3,570	4,446	4,561	4,650	5,134	5,656	7,188	9,031

Source: International Trade, National Statistics Portal, Korean Statistical Information Service (KoSIS). http://kosis.kr/statisticsList/statisticsList_01List.jsp?vwcd=MT_ZTITLE&parentId=N.

among Asian countries to protect IP rights, while developing new business models to overcome IP issues.

Power Dynamics between the United States and Korea in the Hallyu 2.0 Era

Another major issue in IP rights is the increasing dominance of the United States. According to the U.S. Department of Commerce (2010), the United States has enjoyed its maximum benefits in the IP sector. The total amount of royalties and license fees[2] in the major creative industries that the United States received from foreign countries constituted $93.9 billion in 2008, while the amount that the United States paid to foreign countries was $25.7 billion. Net profits in 2008 were therefore as much as $68 billion, which is the major reason why the United States has tried to establish a rigorous global standard in IP rights. The United States believes that its net profits would increase significantly if it could regulate illegal usage of American-origin intellectual properties. Both the creative industries and the digital industries are vital for the U.S. economy, because they are among the few U.S. industries that generate substantial trade surpluses in the midst of growing U.S. trade deficits. Technological innovation drives industrial growth and helps raise living standards. Thus, the importance of IP rights in the creative industries in the twenty-first century cannot be doubted.

More specifically, royalties and license fees, including those for books, music recordings, and film and television distribution between the United States and Korea proves the one-sided dominance. As table 4 shows, the United States expanded its revenues in royalties and license fees from $79 million in 2000 to $280 million in 2007, although revenues slightly decreased to $203 million in 2009. However, during the same period, Korea only expanded its revenue through royalties and license fees from $1 million in 2000 to about $5.5 million in 2010. The net loss of Korea to the United States in this category has easily surpassed $200 million in recent years, which is a clear indicator of the lopsided balance between the two countries. IP rights largely reside with Western TNCs (transnational corporations), allowing them to establish monopolies (Rønning et al. 2006).

Digital technologies and culture have become among the most significant venues for many countries, including Korea, in the twenty-first century. However, the United States has swiftly expanded its dominance in digitally driven technologies and cultural products. The United States has intensified its dominance in the IP sector through its advanced position in developing software in both media and telecommunications. Although Korea has developed its own software and platforms in conjunction with several popular genres, not to mention several massively multiplayer on-line role playing games (MMORPGs), the lopsided interaction between the United States and developing countries, including Korea, remains un-changed and even exacerbated. Korea is slowly exporting its cultural products to the U.S. market, although this commerce is still marginal; however, when the issue is IP rights, the flow of revenue from the United States to Korea is almost nothing. In particular, the formation of U.S. he-gemony in IP rights has been extended through the efforts of international IP regimes, such as WIPO (Lu and Weber 2009). Again, copyright is the most significant resource of profit for cultural industries, which is eventu-ally monopolized by Western cultural industries with the support of state regulation (Iwabuchi 2010, 204). As Hesmondhalgh (2008) argues, the copyright monopoly by Western cultural industries works as the neolib-eral operation of imperialism.

Arguably, global flows of culture and technology have been asymmet-rical. The recent growth of an IP regime based on new platforms shows an asymmetrical relationship of interdependence between the West, primar-ily the United States, and many developing countries. It is characterized in part by unequal technological exchanges and therefore cultural and capi-tal flows. In the early twenty-first century, the United States has extended

TABLE 4. Royalties and License Fees between United States and Korea, 2000–2010 (unit: millions)

		2000	2001	2002	2003	2004	2005	2006	2007	2008	2009	2010
Receipts	Books, music records and tapes	6	7	9	6	6	6	2	6	6	6	14
	broadcasting and recording of live events	4	5	D	5	1	1	1	9	9	9	D
	Film and television tape distribution	69	77	87	92	80	65	148	265	197	188	181
Payments	Books, music records and tapes	1	*	*	*	1	2	1	2	1	1	4
	Broadcasting and recording of live events	0	*	*	*	1	2	0	1	*	1	1
	Film and television tape distribution	0	0	1	1	0	4	*	*	7	4	*

Source: U.S. Department of Commerce (2011, 2008, 2006, 2003); Survey of Current Business, Washington, DC: U.S. Department of Commerce.

Note: D means no disclosure and * means less than $500,000.

its dominance in global markets, not only with cultural products, but also with intellectual properties based on its advanced technologies. The dramatic changes ushered in by cutting-edge digital/social technologies have significantly increased the magnitude and relevance of the phenomenon of the diffusion of IP rights infringement. Therefore, as global computer networks and global trade in software products and cultural genres develop, there is an increasing tension between developed countries as IP owners and developing countries as IP users. This is due to these commodities' unique role not only as computational infrastructure, but also as framework that allows software to run (Jin 2013). Admitting the significance of innovative designs as a form of open source for platforms, IP becomes important for designers and corporations because of platforms' commercial imperatives for massive capital gains. The Hallyu 2.0 period has shown unique development in the digital/social media era; however, in order to assure balanced power relations with the West, it is crucial that Korea acknowledge the significance of IP rights, and promote the creation of cultural products. Korea needs to advance social media and digital technologies so that the country grows not only as the exporter of cultural products but also as the beneficiary of domestic-based platforms and IP rights. The promise of Hallyu cannot be fulfilled without the growth of these key areas in the global market.

Conclusion

This chapter has analyzed the construction of Hallyu 2.0 within the notion of creative industries and examined IP rights issues as one of the most significant aspects in the new Korean Wave phenomenon. Unlike Hallyu 1.0, the new Korean Wave has focused on the relationship between digital technologies, their techniques and practices, their uses and the affordances they provide, and Korea's compressed modernity and swift industrialization. Hallyu 2.0 underscores a range of groundbreaking developments and innovations within Korea's digital mediascapes and its creative industries (Goldsmith, Lee, and Yates 2011, 70). With rapid convergence between previously separate technologies and culture, digital content industries are increasingly valuable to national economies. While digital technologies have influenced the production and distribution of domestic popular culture, social media have played a major role in spreading several popular genres—particularly K-pop—worldwide, including Europe and North America. For the last few years, digital technologies and social media have boosted the dissemination of Korea's popular media content. Hallyu 2.0 needs to comprehend and interpret the meaning of this new and powerful cultural industry.

The new Korean Wave has been successful; however, the Korean creative industry faces challenges ahead. One main issue is the illegal distribution of cultural products and software. Pirated copies of DVDs and CDs, as well as illegally circulated content, are rampant in the regional markets and online. It is certain that an efficient and fair international IP system is in the interests of creators, creative industries, governments, and consumers in all countries (UNCTAD 2008). Increasing awareness of the contribution and potential of the creative sector for development is a major task for the government. Protecting IP is a public policy goal of countries seeking sustained growth in the creative economy. Conversely, the inefficiency of IP legislation and enforcement systems imperils the economic growth to which the creative industries contribute. Enforcement is as important as education and awareness. The Korea that wishes to see its creative industries prosper must take a strong stance for the promotion of the full spectrum of copyrights and their licenses, for the best way to expand the creative economy is to implement a balanced copyright framework that realizes their developmental potential (UNCTAD 2008, 156). The notion of creative industries certainly pushes the Korean Wave to be more a market-driven cultural phenomenon, as Miller (2009) argues; however, as long as we admit the importance of IP rights in conjunction with cultural flows, it is a natural step to fairly actualize IP rights in the digital economy era.

Of course, it is vital to approach the IP issues with caution, because excessively strict IP rules may hold the new Korean Wave back. As Frank Kogan (2012) aptly puts it, the Japanese music industry has experienced a tangible decline over the last decade, and one of the major reasons for this setback is stringent IP rules. Indeed, Japanese music labels keep trying to prevent us from seeing full videos on YouTube. In contrast, Korean labels give fans full access to their videos. In general, Korea has opened itself up to the international eye and ear via YouTube, which has partially resulted in the current boom of local popular culture in global markets (Kogan 2012).

Finally, Korea has competed with Western countries, and the country is supposed to build a new global order. However, there are some doubts about whether Korean corporations have reorganized the global flow and constructed a balance between the West and the East. A critical interrogation of the global hegemony of IP rights shows that these are primarily dominated by the United States, and that they have intensified an increasingly unequal relationship between the United States and the majority of non-Western countries.

In promoting cultural and creative industries, the government needs to play a strategic role. While its major mission is to form a model with creative industries and commercial businesses and to use policy to enable commercial collaboration, the Korean government should try to increase the level of policy implementation, strengthen budgeting and integration, and conduct interministerial coordination (Huang 2011).

NOTES

1. For example, the Korean government has changed the title of its annual white paper from Cultural Industries Whitepaper to Content Industry Whitepaper in 2009.

2. Royalty and license fees are payments and receipts between residents and non-residents for the authorized use of intangible and nonfinancial assets as well as proprietary rights (such as patents, copyrights, trademarks) and for the use, through licensing agreements, of produced originals of prototypes (such as films and manuscripts) (World Bank 2011).

WORKS CITED

British Council. 2010. "The Creative Economy: An Introductory Guide." Accessed October 24, 2012. http://www.britishcouncil.org/the_creative_economy_an_introductory_guide_1-2.pdf.

Choe, Sang-hun, and Mark Russell. 2012. "Bring K-Pop to the West." *New York Times*, May 4.

Chun, Su-jin. 2004. "A Korean Wave in Japan." Accessed October 23, 2012. http://www.hancinema.net/a-korean-wave-in-japan-1203.html.

Cunningham, Stuart. 2005. "Creative Enterprises." In *Creative Industries*, ed. John Hartley, 282–98. Malden, MA: Blackwell.

Cunningham, Stuart. 2009. "Creative Industries as a Globally Contestable Policy Field." *Chinese Journal of Communication* 2 (1): 13–24.

Flew, Terry. 2012. *The Creative Industries*. London: Sage.

Garnham, Nicholas. 2005. "From Cultural Industries to Creative Industries: An Analysis of the Implications of the 'Creative Industries' Approach to Arts and Media Policy Making in United Kingdom." *International Journal of Cultural Policy* 11 (1): 16–29.

Goldsmith, Ben, Kwang-suk Lee, and Brian Yates. 2011. "In Search of the Korean Digital Wave." *Media International Australia* 141: 70–77.

Hesmondhalgh, David. 2007. *The Cultural Industries*. 2nd ed. London: Sage.

Hesmondhalgh, David. 2008. "Neoliberalism, Imperialism, and the Media." In *The Media and Social Theory*, ed. David Hesmondhalgh and Jason Toynbee, 96–111. London: Routledge.

Hesmondhalgh, David, and Andy C. Pratt. 2005. "Cultural Industries and Cultural Policy." *International Journal of Cultural Policy* 11 (1): 1–14.

Horkheimer, Max, and Theodor Adorno. 1969. *Dialectic of Enlightenment.* Trans. Edmund Jephcott. Stanford, CA: Stanford University Press.

Huang, Yen Shin. 2011. "An Exploratory Study of the Competitive Strategy of Cultural and Creative Industries in Taiwan." *European Journal of Social Sciences* 20 (3): 391–400.

IFPI (International Federation of the Phonographic Industry). 2012. *Digital Music Report 2012.* IFPI.

Iwabuchi, Koichi. 2010. "Globalization, East Asian Media Cultures and Their Publics." *Asian Journal of Communication* 20 (2): 197–212.

Jin, Dal Yong. 2010. *Korea's Online Gaming Empire.* Cambridge: MIT Press.

Jin, Dal Yong. 2011. "Cultural Politics in Japanization and the Korean Wave: The Changing Role of Nation-States in the Midst of Cultural Globalization." In *Hallyu: Influence of Koran Popular Culture in Asia and Beyond,* ed. Do-kyun Kim and Min-sun Kim, 91–132. Seoul: Seoul National University Press.

Jin, Dal Yong. 2013. "The Construction of Platform Imperialism in the Globalization Era." *Triple C: Communication, Capitalism & Critique* 11(1): 145–172.

Jung, Sun. 2011. "Race and Ethnicity in Fandom: Praxis K-Pop, Indonesian Fandom, and Social Media." *Transformative Works and Cultures* 8.

Kaplan, Andreas, and Michael Haenlein. 2010. "Users of the World, Unite! The Challenges and Opportunities of Social Media." *Business Horizons* 53 (1): 59–68.

Ki, Eyun-jung, Byeng-Hee Chang, and Hyoungkoo Kang. 2006. "Exploring Influential Factors on Music Piracy across Countries." *Journal of Communication* 56: 406–26.

Kim, Do-kyun, and Se-jin Kim. 2011. "Hallyu from Its Origin to Present: A Historical Overview." In *Hallyu: Influence of Koran Popular Culture in Asia and Beyond,* ed. Do-kyun Kim and Min-sun Kim, 13–34. Seoul: Seoul National University Press.

Kim, Youna. 2011. "Globalization of Korean Media: Meanings and Significance." In *Hallyu: Influence of Korean Popular Culture in Asia and Beyond,* ed. Do-kyun Kim and Min-sun Kim, 35–62. Seoul: Seoul National University Press.

Kim, Young-hoon. 2008. "Developing Content Economics into Core Industry." *Korea Herald,* December 12.

Klein, Naomi. 2000. *No Logo: Taking Aim at the Brand Bullies.* Toronto: Vintage Canada.

Kogan, Frank. 2012. "Dear Japan—There Are Reasons Why K-Pop Is Breaking Big Internationally and J-Pop Is Not." Accessed August 18, 2014. http://koganbot.livejournal.com/314418.html.

Korea Creative Contents Agency. 2011. "K-Pop Driven New Korean Wave: Current Trends and Issues." *KOCCA Focus* 31 (3): 1–23.

Lee, Jung-yup. 2009. "Contesting Digital Economy and Culture: Digital Technologies and the Transformation of Popular Music in Korea." *Inter-Asia Cultural Studies* 10 (4): 489–506.

Lie, John. 2012. "What Is the K in K-Pop? South Korean Popular Music, the Culture Industry, and National Identity." *Korea Observer* 43 (3): 339–63.

Lu, Jia, and Ian Weber. 2009. "Internet Software Piracy in China: A User Analysis of Resistance to Global Software Copyright Enforcement." *Journal of International and Intercultural Communication* 2 (4): 296–317.

Miller, Toby. 2009. "Albert and Michael's Recombinant." *Continuum* 13 (2): 269–75.

Ministry of Culture, Sports, and Tourism. 2012. *2011 Contents Industry Results and 2012 Expectations*. Seoul: MCST.

Ministry of Culture and Tourism. 2002. *Cultural Industry Whitepaper*. Seoul: Ministry of Culture and Tourism.

Ministry of Culture and Tourism. 2006. *Cultural Industry Whitepaper*. Seoul: Ministry of Culture and Tourism.

Ministry of Culture and Tourism. 2011. *Cultural Industry Whitepaper*. Seoul: Ministry of Culture and Tourism.

Rønning, Helge, Pradip Thomas, Keyan G. Tomaselli, and Ruth Teer-Tomaselli. 2006. "Intellectual Property Rights and the Political Economy of Culture." *Contemporary Arts* 20 (1): 1–19.

Rosnan, Herwina, and Mohd N. Ismail. 2010. "The Impact of Cultural Industries on National Economy." *BMQR* 1 (2): 33–42.

Schiller, Herbert. 1989. *Culture Inc*. New York: Oxford University Press.

To, An-gu. 2002. "2001 Character Market Overpassed 4 Billion Won." *ZDNet*, March 25. Accessed October 24, 2012. http://www.zdnet.co.kr/news/news_view.asp?artice_id=00000010047414&type=det.

UNESCO (United Nations Educational, Scientific, and Cultural Organization). 2005. *Asia-Pacific Creative Communities: Promoting the Cultural Industries for Local Socio-economic Development: A strategy for the 21st Century*. Bangkok: Office of the UNESCO Regional Advisor for Culture in Asia and the Pacific.

UNCTAD (United Nations Conference on Trade and Development). 2008. *Creative Economy Report 2008: The Challenge of Assessing the Creative Economy towards Informed Policy Making*. New York: UNDP.

U.S. Department of Commerce. 2003. *Survey of Current Business*. Washington, DC: U.S. Department of Commerce.

U.S. Department of Commerce. 2006. *Survey of Current Business*. Washington, DC: U.S. Department of Commerce.

U.S. Department of Commerce. 2008. *Survey of Current Business*. Washington, DC: U.S. Department of Commerce.

U.S. Department of Commerce. 2010. *Survey of Current Business*. Washington, DC: U.S. Department of Commerce.

U.S. Department of Commerce. 2011. *Survey of Current Business*. Washington, DC: U.S. Department of Commerce.

VITALSIGN. 2010. "Hallyu 2.0 Has Begun." September 24. Accessed October 24, 2012. http://www.allkpop.com/2010/09/hallyu-2-0-has-begun.

WIPO (World Intellectual Property Organization). 2003. *Guide on Surveying the Economic Contribution of the Copyright Industries*. Geneva: WIPO.

World Bank. 2011. "Royalties and License Fees, Receipts." Accessed October 24, 2012. http://data.worldbank.org/indicator/BX.GSR.ROYL.CD.

PART 2.

Rethinking K-Pop

3

New Wave Formations

K-Pop Idols, Social Media, and the Remaking of the Korean Wave

Eun-Young Jung

Contemporary transnational popular cultural flows constitute an increasingly fluid terrain as boundaries between nations, regions, and cultures are rapidly imploding. With the ubiquity of the Internet and the recent explosion of "social media," the global cultural environment is constantly being reconfigured by flows that are instant, momentary, pervasive, and unremitting. It is this environment in which Korean popular culture is spreading in ways unimaginable only a decade ago.

Social media, defined by Kaplan and Haenlein (2010, 61) as "a group of Internet-based applications that build on the ideological and technological foundations of Web 2.0, and that allow the creation and exchange of User Generated Content," have brought profound changes to society, economy, and culture, including the industry practices of production, distribution, and consumption. Among the various cultural industries, the music industry has been particularly impacted by the availability of user-generated and peer-to-peer applications. For example, Napster, the revolutionary music-sharing site operating from late 1999 through mid-2001, challenged the copyrights and distribution hegemony of the world's dominant record labels (Menn 2003, 1–3), and its innovative technology became a model for numerous Napster-like streaming music services (Levy 2011), including Korea's Soribada (2000–2002), among many others. While a number of academic studies have examined the latest developments in social media and their relationships to digital technology, marketing, politics, media, popular culture, and education (Burgess and Green 2009; Behnke 2010; Fisher 2010; Kackman 2010; Scott 2010; among others), only a few studies thus far have specifically dealt with issues of music and social media relations. These include Sun Jung's article on K-pop and social media in Indonesia (2011b) and Kiri Miller's book on music video games (2012).[1] As social media become an increasingly important cultural space in many people's everyday lives, the close relationship between music and social media becomes an inevitable twenty-first century sociocultural reality.

This chapter intends to highlight a very narrow sector of the world's transnational popular music flows by investigating a few recent K-pop boy bands and girl groups whose managing companies and fans around the world have been successfully utilizing popular social media platforms like Facebook, Twitter, and, most importantly, YouTube. What is now widely referred to as the *Korean Wave* or *Hallyu*—the international popularity since the late 1990s of Korea's popular cultural products such as television dramas, films, music, fashion, and computer games—has been actively discussed internationally in both popular and academic circles. While the earlier phase of Hallyu (from the late 1990s to mid-2000s) was driven mainly by numerous television drama hits throughout Asia and among overseas Asian communities, the latest Hallyu development has been led by a relatively small sector of Korean pop music known as aidol (hereafter idol)[2] bands, which have been attracting a broader range of fans around the world.

By examining exemplary K-pop idol bands and their fast-growing visibility in major social media spaces, where the viewers' reception is instant and often verbalized, this work traces how the K-pop music industry, K-pop idols, and their transnational fans have successfully deployed social media and accelerated transnational K-pop presence, placing it under a bright spotlight in the contemporary transnational popular culture scene. As background, this chapter reviews earlier K-pop idol bands and singers, including those who attempted to break into the United States pop market during the years prior to the social media explosion, and discusses the changes in promotion strategies and market environments of the latest K-pop idol bands over the last fifteen years. Although this chapter clearly acknowledges the importance of K-pop idol bands' strong presence in Asia and Asian fans' active deployment of social media, it focuses on tracking their presence beyond Asia, including the United States and Europe—a *new* dynamic phase in transnational K-pop.

Hallyu and K-pop

The unexpected emergence of Hallyu in the late 1990s serves as a good example of the often unpredictable and uneven transnational flows of culture, contrasting with center-periphery cultural distribution models of American pop culture dominance. As Arjun Appadurai states:

> The crucial point, however, is that the United States is no longer the puppeteer of a world system of images but is only one node of a complex transnational construction of imaginary landscapes. The world we live in today is characterized by a new role for the imagination in social life . . . now mediated through the complex prism of modern media. (2006, 587)

Until the late 1990s, Korea's popular culture was primarily produced, distributed, and consumed by Koreans in Korea and was mostly unknown outside Korea (with a few exceptions: e.g. some films, including *Red Muffler* [Ppalgan mahura, 1964], and film stars were popular in Taiwan and Hong Kong in the 1960s; also, pop musicians like Cho Yong-pil were popular in Japan in the 1980s). However, new media technology created novel transnational media circulations and enabled a sudden surge of Korean television dramas and pop music in Taiwan and China in the late 1990s and subsequent success in other Asian countries and overseas Asian communities elsewhere. Within years, Korea became an important transnational cultural player.

Due to the overwhelming popularity of television dramas from the late 1990s to mid-2000s in Asia, most Hallyu scholarship has been devoted to various aspects of television dramas and Korea's cultural relations to regional dynamics in Asia (e.g. cultural policy, economy, political history, audiences' gender, class, age).[3] Though K-pop has been playing a crucial part in the overall development of Hallyu from the early stages, Hallyu studies on pop music both in Korean and in English are relatively limited in volume and scope.[4]

The following sections first offer a brief look at the K-pop idol bands and singers from the earlier stages of Hallyu (pre-social media explosion), and then examine the current K-pop phenomenon, particularly outside Asia, traveling through the popular social media spaces Facebook, Twitter, and YouTube. The history of Hallyu K-pop from the last fifteen years is divided roughly into four waves, the first three preceding the period social media dominance: 1) young boys and girls bands, including H.O.T., NRG, S.E.S., Baby V.O.X., and Shinhwa; 2) solo singers, including BoA, Rain, and Se7en; 3) return to young boys and girls bands, including TVXQ, Super Junior, and Wonder Girls; and 4) riding the current social media boom, featuring the latest idol boys and girls bands, Big Bang, 2PM, 2NE1, Girls' Generation, SHINee, JYJ, and others (including some active earlier). Though each individual band and singer is an important player in the Hallyu K-pop wave formations and deserves an independent in-depth study, my focus here is limited to several representative bands and singers and to the social media relevant to new developments.

Hallyu K-Pop in the Pre-Social Media Explosion Era

The First Wave (Late 1990s to Early 2000s)

Prior to the first wave of Hallyu K-pop, there were initial developments that signaled an emergence of Korean pop music. The Korean pop music industry in the late 1980s and early 1990s was going through a major transformation as it grew rapidly with Korea's political, social, economic, and cultural changes. Most noticeably, the mainstream pop music scene, dominated by non-age-specific, sentimental love songs, palladŭ, was diversified by younger musicians' introduction of dance-oriented genres (including hip-hop), which were instantly favored by Korean youth. After conquering the mainstream Korean pop music scene in 1992, the legendary male trio Seo Taiji and Boys gained a noticeable following in Japan with very little strategic promotion, in contrast to the norm these days, and released their albums (in Korean language) in 1994 and 1995.[5] Other examples of the initial wave occurred in Taiwan with female solo singer Kim Wan-sun in the mid-1990s and the male duo Clon in the late 1990s, both with dance-oriented music (Sung 2006, 170–72).

The first wave of Hallyu K-pop was led by the first generation of young teenage idol groups, including H.O.T., NRG, S.E.S., Baby V.O.X., and Shinhwa, all systematically produced by major entertainment companies' exclusive audition processes and in-house training systems. Initiated by Lee Soo-man (CEO of the Hallyu K-pop powerhouse S.M. Entertainment, hereafter S.M.) and following typical Japanese aidoru pop genre practice, S.M.'s production style of manufacturing boy bands and girl groups for both local and foreign markets was soon adopted by other Hallyu K-pop leaders, such as YG Entertainment and JYP Entertainment (hereafter YG and JYPE). By implementing the typical Japanese aidoru production system, S.M. fully systemized the total procedure of young pop star making, with breakthroughs by boy band H.O.T. and girl group S.E.S. After becoming the most popular boy band in Korea, H.O.T. was particularly popular in China from 2000 to 2001 through the conventional media (television, radio) and online spaces (music-download sites, online broadcasters, personal homepages) as they formed active virtual fan communities (Pease 2006). S.E.S., the most popular girl group in the late 1990s and early 2000s in Korea, was carefully formed to be marketable internationally—in Japan, in particular, by including the Japanese Korean member Shoo (see Roald Maliangkay's chapter, this volume). Like the typical Japanese female *aidoru* group SPEED (immensely popular in Japan from 1996–2000), S.E.S.'s cutesy musical and visual style led them to gain initial popularity in Japan relatively easily. In short, the first wave of Hallyu K-pop was initiated by S.M.'s idol groups and found audiences mainly in the East Asian region by offering music and performance based on catchy melodies, simple harmonic progressions, group dance movements, English words and short phrases, and trendy fashion styles.

The Second Wave (Early 2000s to Mid-2000s)

The second wave of Hallyu K-pop differs from the other stages in that it was led by a few solo singers—BoA, Rain, and Se7en—who attempted to enter the U.S. market after gaining success in Asia. It was a considerably bigger wave, reaching a much broader region in East and Southeast Asia and coinciding with the peak of the television drama boom. Though not as successful as television dramas, Korean pop became fairly visible, especially within the Asian pop music loop, and *K-pop* became a generic term to refer to Hallyu K-pop internationally, just as the term *J-pop* (referring to contemporary mainstream Japanese popular music) had emerged in the 1990s (de Ferranti 2002).

The female pop star BoA has been closely followed by popular media in Korea, Japan, Asia, and beyond since her successful Japan debut in 2002 as a singer of J-pop. As I have discussed elsewhere (2010), the choice to debut as a J-pop star in the early stage of her singing career complicated her identity as a Hallyu K-pop star, at least until a few years later when she became popular throughout Asia and eventually made her not-so-glorious American debut in 2008. Carefully trained (including foreign language education), groomed, and promoted from an early age by S.M., BoA achieved great success in Japan in the mid-2000s and was frequently touted as "Asia's Star" by Korean media. The dramatically changed cultural relations between Korea and Japan, through Korea's Open-Door policy (1998–2004), the 2002 FIFA World Cup being cohosted by Korea and Japan, and the exploding Hallyu boom in Japan from 2004 clearly contributed to her success in Japan. While S.M.'s calculated collaboration with the powerful Japanese company AVEX Entertainment was clearly the right strategy, the ambitious but premature plan for BoA's American debut resulted in severe damage to her career. Her American debut song "Eat You Up" (2008) flopped, and low sales of her subsequent Japanese album and singles suggest a singing career in decline.

The male R&B/hip-hop singer and actor known as Rain gained extraordinary popularity throughout Asia and beyond in the mid-2000s. His fame came first not from singing, but from acting in the hit Korean television drama *Full House* (P'ul hausŭ, 2004). Although Rain's showcase performance at Madison Square Garden in New York in 2006 was criticized for its "unoriginality" (Pareles 2006), Rain soon became the most successful Korean entertainer in history, even winning the male protagonist role in a Hollywood movie, *Ninja Assassin* (2009). In 2007, Rain became the first Korean singer to hold a concert at the Tokyo Dome, the largest and most prestigious concert venue in Japan (Garcia 2007), without the years of preparation invested by BoA. Another R&B/hip-hop male singer, Se7en was often compared to Rain during the mid-2000s, when he also gained wide international success as a singer. Like BoA, Se7en also moved to the United States in 2007 to prepare for his American debut, but after his debut single "Girls" (2009) flopped, he returned to Korea.

These three solo pop stars reached their career peaks by contributing to and taking advantage of the widespread Hallyu boom in East and Southeast Asian regions in the mid-2000s. But their attempts in the United States, despite elaborate preparations, all fell short, confirming the complexity and unpredictability of contemporary transnational flows and the challenges of entrenched notions of race, ethnicity, sexuality, as well as musical sound in the mainstream American pop music market environments. Along with their lackluster results in the United States by the end of the second wave, the overall Hallyu boom in Asia and overseas Asian communities was also fading as fewer television drama hits were produced.

The Third Wave (Mid-2000s to Late 2000s)

Reinvigorated by S.M.'s boys band TVXQ, the third wave of Hallyu K-pop represented a return of young boys and girls bands (idol pop), and K-pop became the central force of Hallyu. Compared to the earlier cases, with much more refined performance, high-quality music video production, and vibrant domestic entertainment industry with the government's enthusiastic support, the third-wave bands were able to build their international fans (still mostly in East and Southeast Asia) within a shorter period time.

The five-boy band TVXQ expanded its career throughout Asia soon after its domestic success. Based on S.M.'s exclusive partnership with AVEX Entertainment in Japan and a systematic training and promotion strategy, the highly capable TVXQ (also fluent in Japanese) made a smooth and remarkable debut in Japan in 2005, and the band soon became the most successful Korean boy band in Asia, producing a number of top-selling singles, albums, and DVDs, and sold-out concerts throughout Asia in the mid and late 2000s. Another of S.M.'s boy bands is Super Junior, with thirteen members at its peak (including the Chinese member Han Geng). It was particularly popular in China and Southeast Asia (including Thailand, Vietnam, Indonesia) in the late 2000s and made an international breakthrough with the 2009 song "Sorry Sorry" and the members' constant media appearances as multi-entertainers. "Sorry Sorry" differs from the previous Hallyu K-pop songs in some important ways, a few aspects of which have become norms for later Hallyu K-pop groups. It makes near constant use of Auto-Tune (an audio processor that corrects pitch), has short catchy refrains (the beginning phrase "Sorry Sorry Sorry Sorry" is repeated eight times), minimalist lyrics, and synchronized dance movements specific to the song. JYPE's girl group Wonder Girls also exhibited many stylistic trends of idol pop in their hit songs "Tell Me" (2007) and "Nobody" (2008) by including short catchy refrains, synchronized dance movements, and fashion styles specific to each song.

The new formula of Korean idol pop style have become a set of sonic and visual signifiers that are recognized as specific characteristics of Hallyu K-pop by many international fans. Perhaps due to the grand ambition of Park Jin-young (CEO of JYPE), Wonder Girls quickly made their American debut by moving to the United States in 2008. But in contrast to their instant success in Korea, the group's career in the United States did not meet expectations, despite their initial exposure to large American teenage audiences by opening for the popular American boys band Jonas Brothers on their tour in 2009 (Wong 2009).

By the late 2000s these idol groups, though they had gotten their start via the conventional idol-making process and had been systematically packaged by their companies, began to follow the same approach used by the most recently formed Hallyu K-pop idol groups—an intensive adoption of social media. The most significant factor of the third wave is that young all-boys and/or all-girls-band format and their stylistic features—Korean idol pop—began to be identified as the typical Hallyu K-pop internationally.

Hallyu K-Pop Riding the Social Media Wave

The Fourth Wave (Late 2000s to Present)

The fourth wave includes the latest Hallyu K-pop idol groups, such as Big Bang, 2PM, 2NE1, Girls' Generation, SHINee, JYJ (see Seung-Ah Lee's chapter, this volume), and some of the third-wave acts, such as Super Junior and Wonder Girls. Fundamentally, these groups are not different from the third-wave idol groups, as the basic formula—group format, music and dance styles, visual stylistic emphasis, and multimedia presence—is identical. However, the results are quite different. Up to this point, most Hallyu K-pop singers and idol groups were successful predominantly in East and Southeast Asia, and popularity for some was limited to one or two areas outside Korea (e.g., H.O.T. in China, S.E.S. and BoA in Japan, and TVXQ in China and Japan). Although the Hallyu phenomenon as a whole has been considered a remarkable transnational cultural success—as Korea has never been a transnational cultural powerhouse before—that its popularity has been limited to East and Southeast Asia has been viewed as the ultimate shortcoming of Hallyu. Yet, as the following examples indicate, the recent Hallyu K-pop idol bands are generating new waves and reaching different shores, including America and Europe.

In August 2011 Billboard launched a new chart, the Billboard K-Pop Hot 100.[6] In November 2011, boy band Big Bang won the 2011 MTV Europe Music Awards' Best Worldwide Act Award, hosted in Belfast, Northern Ireland. Its EP album *Tonight*, released in February 2011, became the first K-pop album to reach the top 10 on the U.S. iTunes chart and is the only non-English-language album in the top 100.[7] Girl group 2NE1 won the MTV Iggy's Best New Band in the World Award for 2011 and gave a performance to honor the award at Times Square in New York in December 2011.[8] In January 2012, another girl group, Girls' Generation, made its official American debut on the stage of CBS's *The Late Show with David Letterman*, and the next day performed its American debut song "The Boys" again on *Live! with Kelly* (Jung 2013). The group's earlier song "Gee" (2009) had exceeded 80 million views on YouTube as of June 2012, making them the first female K-pop group to reach that mark,[9] and their 2013 song "I Got a Boy" won the Video of the Year at the 2013 YouTube Music Awards. In March 2012 Super Junior's hit song "Mr. Simple" (2011) exceeded 40 million views on YouTube, making the band the first current male K-pop group to reach that mark.[10] And also in March 2012, a member of the male trio JYJ, Kim Jaejoong, won his second award as "Best Celebrity in Social Media" in the Shorty Awards. The Shorty Awards is known as the Twitter version of the Oscars and annually "honors the best of social media, recognizing the people and organizations producing real-time short-form content across Twitter, Facebook, Tumblr, YouTube, Foursquare, and the rest of the social web," hosted since 2009 at the New York Times Center.[11] By winning these awards, Kim has surpassed other international pop sensations like Justin Bieber and Miley Cyrus in the social media world.[12]

How has Hallyu K-pop come this far? One of the contributing factors is Korea's intense development of information and communication technologies, leading the K-pop industry to actively utilize user-generated international social networking sites and video sharing sites like Facebook, Twitter, and YouTube to promote and disseminate K-pop from early on. Since the early 2000s, Korea has gone through dramatic market changes, including the pop culture market. In addition to exercising its typical functions of disseminating music videos and responding to fans' (and antifans') feedback, the K-pop industry now exploits these new social media to the maximum, including K-pop flash mob contests and K-pop "cover dance" contests and festivals.

Flash mob ("a public gathering of complete strangers, organized via the Internet or mobile phone, who perform a pointless act and then disperse again")[13] has been a popular fandom activity among K-pop idol fans, as they can dance as a group imitating their favorite bands' group dance movements. Countless K-pop flash mobs from all over the world (Jakarta, Bangkok, Macau, Los Angeles, Chicago, New York, Vancouver, Melbourne, Sydney, Milan, London, Hamburg, Paris, São Paulo, Mexico City, Buenos Aires, Dubai, and more) have been posted on YouTube and simultaneously linked to Facebook and Twitter. Popular ones are instantly acknowledged by the K-pop idols via Twitter, Facebook, and other social media, quickly generating even greater circulation. While most K-pop flash mob videos follow the same basic idea, some of the more elaborated ones show coordinated efforts among the participating fans to create high-quality clips. For example, a popular K-pop flash mob video *Super Junior Flashmob in Milan (KPOP ITALIA) 11.10.16*, shot in front of Milan Cathedral, was posted on YouTube in October 2011, and had been viewed over 160,000 times as of

March 2012.[14] Organized by kpopitalia.net, the fans' flash mob project team posted a teaser and dance tutorial video six days before the flash mob day on Facebook, Twitter, and YouTube. This video is about a wishful message from Super Junior's fans in Milan to the band (as well as to S.M.) as they yearn to see "Super Junior's 2011/12 World Tour-Super Show 4" in Milan. The fans' message in the video is presented as a minimovie that starts with a young Asian girl following handwritten memos given to her by strangers, which lead her to the place where the Super Junior flash mob is happening (for about twelve minutes), and ends by showing the fans holding the placards "Waiting for SS4 Super Junior." As the company was adding new cities and scheduling extra shows if they were assured of strong demand, the fans were posting flash mobs on YouTube and organizing campaigns and rallies[15] in an attempt to sway S.M. to give concerts in their cities before the tour officially ended in May 2012. For example, Super Junior fans in the United States campaigned for concerts in the United States through their Facebook page "Super Show 4: North America" because no city in the United States had been included in the tour.[16] Comments on the Facebook page from March 2012 include these:[17]

LILA DUNK: I want it in New York so bad!!

VANESSA SANTANA: if they came to NY for sure it would be sold out :D I know for sure my friend and I would go in a heartbeat and most likely her other 2 friends :D

SHAYELA HASSAN: the US is so huge that it'd be crazy not to have a concert for each coast—i'm hoping for new york like crazy, but I hope West coast ELFs get a chance to see suju too.

Through these kinds of fan-made flash mob videos and Facebook campaigns circulated in social media, the Hallyu K-pop industry can easily and instantly identify a fan community's location, size, and demographic makeup (e.g., gender, age, race/ethnicity), which can be extremely helpful for current and future marketing strategies. This is market research at no cost.

Another popular practice exercised through social media by the Hallyu K-pop industry is virtually hosting K-pop cover dance contests and festivals—one way to promote newly released songs and albums. As Billboard Korea reports, *K-pop cover dance* is "a term used to describe the imitation of K-pop artist's dance choreography," which is "the latest K-pop global trend."[18] One of the biggest K-pop cover dance contests, 2011 K-Pop Cover Dance Festival, was supported by the Ministry of Culture, Sports, and Tourism, Korean Culture and Information Service, Korea Tourism Organization, and Asiana Airlines, confirming Korea's nationwide support of Hallyu K-pop. The festival was hosted by Visit Korea Committee in Korea as a part of the Hallyu Dream Festival celebration in October 2011.[19] The project director states, "The cover dance boom has created a platform for fans from all around the world to actively participate in and enjoy K-Pop; and therefore, it is helping expand K-Pop as a truly international form of social entertainment."[20] This shows that the Hallyu K-pop industry is clearly aware of the convergence of fan/consumer behavior that is rapidly shifting to being participatory through their daily social networking. For the festival, 1,700 amateur contestants from sixty-four countries submitted video files online, and those chosen for the second round had to go through the regional finals (hosted in Moscow, São Paulo, LA, Tokyo, Bangkok, Madrid, and Seoul) before entering the final competition in Seoul.[21] The semifinal rounds (sixty-six finalists from ten countries) and the final show were broadcast by MBC (Munhwa Broadcasting Corporation) as an entertainment-documentary series, entitled *Cover Dance Festival K-POP Road Show 40120* (40120 being the distance around the globe in kilometers), including sixteen teams from all over the world (Europe: five, Africa: one, the United States: four, Latin America: four, Asia: five).[22]

More common examples of K-pop cover dance contests are usually held by the major Hallyu K-pop companies and their associated acts via various social media. For example, 2NE1 held the "I AM THE BEST—Dance Cover Contest" from July 8 to August 5, 2011, through YG's official event page on YouTube.[23] An announcement was posted on 2NE1's Facebook page, with step-by-step guidelines and tips:[24]

2NE1's 2011 Global Event VER.2!!!!!!!!

Regardless of your nationality or age, everyone from all over the world who loves 2NE1 can participate. Remember the [2NE1 LONELY COVER CONTEST] boom? Now, this is a chance for you to ride a current by participating in 2NE1's 2nd cover event! Please upload a dance cover of "I AM THE BEST." The winner will be invited to 2NE1's first concert!

The official music video of 2NE1's "I'M THE BEST" on YouTube (uploaded on June 27, 2011) alone had over 56 million views as of March 2012, making it one of the most popular Hallyu K-pop videos on YouTube.[25]

By encouraging their international fans to participate in the contest, 2NE1 invited their fans to join the promotion of their new song. At the same time, the fans got the chance to be creative by making their cover dance videos and circulating them through social media. As discussed by media studies scholars such as Henry Jenkins (2006a; 2006b) and Michael Kackman (2010), this chain of media circulation through social media is enabled by "media convergence and participatory culture," allowing both the industry and the consumers to conveniently promote, circulate, appropriate, re-create, and recirculate media contents. In other words, motivated by the opportunities of receiving gift boxes, visiting Korea to see concerts, and meeting the pop idols, fans are eager to participate in these events, handily serving the marketing needs of the company at very little cost. For Hallyu K-pop, the industry's exploiting flash mob and cover dance contests via YouTube works particularly well since most Hallyu K-pop idols focus on dance-oriented songs, presented in styles that emphasize the visual.

The scale of current Hallyu K-pop expansion was simply unimaginable during the periods prior to the current period of social media explosion. As Choe and Russell write:

> The Korean Wave has long conquered Asia, but before the proliferation of global social networks, attempts by K-pop stars to break into Western markets, including the United States, had largely failed. But now YouTube, Facebook and Twitter make it easier for K-pop bands to reach a wider audience in the West, and those fans are turning to the same social networking tools to proclaim their devotion. (Choe and Russell 2012)

Expansion notwithstanding, it is still hard to say that Hallyu K-pop has made the commercial breakthrough hoped for in the U.S. market. Although iTunes Store, the biggest online music store, has recognized K-pop's potential and began selling it in 2009, conventional mainstream American pop media such as music television channels (MTV, VH1), radio, and magazines seem hesitant about including K-pop. Nevertheless, the Hallyu K-pop industry is continuing its efforts in the United States, as the latest attempt by S.M.'s nine-girl group Girls' Generation shows. After all, the American music market is still the biggest and the most powerful one, the ultimate confirmation of true transnational cultural success for which the Hallyu K-pop industry has been yearning.

The Girls' Generation's case is telling. Signed with Interscope Records

(Universal Music Group), Girls' Generation made its American debut performances on two major television talk shows. These appearances would not have been booked if the group had not already gained a following in the United States. As is evident on the Google Trends graph, the group as a "trend" in the United States jumped sharply right after the appearances.[26] Yet this alone does not guarantee that the group will be able to break into the United States market. Their American debut song "The Boys" (in English) follows the conventions of Hallyu K-pop songs, dance-oriented, minimalistic lyrics, and short catchy refrains ("bring the boys out" repeated twenty-one times). In a manner slightly different from their usual styles, the girls dressed more sexily, particularly on the *Late Show with David Letterman* appearance (in fishnet stockings), and their dance moves were much more suggestive and less cutesy than their earlier dancing styles. Responses to the YouTube clips of the music video and the David Letterman show performance addressed the girls' sexy dance moves, but did not seem to like the song itself (Jung 2013). Both the music video and the Letterman clip barely made a few million views upon their releases, contrasting sharply with the over 80 million views for their earlier song "Gee," for example.

Girls' Generation has not securely established itself in the United States music market.[27] However, given its immense following all over Asia and Europe, which continues to grow through social media, the group's career in the United States may take off if the right momentum is formed by their American fans' active social networking.

Conclusion

Hallyu K-pop has recently been gaining worldwide recognition and success largely thanks to the major social media spaces like Facebook, Twitter, and YouTube. This development provides very strong support for the proposition that, with the revolutionary emergence of media convergence and participatory culture, cultural products from a small country like Korea can also be circulated and consumed extensively, rapidly, and massively, on a par with American popular cultural products. The current wave formation of Hallyu K-pop is an intriguing example of how both the industry and the consumers successfully transform themselves into equally important players in the global game of social networking. However, it certainly has not happened by chance. The Hallyu K-pop industry took more than a decade to establish its current status by actively adopting new digital technologies and utilizing newly available social media spaces like Facebook, Twitter, and YouTube. By expanding engagements with fans, actively encouraging K-pop fans all over the world to participate in fandom activities through social media, the Hallyu K-pop industry exploits its potential to the maximum with very little investment of either time or money.

As marketing experts Turner and Shah argue, "Social media is similar to a snowball. When it gets going, it builds and builds. With a little bit of luck and a good amount of work, your social media campaign will eventually create its own circular momentum. When that happens, you're off to the races" (2011, 94). As more and more K-pop singers and groups such as 2NE1 and Big Bang attempt to expand their careers internationally, including in the United States and Europe, it is clear that Hallyu K-pop is still forming new waves, and attempts to form that snowball effect may actually result in the kind of mega-momentum needed for a true transnational breakthrough of Hallyu K-pop as a whole. In the meantime, scholars of popular music, of Korea, and of new media can benefit from recognizing the enormous significance of the powerful forces put into motion in these music-social media confluences, and the unpredictable directions in which they can go.

NOTES

1. Pease (2006) offers a pre-social-media-age examination of the triangular relation between digital media technology, K-pop, and fandom.

2. Editors' note: As a term originated from Japan's aidoru system, a K-pop idol (aidol) is a popular K-pop celebrity and media personality under the age of thirty who has trained several years under a "factory-like" talent agency system in Korea. For more about Korea's K-pop idol system, see Seung-Ah Lee's and Roald Maliangkay's chapters in this volume. Throughout the volume, the English spelling *idol* will be used in place of *aidol*.

3. In addition to a number of books on television dramas in Korean, the major edited volume on Hallyu in English, *East Asian Pop Culture*, is devoted solely to television drama-related issues (Chua and Iwabuchi 2008).

4. The several academic sources available in English include Sung 2006; Pease 2006; Jung 2009a; 2009b; 2010; and 2013; and two chapters in Jung 2011a.

5. See further Yi (1999).

6. "Billboard K-Pop Hot 100 Launches; Sistar Is No. 1 on New Korea Chart," Billboard, accessed March 25, 2012, http://www.billboard.com/charts/k-pop-hot-100#kFUkJlXTEYt5ulr3.99.

7. "Tonight Reaches #7 on the US iTunes Top Albums," Soompi, accessed March 25, 2012, http://www.soompi.com/2011/02/24/tonight-reaches-top-ten-on-us-itunes-top-pop-albums/.

8. "K-Pop Superstars 2NE1 Crowned Best New Band in the World!" MTV, accessed March 25, 2012, http://www.mtviggy.com/best-new-band/.

9. "Gee," YouTube, accessed July 15, 2012, http://www.youtube.com/watch?v=U7mPqycQ0tQ.

10. "Mr. Simple," YouTube, accessed March 29, 2012, https://www.youtube.com/watch?v=r6TwzSGYycM.

11. "Hollywood Has the Oscars. Broadway Has the Tonys. Now Twitter Has the . . . Shorty Awards," Shortyawards, accessed March 27, 2012, http://shortyawards.com/about.

12. "Celebrity of the Year," Shortyawards, accessed March 27, 2012, http://shortyawards.com/category/celebrity.

13. "Flash mob," Oxforddictionaries, accessed March 27, 2012, http://oxforddictionaries.com/definition/english/flash%2Bmob#m_en_gb0972977.

14. http://youtu.be/cZasjtF389s

15. On May 1, 2011, over one thousand K-pop fans protested at Le Louvre to sway S.M. Entertainment to add another date to the "SM Town Live" in Paris concert because they did not have the chance to buy tickets to attend the concert on June 10, 2011, at Le Zenith (only 6,000 seats). Soon after the initial protest, a series of K-pop fans' protest-plus-flash mobs were organized throughout Europe. http://www.koreaboo.com/index.html/_/concerts/protest-at-the-louvre-attracts-over-1000-kpop-r5948; http://www.hellokpop.com/2011/05/02/1000-kpop-fans-protest-at-le-louvre/.

16. http://www.facebook.com/pages/Super-Show-4-North-America/223367677674973.

17. http://www.facebook.com/pages/Super-Show-4-North-America/223367677674973.

18. "A Look inside the 'K-Pop Cover Dance' Trend," Billboard, accessed March 27, 2012, http://www.billboard.com/news/a-look-inside-the-k-pop-cover-dance-trend-1005420832.story#/news/a-look-inside-the-k-pop-cover-dance-trend-1005420832.story.

19. http://www.hallyudreamfestival.or.kr/main.html.

20. http://www.hallyudreamfestival.or.kr/main.html.

21. "Round 2 of '2011 K-Pop Cover Dance Festival' to Be Directly Judged by Hallyu Idol Stars," Allkpop, accessed March 30, 2012, http://www.allkpop.com/2011/08/round-2-of-2011-k-pop-cover-dance-festival-to-be-directly-judged-by-Hallyu-idol-stars.

22. "Idol Groups to Judge New Show, 'Cover Dance Festival K-POP Roadshow 40120," Allkpop, accessed March 30, 2012, http://www.allkpop.com/2011/09/idol-groups-to-judge-k-pop-cover-dance-festival.

23. http://www.youtube.com/ygevent

24. "2NE1 'I AM THE BEST' DANCE COVER CONTEST !!!" Facebook, accessed March 30, 2012, http://www.facebook.com/notes/2ne1/2ne1-i-am-the-best-%EB%82%B4%EA%B0%80-%EC%A0%9C%EC%9D%BC-%EC%9E%98%EB%82%98%EA%B0%80-dance-cover-contest-/189441577780003.

25. The cover dance contest winner was a team from Vietnam, L.Y.N.T, whose contest entry video gained over 840,000 marks. See "[2NE1 'I AM THE BEST' DANCE COVER] L.Y.N.T from Vietnam" available at http://www.youtube.com/watch?v=ScFCRm7tfbs.

26. "Girls Generation in the U.S.," Google Trends, accessed March 29, 2012, http://www.google.com/trends/?q=Girls+Generation&ctab=0&geo=us&geor=all&date=all&sort=0.

27. In his February 6, 2012, *Wall Street Journal* article, "Can Girls' Generation Break Through in America?" Jeff Yang notes that having Korean American members fluent in English in the group is definitely important for their career-building in the United States even though America's issues of racial and ethnic identities of Asians may cause some disruptions.

WORKS CITED

Appadurai, Arjun. 2006. "Disjuncture and Difference in the Global Cultural Economy." In *Media and Cultural Studies: Keyworks*, rev. ed., eds. Meenakshi Gigi Durham and Douglas M. Kellner, 584–603. Malden, MA: Blackwell.

Behnke, Philip, ed. 2010. *Social Media and Politics: Online Social Networking and Political Communication in Asia.* Singapore: Konrad-Adenauer-Stiftung.

Burgess, Jean, and Joshua Green. 2009. *YouTube: Online Video and Participatory Culture.* Malden, MA: Polity Press.

Choe, Sang-hun, and Mark Russell. 2012. "Bring K-Pop to the West." *New York Times,* May 4.

Chua, Beng Huat, and Koichi Iwabuchi, eds. 2008. *East Asian Pop Culture: Analysing the Korean Wave.* Hong Kong: Hong Korean University Press.

de Ferranti, Hugh. 2002. "'Japanese Music' Can Be Popular." *Popular Music* 21 (2): 195–208.

Fisher, Eran. 2010. *Media and New Capitalism in the Digital Age: The Spirit of Networks.* Basingstoke: Palgrave Macmillan.

Garcia, Cathy Rose A. 2007. "Rain Becomes First K-Pop Star to Perform at Tokyo Dome." *Korea Times,* May 27.

Jenkins, Henry. 2006a. *Convergence Culture: Where Old and New Media Collide.* New York: New York University Press.

Jenkins, Henry. 2006b. *Fans, Bloggers, and Gamers: Exploring Participatory Culture.* New York: New York University Press.

Jung, Eun-Young. 2009a."Korean Wave in Japan vs. Japanese Wave in Korea." *Asian Musicology* 14: 5–40.

Jung, Eun-Young. 2009b. "Transnational Korea: A Critical Assessment of the Korean Wave in Asia and the United States." *Southeast Review of Asian Studies* 31: 69–80.

Jung, Eun-Young. 2010. "Playing the Race and Sexuality Cards in the Transnational Pop Game: Korean Music Videos for the US Market." *Journal of Popular Music Studies* 22 (2): 219–36.

Jung, Eun-Young. 2013. "K-Pop Female Idols in the West: Racial Imaginations and Erotic Fantasies." In *The Korean Wave: Korean Media Go Global,* ed. Youna Kim, 106–19. New York: Routledge.

Jung, Sun. 2011a. *Korean Masculinities and Transcultural Consumption: Yonsama, Rain, Oldboy, K-Pop Idols.* Hong Kong: Hong Kong University Press.

Jung, Sun. 2011b. "K-Pop, Indonesian Fandom, and Social Media." *Transformative Works and Cultures* 8. http://journal.transformativeworks.org/index.php/twc/article/view/289/219.

Kackman, Michael, ed. 2010. *Flow TV: Television in the Age of Media Convergence.* New York: Routledge.

Kaplan, Andreas M., and Michael Haenlein. 2010. "Users of the World, Unite! The Challenges and Opportunities of Social Media." *Business Horizons* 53 (1): 59–68. http://dx.doi.org/10.1016/j.bushor.2009.09.003.

Levy, Stephen. 2011. "Steven Levy on Facebook, Spotify and the Future of Music." *Wired*, October 21. http://www.wired.com/magazine/2011/10/ff_music/all/1.

Menn, Joseph. 2003. *All the Rave: The Rise and Fall of Shawn Fanning's Napster*. New York: Crown Business.

Miller, Kiri. 2012. *Playing Along: Digital Games, YouTube, and Virtual Performance*. New York: Oxford University Press.

Pareles, Jon. 2006. "Korean Superstar Who Smiles and Says, 'I'm Lonely.'" *New York Times*, February 4.

Pease, Rowan. 2006. "Internet, Fandom, and K-Wave in China." In *Korean Pop Music: Riding the Wave*, ed. Keith Howard, 176–89. Kent, UK: Global Oriental.

Scott, David Meerman. 2010. *The New Rules of Marketing and PR: How to Use Social Media, Blogs, News Releases, Online Video, and Viral Marketing to Reach Buyers Directly*. Hoboken, NJ: John Wiley & Sons.

Sung, Sang-yeon. 2006. "The Hanliu Phenomenon in Taiwan: TV Dramas and Teenage Pop." In *Korean Pop Music: Riding the Wave*, ed. Keith Howard, 168–75. Kent, UK: Global Oriental.

Turner, Jamie, and Reshma Shah. 2011. *How to Make Money with Social Media: An Insider's Guide on Using New and Emerging Media to Grow Your Business*. Upper Saddle River, NJ: Pearson Education.

Wong, Aileen. 2009. "5 Things to Know about the Wonder Girls." *People's Magazine*, October 25.

Yi, Tong-yŏn. 1999. *Sŏ T'ae-ji nŭn uri ege muŏt iŏnna* (What has Seo Taiji Meant to Us?). Seoul: Munhwa Kwahaksa.

4

Uniformity and Nonconformity

The Packaging of Korean Girl Groups

Roald Maliangkay

Hallyu has set new criteria for the presentation of male and female pop idols across a significant part of the Northeast and Southeast Asian region. The Korean entertainment companies that create and promote K-pop acts pay careful attention to the positioning of their stars, both on the competitive music scene in the region vis-à-vis similar acts, and within their own formations.[1] Boy bands and girl groups have proven to be the most successful K-pop formula. It appears that in order to maximize their commercial potential, agencies eschew deviating from an established set of expectations that comprise synchronized dance routines, a mixture of contemporary R & B, rap and hip-hop with a heavy beat, good looks, and the latest fashion, as well as high-quality music videos and conservative lyrics that suit the predominantly teenage fan base. Many have either noted or criticized the homogeneity of K-pop acts' look and sound (Willoughby 2006; Ch'oe 2012; Seabrook 2012, 91), but the uniformity in presentation is no new phenomenon and was first introduced to Korea in the 1910s (Maliangkay 2014, 21). What is more, this standard helped generate US$177 million worth of exports in 2011, and is a major factor in the expansion of K-pop's overseas fanbase today.[2] The various production agencies closely monitor their ever-diversifying markets and will do what they can to avoid jeopardizing their multi-million-dollar investments. It is partly due to the constant repositioning of existing acts and careful positioning of new ones that apart from a number of anti-Hallyu incidents and campaigns, there are few noticeable signs of K-pop fatigue as yet.

Like those in the West, Korean all-boy and all-girl acts are tailored mostly to teenage fans. Whereas all groups are ultimately distinct, the musical and stylistic differences can be fairly small. There appears to be considerable conformism among fans whose affection for a specific group often lies in the look of one or more of its members. Many comments on YouTube and SNSs relate to their physical beauty rather than their ability to dance or sing. In comparison to girl groups, boy bands generally display a greater degree of individualism. Their members tend to be styled more independently, and they have longer solo sections within songs and videos. The members of girl groups, on the other hand, often appear interchangeable. On many occasions they not only dress identically, but often sing in unison, performing the same dance routine, in seemingly egalitarian fashion.

The high degree of uniformity in both look and performance can, however, make the girls look like mere marionettes. One would expect agencies to do their best to avoid ostracizing fans, but all too blatant control of the acts can make their audiences feel manipulated and patronized. As a precaution, they have begun to incorporate elements that express resistance to the cultural hegemony through modest symbols of nonconformity. By adding a teaspoon of attitude or "street cred," the suggestion is created that the idols involved wish to break the mold and take some ownership of their act. The elements add a veil of fallibility and individualism to their picture-perfect looks and presentation and help avoid distancing those fans unable to emulate the ideals of beauty and affluence that the acts represent.[3] Even though the elements of resistance appear to be novel, they do not constitute a significant departure from the well-tested formula of the Korean girl group. The only major differences between past girl groups and contemporary ones can be found in their audiences, and the ways in which the various products are enjoyed and shared. In this chapter I analyze how in recent years Korean all-girl acts have been packaged in order to target specific audiences and meet their expectations. I deliberate on how such formations manage to compete in conformist environments by paying particular attention to styling and performance and the inclusion of modest symbols of resistance.[4]

Why Uniformity?

Videos showing girl groups in uniform performing in perfect sync abound among contemporary K-pop videos, examples including Gangkiz's song

"MAMA" (2012), Crayon Pop's song "Bar Bar Bar" (2013) and AOA's (Ace of Angels) "Miniskirt" (2014). Acts involving girls in identical costumes singing in unison and dancing in perfect sync have, however, been around since the colonial period (1910–45). Along with popular Western examples, such as the Andrews Sisters, international Korean all-girl acts, such as the Chŏgori ("Jacket") Sisters in the 1930s and the Kim Sisters in the 1950s and 1960s, provided much inspiration for later Korean girl groups. Although the style of music and performance of the acts would differ considerably over the years, many of them would cater to predominantly male audiences, who tended to forgive the frequent lack of musical talent among of the groups as long as they looked the part. Apart from a degree of eroticism, that part entailed a presentation that eschewed individualism and expressed solidarity toward the many men in uniform for whom they performed in identical costumes—including short skirts and hot pants—in Korea, Japan, China, and Vietnam (Maliangkay 2014).

Cynthia Cyrus shows that in the United States in the 1960s the vast majority of girl groups were characterized by uniformity in appearance and performance. She argues that it served to make the acts more familiar to fans by emphasizing that the girls were not individual stars in their own right, but, rather, team members of equal importance to the group act (Cyrus 2003, 179):

> The visual cohesion of the girl groups, the emphasis on group over individual, facilitated this kind of interchangeability, both within acts and between them. . . . Close analysis of the visual images which chronicle girl group success demonstrates the remarkable extent to which girl groups relied on a communal look. Their visual representations emphasised their sameness, their interchangeability. (Cyrus 2003, 183)

Cyrus argues that the interchangeability was intentional as it allowed fans to imagine being one of the girls. An album such as *We Are the Chantels* (1958) implied that fans could one day be part of the act, or an act exactly like it (Cyrus 2003, 184). This aspect is also an important factor in the appeal of K-pop girl groups today. A number of girl groups, such as T-ara, After School, and Nine Muses, have added, replaced, or lost members, sometimes in the space of several months. Although fans have on occasion expressed their strong dislike of such changes (Kim and Im 2012)—presumably for the harmful effect they can have on the team spirit among group members, so crucial to the fandom experience—changes in the composition of groups rarely have an immediate effect on their over-all sound.

The agencies recognize the importance of building loyalty among fans and allowing them to fantasize about being a group member. Apart from ensuring the synergy among members looks strong, they present them as being modest and approachable girls next-door who despite their various talents, have had to earn their place in the group. They therefore release videos of their stars practising their dance routines in front of a mirror without makeup or uniform. These "mirrored dance" videos encourage fans to try the dance routines and become more involved in the act, while indirectly highlighting the difficulty of the synchronized performances and the many hours of hard work put in by the stars.[5] The raw footage is intended to nurture fandom and encourage fans to upload a similar video of their own and circulate it via social networking systems (SNSs), just like they do with official videos.

Today, SNSs are one of K-pop's most important marketing tools. As with other forms of popular music, K-pop is increasingly consumed through social media, where the still or moving image of an act, rather than a "blind" sound bite, invites people to explore it. Record, video, and game stores have become a rarity in Korea, and the small number of phys-ical copies that are sold through conventional retail stores quickly sell out. The primary market for all forms of Korean popular entertainment is on-line. Since 2008, when Korea became the first country to see sales of digi-tal music media overtake those of physical copies, the growth of digital consumption in Korea has grown steadily, due, in part, to its high-speed mobile network (IFPI 2008, 8). A fast-growing number of Koreans use SNSs, such as KakaoStory, Facebook, and Cyworld, which allow easy shar-ing of entertainment media, including those available on YouTube. The importance of SNS to non-Korean fans of K-pop will be equally signifi-cant (Kim 2012, 3, 5).

The visual aspect of K-pop is a major part of its attraction. Inspiration for the styling and choreography of girl groups is drawn from a wide range of acts, including boy bands. In Korea, the first "real" boy bands—bands whose members have little creative input, such as by playing an instru-ment or by being involved in the composition of songs—emerged in the mid-1990s. Like girl groups, they offer synchronized dance routines, con-temporary R & B songs with a heavy beat and rapped bridge sections, and good looks, but there is greater diversity between the members' perfor-mances overall. While their outfits may be based on the same or a similar fabric, there is usually some variation in how the patterns are tailored and arranged, and members rarely share the same hairstyle.[6] Seduction is just as important an aspect of their performance as it is for girl groups, and many male idols take off their shirt during live performances. Even so, their music videos remain conservative. They are sometimes romantic, but unlike those for girl groups they contain few erotic elements.

The videos for girl groups, on the other hand, can be very erotic. Presumably because the eroticizing of women is so common, however, they have not raised many censorship issues as yet. Whereas cleavage has remained largely unused in both live performances and videos, in the next few years the surgically enhanced chests of a growing number of female idols may well be called to duty. Until then, girl groups like Girls' Generation, Sistar, miss A, AOA, and T-ara offer plenty of leg, tight pants, and bums for men and women to gawk at. In videos for these groups, the gaze of the camera often targets the hips directly or segues up slowly from the bare heels to the rim of their hot pants or miniskirt. In these cases, the groups' relative uniform look adds power and impact to the choreography while diminishing the remnants of individualism. Despite the eroticism and sometimes diva-like elements in the performances of some girl groups, the similarity in presentation associates innocence and compliance. The idols are portrayed as cheeky girls who love the camaraderie and despite being liberated have no ambition to stand out or dominate. The displays of individualism are thus subtle and they often express a subservience that is intended to underline the members' femininity (see also Kim 2011, 340).

In a study of music videos from the mid-2000s Kim Hoon-Soon argued that the images projected were either that of "a sweet and innocent girl (angelic) that stirs a sense of protection and is non-threatening to men" or that of a "provocative and sensual femme fatale (seductress) that threatens men with sex appeal as a weapon" (2005, 206). Many videos nevertheless incorporate the two images, while those that project only the second image are small in number. In the videos, which often comprise dance routines, all too powerful dance moves are generally avoided as they would jeopardize the notion of femininity and the suggestion of innocence, which remains oddly untainted by the fact that the girls' legs, arms, and/or abdominal areas are often left uncovered. Many idols wear white or black lingerie—such as in AOA's "Miniskirt" or Girls' Generation's 2009 video for "Chocolate Love," which shows a few of the girls peeking into a room where the full group is performing in negligees—but rather than projecting the girls as promiscuous it is steered toward an eroticized naïveté. Despite the large amounts of skin shown it is suggested that the women are unaware of the possible impact their revealing clothing may have on the male gaze. Another example is Starship Entertainment's video for the Sistar (Ssisŭt'a) song "Ma Boy" (2011). While the two girls sing that boys need to treat girls better, Bora is shown sitting on a bed in hot pants and a singlet looking somewhat glum next to a fully dressed, troubled-looking young man, sitting on a chair, who we may presume is her love interest. Her fellow band member, Hyolyn, meanwhile, is shown standing in a kitchen wearing an identical outfit and high heels while a young man faces her leaning against the opposite wall of the kitchen with a look on his face that tells the viewer he's been told off. Since the dance sequences later in the video are fairly sexually provocative, with the two singers repeatedly curling their bodies in a wave-like motion standing sideways in order to show off their curves, the previous scenes appear intended to show that the young women remain chaste in their romantic lives.

The groups' management agencies which create the images that the acts project, whether they are submissive or empowered, or a combination thereof, do so in an attempt to exploit the girls' sexuality.[7] It warrants a thorough questioning of the notion of "girl power," which Kim Hoon-Soon appears to allude to. The concept is often adopted when girl groups gain popularity, and discussions consider the social pressure on women to conform to the standards of desirability and the genuine empowerment that may come from it (Cyrus 2003, 190).[8] Among the issues that complicate the notion of power is the male ownership of most girl groups, their exploitation of the girls' sexuality, and the fact that the all-girl acts represent the power of the group over that of the individual. Since music videos affect young women's views on gender and sexual relationships, entertainment companies wield considerable power over young women's self-confidence in the face of social pressures to conform (Kim 2011, 334).[9]

The image of girl groups is not, however, intended for the male gaze only. Considering female fans between the ages of ten and twenty make up the majority of the fans of both the boy bands and girl groups,[10] the diversity in the styling of some female acts may be intended not only to help fans identify their idols and—more importantly—identify with them, but also to show the possibilities of different forms of styling in a diverse range of settings (Willoughby 2006, 103). K-pop videos are like four-minute catwalk skits that have a strong impact on notions of both male and female beauty and are foremost visual forms of entertainment. The videos showcase not only clothing combinations and hairstyles, but also dance styles and ways of interacting with others. Considering the girl groups' common offer of variations on a single fashion style, the reason behind the female consumption of the videos of girl groups will therefore lie not so much in any homoerotic fantasy—although this ought not be ruled out, especially when considering the boyish look or uncharacteristically tomboyish attitude of some of the girls mentioned later in this chapter—but, rather, in the fact that women enjoy "eye shopping" more than men. The positive impact of K-pop on Korea's fashion industry is significant. In November 2010, the Towers Records store in Tokyo's fashion district Shibuya had a set up of mannequins wearing the uniforms of the girl group 4Minute and boy band Smash that took over most of its main floor space.

A good example of the function of a video as a fashion show is the video for f(x)'s song "Pinocchio Danger" (P'inok'io, 2011) (figure 4). In a rhythmic stop-motion sequence between 1:40 and 1:50 into the video, the five members are lined up next to each other in white boxes, with each of them wearing a different outfit every few seconds. Another example of this musical display of styling options is S.M. Entertainment's video for the 2009 hit song "Gee" by Girls' Generation. This video, the various versions of which together had been viewed on YouTube more than 125 million times at the time of writing, starts with a young man arranging the members as lifeless mannequins in a shop window wearing very similar colourful jeans and sleeveless shirt-based combinations.

Controlled Rebellion within Uniformity

Music videos are not merely style indicators, but they also provide information on the singers' lifestyle and allow fans to imagine how their idol would express his or her affection in a relationship. Adopting an act's specific style signifies a set of sociopolitical preferences, and as Zillmann and Bhatia have shown (1989, 263–88), that set—as expressed directly, as in their study, or as associated with the style adopted by the individual—affects the degree of his or her attractiveness to others. Equally, Simon Frith has argued that music is worn as a badge informing others of the wearer's values and opinions and that this may result in the formation of subcultures (North and Hargreaves 1999, 76). The argument that leading styles in Korean popular culture represent subcultures seems, however, untenable. Kim Yeran posits that earlier acts such as Fin.K.L. and Baby V.O.X. were intended for female subcultures, but if Dick Hebdige's concept of subculture as "a form of resistance in which experienced contradictions and objections to the ruling ideology are obliquely represented in style" is applied, it is doubtful that the term applies (Hebdige 1979, 133; Lee 2007, 65; Kim 2011, 338). Perhaps it should be used only with reference to

Fig. 4. A sequence from f(x)'s song "Pinocchio Danger" shows various styling options. (From https://www.youtube.com/watch?v=kKS12iGFyEA.)

music acts that resist conformity as well as any form of ownership by a major economic or sociopolitical entity, and not, in other words, to any mainstream music act that along with its local fan base falls perfectly in the mainstream with its nonconformist style.[11]

Although there is a punk subculture in Korea that may well offer forms of genuine resistance to the dominant social norm (see Epstein 2000, 1–34), it seems that there are few others. Indeed, one may occasionally run into a small group of students sporting rockabilly-type hairstyles and outfits, but they only do so on special occasions and they will return home in their usual clothes. Kim Yeran contends that in spite of their girl-power image, idols always have to conform to the industry's set of norms (2011, 338). Indeed, if the idols, who are generally expected to conduct themselves both publicly and privately according to specific standards outlined in their contracts, were to reject the mainstream norms, they would risk ostracizing the many young teenage girls that make up their main fan base. They ought to flirt with resistance, therefore, not insist on it. The girls may tantalize as divas, but they cannot disturb the group synergy by way of too much individualism. Judy Park argues that the importance of maintaining the image of humble and approachable stars has been paramount in the success of Korean pop acts in Japan (2011, 23–34). Whereas in music videos the look and behavior of girls sometimes seem confrontational and flirt with resistance to the social norm, the stars do indeed remain courteous and unassuming in public life. It is this trait that allows fans to feel a connection with their idols, and it is this aspect that distinguishes Korean idols from most Western ones.

Susan Douglas argues that despite the inherent contradictions that girl groups generally represent, they have long managed to appeal to girls by taking on their plights:

> While girl group music celebrated love, marriage, female masochism, and passivity, it also urged girls to make the first move, to rebel against their parents and middle-class conventions, and to dump boys who didn't treat them right. Most of all, girl group music—precisely because these were groups, not just individual singers—insisted that it was critically important for girls to band together, talking about men, singing about men, trying to figure them out. (Douglas 1994, 97; see also Stos 2012, 119)

Epstein and Turnbull (2014) have found that in recent years many of the girl groups' music videos show the idols taking revenge on misbehaving boyfriends. Among the videos they mention are Wonder Girls' debut song "Irony" (2007), 2NE1's "I Don't Care" (2009) and "Go Away" (2010), and 4minute's "Heart to Heart" (2011). Despite the seemingly empowering actions of the idols in these videos, the videos for the Wonder Girls and 4Minute songs do little to change the groups' overall image since their performance and presentation remain girlish and seductive overall. The underlying message of the video for miss A's song "Good-bye Baby" (2011) appears to be similar: attitude is just sexy. The singers are shown taking revenge on an arrogant young male producer. After performing (in sexy, tight black outfits with high heels) around a glass cabin that shows him slowly drowning in fast-rising water, they blow up the stage. When the camera zooms in on the man lying hurt and soaked on the floor, he slowly smiles as if to show his approval of the girls' feistiness.

Videos by 2NE1 go quite a bit further. In the video for their song "I Am the Best" (Naega cheil chal naga, 2011), the very Lady Gaga-like glam-punk fashion and stage sets as well as the recalcitrant and masculine vocal style and performance are interrupted from 2:25 by a scene in which the styling of the girls is street-punk, albeit with lots of makeup and fake eyelashes, polished chrome spikes and perfectly groomed punk hairdos. In the scene, the girls sit on black stairs looking both aggressive and bored; to prove they're serious about their contempt for the industry the two girls holding baseball bats smash a few vitrines displaying their platinum albums. In another video from that year for their song "Ugly," the girls are shown trespassing into a fenced-off neighborhood to which "ugly girls [are] not allowed."

Soon after one of the singers has hurled a television through a shop window and another kicked over a trash bin, the girls spray-paint a few cars before turning the spray onto each other.[12] In videos like this the singers may appear boisterous and rebellious, but the likelihood that the teenage girl fans of 2NE1, whose styling and performance have always been about girl power, belong to a subculture with values and opinions that challenge those of the mainstream remains very small.[13] Even when one considers that a song like "Ugly" deals with the pressure on girls to conform to Korea's beauty standard, one must acknowledge that this is one of Korea's biggest all-girl acts and that it is itself under considerable pressure to conform. It has clearly been marketed as a music act for those who tire of the perfect and cutesy uniformity of so many other mainstream acts, be it because they don't like the music, the styling, or the message, or because they are unable to emulate their look. What the band represents in Korea, where social conformism and heteronormativity remain strong and would

Fig. 5. A second illuminated billboard spells out the song's message. (From
http://www.youtube.com/watch?v=NGe0hHvAGkc.)

certainly not allow vandalism by women for the sole purpose of expressing discontent over social norms, is therefore not so much a genuine alternative, but an alternative mainstream. Mainstream girl groups promoting
rebelliousness for the purpose of commercialism is not, however, new.
Referring to the all-girl acts popular in the United States in the 1960s,
Douglas (1994, 98) says,

> [They] mattered because they helped cultivate inside us a desire to
> rebel. The main purpose of pop music is to make us feel a kind of
> euphoria that convinces us that we can transcend the shackles of
> conventional life and rise above the hordes of others who do get
> trapped. It is the euphoria of commercialism.

The need for diversity is nevertheless a genuine one. With more and
more similar-looking girl groups coming on the scene each year, there is a
danger that the acts become too easily associated with one-size-fits-all
products that are created and launched as opposed to formed out of creative talent. In an interview in January 2013, YG Entertainment's CEO
Yang Hyun-suk acknowledged that "too many similar groups" had satu-
rated the market and reduced demand (Yi 2013). There is nevertheless
some irony in the fact that while it is generally understood that the indus-

try needs to be competitive, fans are under the same pressure as their idols to conform to various social norms. Nonconformity allows the suggestion of creative input and avoids the image of complacency, but the euphoria Douglas speaks of must be nurtured carefully. Rather than allowing all group members to express degrees of nonconformity and risk ostracizing the mainstream fan base, management companies have in a number of cases carefully tailored a single group member's styling and performance to express a controlled measure of resistance. Well-known examples of members whose physical appearance and performance represents resistance include f(x)'s rather tomboyish Amber Liu, 4Minute's Jeon Ji-yoon, and 2NE1's CL (Lee Chae-rin), who usually presents herself as having a tough attitude and recites her lines with a cynical smile and posing in that typical hip-hop-like fashion that tells the viewer that respect is earned and not a given.[14]

In February 2012, Thomas Entertainment and CJ E&M released the debut single "Never Say Goodbye" for their jointly produced girl group Tomboy Girls. Despite the title, however, there does not appear to be anything nonconformist about the group. The song is undeniably a romantic ballad, sung by a pretty singer with long wavy hair, who in the accompanying video carries a pink suitcase toward a caravan. In the comments section on YouTube where one version of this video was uploaded, a visitor wrote, "amber, u needa smack these chiks cuz they sure as hell aint tomboys!"[15] In April 2013, SimTong Entertainment's tomboy girl group GI (Global Icon) debuted with the song "Beatles." In the video for the song, which opens with a skull opening its mouth, the girls are shown performing with boy band-like attitude against a dark background. The girls all have an unmistakeably tomboyish look, much like f(x)'s Amber, and they wear different clothing combinations. Although the band's label initially planned to form a boy band (Jackson 2013), it eventually sought to fill a niche with a boyish girl band instead. It commented that it was going to be different "from the cute and sexy girl groups that come out almost once every week."[16]

Although GI set out to bring some change to the all too standard format of girl groups, an arguably more serious attempt to do so had preceded it in the form of the Taiwanese girl group MissTER. The girls in this group also sport very androgynous looks. In the video for their song "Super Lover" (2011) the synchronized styling and performance is more masculine and sporty, but the girls nevertheless remain dressed in the same uniform, albeit with slight variations. Throughout the video, female models appear in strapless dresses and high heels with long hair to offset the androgynous singers who appear to show their affection for the ladies when short sequences of them singing the chorus "and I'll always be your super lover" are edited in between close-ups of the ladies. The group, which on its official page (http://misster.pixnet.net/blog) claims to pursue a "gender neutral" (zhongxing) image "with a teenage girl heart inside" (zaishaonuxin) has not been very successful so far, which may be because of the quality of the act or its marketing, or because the act has become widely regarded as a lesbian one.[17] After all, new girl groups may flirt with or incorporate elements of nonconformity, but they venture onto thin ice when challenging society's heteronormative foundations.

Conclusion

In Korea, the girl group formula has long been a popular format. Because of the eye candy that contemporary acts offer, and their great exposure, a growing number of adults are finding entertainment in girl groups. It is likely that adult men are drawn more to the videos than the music itself, but this is not clear, especially since teenage girls make up the vast majority of K-pop fans. The inclusion of elements of attitude or resistance are perhaps not intended for adult men per se, but they may enjoy deviously interpreting the girls' actions as playful, sexual provocation. Considering most girl groups have a very large number of teenage girl fans, one might expect greater constraint in the depiction of sexualized femininity than one can currently find. The groups' performances place great emphasis on the members' bodies and movements. They are statements that advertise the idol collective as an ideal of female beauty and young women's potential. Although the picture-perfect girl groups would appear to add to the pressure on young women to conform to what is an increasingly unnatural beauty ideal, they also allow girls to dream of being part of the act. They embed in young girls' minds the notion that they, too, can be both the objects and subjects of the fantasy, regardless of whether that affords them any genuine empowerment. SNSs allow fans to form the camaraderie that constitutes such a crucial aspect of the girl group formula. They let them share ideas and experiences in regards to specific girl groups, as well as information that draws them closer to the acts.

Conformism and nonconformism are two important factors driving Korea's pop music industry. The entertainment industries must position and reposition their acts carefully, in order to avoid the image of complacency and mimicry, on the one hand, and too much individualism and attitude on the other. Whereas the strong conservatism and conformity have given rise to specific expectations in terms of performance, the industry still relies on innovation and the element of surprise. By avoiding attitude and conforming to social norms, idols show that they are respectful, approachable individuals that merely enjoy pushing the boundaries of normative behavior a little. Since their primary audience consists of teenagers, they cannot push hard. Korea's younger generations are under considerable pressure to meet set expectations that are specific to their gender, including success in education and at securing a desirable job or partner. A number of girl groups therefore express no more than a cosmetic degree of resistance; they do not advocate a true departure from those expectations. Since many picture-perfect acts have numbed the palates of many consumers, the industry has begun to create acts that can once again intrigue and captivate them. YG Entertainment's Yang Hyun-suk commented that in contrast to the early years of the Wave, his company is now looking for people who are not necessarily good-looking but have something special about them (Yi 2013).

When girl groups incorporate elements of attitude, they appear to have greater ownership of their own act. It is possible that those elements will resonate in particular with the growing number of somewhat older fans of K-pop who find the image of a subservient femininity less interesting. The girl groups' expressions of resistance can be empowering to teenage girls, their primary fan base. But unless both the acts and their fans resist the hegemony of the groups' management or the culture it represents, even if only in style or performance, they cannot be regarded as representing an alternative, or even a subculture. What is more, the various elements of the acts are difficult to separate entirely, and it would be wrong to automatically label any band that does not follow the standard format of the Korean girl group as nonconformist, even if it symbolizes resistance against the objectification of women let alone heteronormativity (see Stos 2012, 122).

The examples and factors presented in this chapter may suggest an outright denial of group members' individual talent or creative input, but this is unintentional. Many of the girls are not only talented, but they must work very hard and be extremely dedicated, endure public scrutiny, and sacrifice their private lives. It is highly unlikely that in spite of the fact that young talents are eager to sign contracts with the major entertainment agencies, they have no issues with the many professional and social demands their work and status demands. This is, after all, a music scene that is driven in particular by music videos, television shows, advertising and

SNSs, as opposed to merely a network of live stages. As a result its idols are not judged only on the basis of their individual talent, but on how well they perform as singers, dancers, models, actors, and celebrities. I expect that as K-pop further develops, a greater number of female idols will seek ownership of their work and by doing so actually resist the hegemony, much like the boy band JYJ has done in recent years.[18] Although this may not result in a dramatic change in the formula of the girl group, it may lead to a greater exposure of the collectives' individual singers, thereby drawing the focus away from the chorus line of legs to the personalities of the individual members. But such a change would not last, whatever the gender of the people in charge: why mess with a winning formula?

NOTES

1. The changes the careful positioning of K-pop acts has brought about are arguably most noticeable among male idols: despite sporting chiseled physiques, many of them have begun to use color foundation creams and lip gloss. They pluck their eyebrows, wear longish, labor-intensive hairstyles, and generally present themselves both verbally and nonverbally in a soft and gracious, arguably vain fashion that in Korea two decades ago would have been uncommon and probably considered unacceptable.

2. Overall sales of Korean music grew faster than those of other entertainment-related products, from approximately US$2.4 billion in 2008 to US$3.5 billion in 2011. Between 2010 and 2011, export sales of K-pop increased by 112.9 percent to US$177 million (Han'guk K'ont'ench'ŭ Chinhŭngwŏn 2012, 13).

3. On Korean Internet message boards one regularly comes across the recently coined terms *kkonminam*, *chimsŭng*, and *ŏltchang*, which commonly relate to the styling, physical fitness, and facial perfection of male idols respectively. Whereas the latter term is also applied to female stars, overall, the pressure on female performers to conform to a nigh-unnatural beauty standard remains high and shows no sign of waning as that on their male counterparts increases.

4. This work was supported by the Academy of Korean Studies (KSPS) Grant funded by the Korean Government (MOE) (AKS-2011-BAA-2106).

5. The intention behind the practice videos is somewhat similar to that of gaming software companies releasing "cheat codes" that allow users easy access to higher levels or additional features otherwise hidden. Although they would appear to do more harm than good to sales of the game, the codes generate additional revenue through the sale of various gaming news media and the advertising this generates, and, most importantly, they allow gamers to experience a greater sense of ownership and, thus, affinity.

6. In S.M. Entertainment's 2005 video for TVXQ's song "Tonight," for example, four of the five band members are wearing dark-colored jumpers left unzipped over white dress shirts with brightly colored neckties. Although there is great consistency in the styling, none of the members' outfits is identical. The idols all remain unique and identifiable. In the company's 2012 video for SHINee's song "Sherlock," the casual styling is so diverse, in fact, that the singers are like dancing mannequins showing off a designer's

line of street wear. In the various short cutaway scenes, different, more formal clothes are worn, but the combinations nevertheless offer an equal measure of divergence.

7. One recent phenomenon is the use of the term *samch'on* (uncle) fan for male fans of girl groups in their thirties and forties. Whereas I do not deny that the use of the term *samch'on* allows these men to solve what would otherwise be a socially unacceptable issue because of the sometimes near-pedophiliac nature of their affection, I doubt that the majority of these men who adopt the term do so without a sense of irony, nor do I understand why the attraction of young male idols with elder female fans shouldn't raise many eyebrows (see Kim 2011, 340; Kim 2010, 79–119).

8. For various approaches towards the notion, see Kim 2011, 334, 336.

9. For a study of the impact music videos can have on African American high school students' attitudes towards gender roles, see Ward, Hansbrough, and Walker 2005, 143–66.

10. See also Na 2011, 143. On February 2, 2013, the author attended a United Cube concert at Seoul's Jamsil Indoor Stadium, which featured, besides the boy bands BTOB and BEAST, the female acts G.NA, 4Minute, 2Yoon, and HyunA. Teenage girls made up approximately 90 percent of the audience.

11. Aoyagi argues that pop idols serve as "lifestyle role models" (Aoyagi 2005, 3).

12. The music video is very similar to the last four minutes of the original version of the video for Michael Jackson's song "Black or White" (1991).

13. In 2011, 65 percent of the fans on 2NE1's website were female, while 58 percent of the fans on Girls' Generation's website were male (Na 2011, 143).

14. Among boy bands, Super Junior's somewhat obese Shindong, SHINee's Taemin, and NU'EST's Ren could be considered to resist the norm. The latter have for some time sported long, blonde hair and as a result a rather effeminate look, unlike their fellow band members.

15. See comment by "untiliget1" at http://www.youtube.com/watch?v=9recWdoVfOQ.

16. From http://www.allkpop.com/2013/03/new-tomboy-girl-group-gi-global-icon-releases-member-images, accessed on January 6, 2013.

17. On July 27, 2012, the band's official fan forum (http://go.to/lovelymisster) had 1,436 registered members. By January 2014, the forum had been closed.

18. See Seung-Ah Lee's chapter on JYJ in this volume.

WORKS CITED

Aoyagi, Hiroshi. 2005. *Islands of Eight Million Smiles: Idol Performance and Symbolic Production in Contemporary Japan.* Cambridge: Harvard University Asia Center.

Ch'oe, Chi-ye. 2012. "'Nuga nugunji morŭge saengginŭn' kŏl kŭrup, idaero choŭn'ga" (Are Girl Groups That People Say "Come Out Looking Exactly the Same" Desirable Like That?). *Maideilli* (My Daily), August 29. Accessed May 15, 2013. http://www.mydaily.co.kr/new_yk/html/read.php?newsid=201208290827411130.

Cyrus, Cynthia J. 2003. "Selling an Image: Girl Groups of the 1960s." *Popular Music* 22(2): 173–93.

Douglas, Susan. 1994. *Where the Girls Are: Growing Up Female with the Mass Media.* New York: Times Books.

Epstein, Stephen. 2000. "Anarchy in the UK, Solidarity in the ROK: Punk Rock Comes to Korea." *Acta Koreana* 3: 1–34.

Epstein, Stephen, with James Turnbull. 2014. "Girls' Generation? Gender, (Dis)Empowerment and K-Pop." In *The Korean Popular Culture Reader*, ed. Kyung-Hyun Kim and Young-Min Choe, 314–36. Durham: Duke University Press.

Han'guk K'ont'ench'ǔ Chinhǔngwǒn (Korea Creative Content Agency). 2012. "2012-yǒn k'ont'ench'ǔ sanǒp chǒnmang II-p'yǒn: sebu sanǒpp'yǒn—2011-yǒn kyǒlsan kwa 2012-yǒn chǒnmang" (Korean Creative Content Outlook II: Details of Production—Results and Prospects). Han'guk K'ont'ench'ǔ Chinhǔngwǒn, Published online, January.

Hebdige, Dick. 1979. *Subculture: The Meaning of Style*. London: Methuen.

Jackson, Julie. 2013. "Global Icon Plays Up Boyish Charms." *Korea Herald*, May 16, p. 17.

IFPI (International Federation of the Phonographic Industry). 2008. "IFPI Digital Music Report 2008." Published online, January.

Kim, Ch'ang-gwǒn. 2012. "Mobail intǒnet t'ǔraep'ik" (Mobile Internet Traffic). KDB Taeu Chǔnggkwǒn (KDB Daewoo Securities). Published online, May 24.

Kim, Hoon-Soon. 2005. "Korean Music Videos, Postmodernism, and Gender Politics." In *Feminist Cultural Politics in Korea*, ed. Oh Jung-hwa, 195–227. Seoul: Prunsasang.

Kim, Su-a. 2010. "Sonyǒ imiji ǔi polgǒrihwa wa sobi pangsik ǔi kusǒng: sonyǒ kǔrup ǔi samch'on p'aen tamnon kusǒng" (The Increasing Objectification and Commercialization of the Image of Young Women: Discussing the Uncle Fans of Girl Groups). *Midiǒ, chendǒ & munhwa* (Media, Gender, and Culture) 15: 79–119.

Kim, Yeran. 2011. "Idol Republic: The Global Emergence of Girl Industries and the Commercialization of Girl Bodies." *Journal of Gender Studies* 20 (4): 333–45.

Kim, Yun-jong, and Hǔi-yun Im. 2012. "Chǒngsonyǒn dǔl kǔdaero ttara halkka musǒmne . . . Sonyǒ Sidae—K'ara iǒ . . . ibǒn en T'iara membǒ wangttasǒl" (How Scary That Young People Just Join In Like That . . . After Girls' Generation and Kara, This Time a Member of T-ara Is Bullied). *Tonga ilbo* [East Asia Daily], July 31, x13.

Lee, Kee-hyeung. 2007. "Looking Back at the Cultural Politics of Youth Culture in South Korea in the 1990s: On the 'New Generation' Phenomenon and the Emergence of Cultural Studies." *Korean Journal of Communication Studies* 15 (4): 47–79.

Maliangkay, Roald. 2014. "Same Look through Different Eyes: Korea's History of Uniform Pop Music Acts." In *K-pop—The international rise of the Korean pop music industry*, ed. JungBong Choi and Roald Maliangkay: 19–34. London: Routledge.

Na, Min-Gu. 2011. "Sinhallyu ǔi ridǒ, K-Pop ǔi 'susahakchǒk him' punsǒk" (An Analysis of K-Pop's Rhetorical Power). *Susahak* (Studies of Rhetoric) 15: 135–63.

North, Adrian C., and David J. Hargreaves. 1999. "Music and Adolescent Identity." *Music Education Research* 1 (1): 75–92.

Park, Judy. 2011. "The Aesthetic Style of Korean Singers in Japan: A Review of Hallyu from the Perspective of Fashion." *International Journal of Business and Social Sciences* 2 (19): 23–34.

Seabrook, John. 2012. "Factory Girls: Cultural Technology and the Making of K-Pop." *New Yorker*, October 8, 88–97.

Stos, Will. 2012. "Bouffants, Beehives, and Breaking Gender Norms: Rethinking 'Girl Group' Music of the 1950s and 1960s." *Journal of Popular Music Studies* 24 (2): 117–54.

Ward, Monique L., Edwina Hansbrough, and Eboni Walker. 2005. "Contributions of Music Video Exposure to Black Adolescents' Gender and Sexual Schemas." *Journal of Adolescent Research* 20 (2): 143–66.

Willoughby, Heather. 2006. "Image Is Everything: The Marketing of Femininity in South

Korean Popular Music." In *Korean Pop Music: Riding the Wave,* ed. Keith Howard, 99–108. Folkestone, Kent: Global Oriental.

Yi, Sŏn-hŭi. 2013. "K'ŏp'i masyŏnnŭnde tto k'ŏp'i ... pungŏppang aidol tŏnŭn ant'onghae" (Another Coffee When You've Just Had One . . . the Demise of Identical Idols Is Misunderstood). *Maeil kyŏngje nyusŭ* (Economy Daily News), January 2, p. 31.

Zillmann, Dolf, and Azra Bhatia. 1989. "Effects of Associating with Musical Genres on Heterosexual Attraction." *Communication Research* 16: 263–88.

5

Of the Fans, by the Fans, for the Fans

The JYJ Republic

Seung-Ah Lee

On July 31, 2009, with their recently released *Secret Code* well on its way to becoming the second best-selling album of the year in Japan, the Korean idol group Tong Bang Shin Ki (hereafter TVXQ) announced that they were leaving the company under whose management they had become international stars in the five years since their debut. Three of its five members—Jaejoong, Yoochun, and Junsu, who would go on to combine their initials and form the group JYJ—had filed for a provisional injunction to void their exclusive contract with S.M. Entertainment (hereafter S.M.) (Ch'oe 2009). Charging that the contract they had signed with S.M., the mammoth Korean record label, music producer, and talent agency widely credited with launching the K-pop portion of Hallyu, was no better than a "slave contract," JYJ entered into a protracted legal and publicity battle with the company. Waged precisely at the moment when K-pop seemed poised to emerge as a truly global phenomenon, announcing the full arrival of the phenomenon that S.M.'s founder Lee Soo-man would term the "New Hallyu" (shin hallyu), the ensuing battle would go on to reveal some of the more somber aspects of the reality behind the celebrated glitter of the K-pop wave. It would establish a new baseline standard for the protection of individual artists in an entertainment industry dominated by a powerful "management system."

The battle would also mobilize fans at an unprecedented scale and with a remarkable degree of organizational intricacy. At the time of the group's split, TVXQ boasted a fandom 800,000 strong, the largest for a Korean idol. Despite the immediate rifts that appeared within this fandom in the aftermath of the announcement, fans who sided with the three members succeeded in consolidating themselves into a significant force as a new entity. Throughout the sustained confrontation between JYJ and S.M. that followed, a confrontation that invited a much larger question about what the proper relationship between an entertainer and his management company ought to be within the rapidly transnationalizing K-pop industry, these fans took on a role of unparalleled importance. Alternately asserting their rights as K-pop consumers and their self-appointed duty as industry watchdogs, JYJ fans organized advertising campaigns, consumer boycotts, and even legal actions against S.M., and threw their collective weight against the existing system of power that heavily favored the entertainment management company over the individual entertainers. Fans' support for JYJ's claim against "slave contracts" further evolved into a discourse of human and labor rights within the fandom, and helped pave the way for a culture of charitable contributions on the one hand and greater political participation on the other among K-pop fans at large.

Following Henry Jenkins, I view these actions as examples of "fan activism." As "forms of civic engagement and political participation that emerge from within fan culture itself," fan activism is "often conducted through the infrastructure of existing fan practices and relationships, and often framed through metaphors drawn from popular and participatory culture" (Jenkins 2012). While much existing literature on the phenomenon of fan activism has focused on the mobilization of fan networks by celebrities through social media toward particular causes they espouse (Lady Gaga against "Don't Ask, Don't Tell," Bono for Africa, etc.), or the mapping of "fictional content worlds onto real-world concerns" (Harry Potter Alliance), the fan activism under analysis in this chapter focuses on a fascinating example of spontaneous mobilization of the fans by themselves aimed at changing the industry infrastructure that they saw as simultaneously infringing on their rights as consumers and violating the rights of the idols as employees, if not as creative agents. In this regard, the mobilization was civic-minded from the start. Spurred into action by a sense of crisis that the idols they love may be permanently expelled from the entertainment industry, JYJ fans played a pivotal role in turning what the Korean media initially described as "a fight between David and Goliath" into a landmark case that helped to shed light on the mechanisms of power within the Korean entertainment industry, establish a new society-wide consensus about fair labor contracts, and set a powerful precedent for civic-minded fan culture that would be imitated in large numbers across different idol fan communities.

In this chapter, I approach the case of JYJ vs. S.M. as a fascinating point of entry into what might be called an ecology of fandom, locating it within multiple Korean contexts: the history of youth culture (chŏngnyŏn munhwa) and its ambiguous relationship to politics, the systematic and institutionalized promotion of Hallyu by the state as a cultural export, the entertainment management system and its practices of both idol and fan production, and practices of online and mobile fan communities. How did the forty-month legal battle that ultimately resulted in a "mutual noninterference" settlement between JYJ and S.M. transform an idol fandom that had been heavily embedded in networks of mobilization and consumption controlled by the management company into a relatively autonomous and self-policed community? How, in other words, did TVXQ fans become members of the JYJ Republic and find themselves politicized in the process of pursuing their pleasure? We will begin with an overview of the place of fans within the idol-centered media environment of K-pop industry, and then trace both the micropolitical and macropolitical contours of JYJ fan activism.

Idol Production

At the heart of the global K-pop phenomenon sings, raps, and dances the idol. Far from being a creative agent in his or her own right, whose popularity is commensurate with the public's appreciation of the artist's skills and talents, the idol is a consummate product of what has been called the "management company system." Indeed, the Korean word for management company is kihoeksa, where kihoek literally means to "design" or "plan" a project.[1] Like the "studio system" or "star system" of old Hollywood—in the famously overconfident words of Louis B. Mayer, "A star is created, carefully and cold-bloodedly; built up from nothing, from nobody. . . . We could make silk purses out of sow's ears every day in the week" (quoted in Basinger 2009, 11)—the management companies that dominate the K-pop industry manufacture idols from scratch, not only through the more overtly commercial operations of distribution and promotion, but by maintaining control over every aspect of the idol's life and work that take place in the public eye. Jimmy Jeong (aka Jeong Wook), the CEO of JYP Entertainment, has commented that idol production occurs through an "in-house system" (Shin 2009, 507–23).

While Hollywood may have pioneered the vertically integrated approach to entertainment, the more temporally and geographically proximate model for the current K-pop industry comes from Japan's so-called agency (jimusho) system. Indeed, the term "idol" itself in Korea's current usage hails from Japanese media culture, where the word was popularized starting in the late 1960s as a name for young performers "designed to contribute to the industry's establishment in the market by virtue of their abilities to attract people and perform as lifestyle role models" (Aoyagi 2005, 3). Idols typically appear on the covers and inside pages of magazines, star in television dramas and variety shows, sing on television and radio and in concerts, and endorse products in numerous commercials. Their hypervisibility in Japan's highly crisscrossed and intertextual media environment makes them the nodal points of the entire entertainment industry, and links entertainment to consumerism. This is the reason why Galbraith and Karlin argue that idols in Japan have long functioned as "interchangeable and disposable commodities . . . produced and packaged to maximize consumption" and as "the currency of exchange in the promotion and advertising of all manner of other products and services" (Galbraith and Karlin 2012, 2). Over these valuable commodities, the agency maintains complete control in terms of production, circulation, and consumption. Indeed, if the idol is the currency, the agency may be the bank and much more. W. David Marx observes that agencies are responsible for "creating performers from zero, full coordination of artistic content by company employees, long-term market planning, and demands to control all media content pertaining to the idol" (Marx 2012, 37).

It was S.M. that imported this business model into Korea in the 1990s and perfected it through multiple iterations of boy bands and girl groups, such that it became the industry standard for the entertainment industry at large. A key aspect of the management system is the labor-, time-, and capital-intensive process that turns what Mayer so uncharitably called "sow's ears" into the highly lucrative "silk purses." This training process typically begins with auditions during which talent scouts seek to spot young girls and boys with the right stuff. The right stuff includes raw talent in singing and dancing, but as these can be acquired later to a large extent, they also look for evidence of personal qualities that are likely to allow the potential idols to withstand the strenuous training regime that is seen as essential to manufacturing idols as commodities. This is a highly selective process. According to Lee Dong Yeon, for every 100,000 teenagers who audition, only 1 percent will go on to become trainees, and only 0.1 percent of the trainees will eventually go on to debut as idols (Lee 2011, 14–48). Training requires daily lessons not only in singing, dancing, acting, and stage manners, but even in foreign languages such as Japanese, Chinese, and English. The training process usually lasts two to three years before the trainees, constituted into specific groups, are allowed to debut. The constitution of the group act follows a typical formula as well: at least one of the members should have strong vocal skills, one member should be good at rapping, one member should be a good dancer, one should be good at speaking, and finally, one must be especially good-looking. The group is then packaged according to a concept chosen by the management company. As this formula reflects, the idol group is from the start a commodity created to appeal to the broadest possible audience within the targeted demographic, and to take the fullest possible advantage of the cross-platform media environment into which it would be inserted.

While the kihoeksa system's indebtedness to the jimusho system is unmistakable, it is the very rigor and intensity of the training process on the one hand and the global ambitions of the industry on the other that distinguish the Korean system from its Japanese counterpart. S.M.'s BoA, for example, was picked up as a trainee at the age of eleven when she accompanied her older brother to S.M.'s break-dancing audition; JYP Entertainment's Jo Kwon underwent eight years as a trainee from the age of twelve to twenty before he was allowed to debut as a member of the four-men act 2AM. The training system and global ambitions go hand in hand with the industry practice of long-term exclusive management contracts. Such contracts are necessary, the companies argue, given the degree of risk that they undertake in order to turn unproven prepubescents into global stars. (S.M. is said to have invested some 300 million won just to bring BoA to her debut.) Asked in 2011 about the practice of long-term exclusive contracts—TVXQ's "slave contract" specified the length of thirteen years, for example—Lee Soo-man defended it as absolutely necessary in order to sustain the Korean Wave: "By thirteen years, we are taking into account three years in Korea, three years in Japan, three years in [other parts of] Asia, and three years [elsewhere] in the world. During this period, the company makes an investment on the future based on trust. It trains [the idol] meticulously in singing, dancing, acting, and even foreign languages. This is what's required to make a star. Agencies in the U.S. are limited in how much they can invest in an entertainer because their relationship is merely contractual" (Chŏng 2011).

What then is the nature of the relationship between Korean management companies and the idols, a relationship that cannot be encapsulated in "merely contractual" terms? Lee Soo-man's comment points to the intangible, less-than-fully-transparent aspects of the management system and idol production in Korea—collectivist ethos, an understanding of K-pop heavily inflected by what Jeongsuk Joo has called "pop nationalism," and a patriarchal management style, to name just a few (Joo 2011, 489–504). The youth of idols when they first sign up as trainees makes them particularly susceptible to the management system's demand that they relinquish their autonomy not only over how their performances and their image is sold, but also how their private lives are conducted. What they receive in return for giving up autonomy is the protection of the "total package." However, what frequently drops out from view in this exchange is the question of labor. As commodities whose consumability is heavily contingent on their youth, idols have limited shelf-life; the fact leads the management system to seek to make most of the idols while their popularity lasts. Because of K-pop's structural dependence on its global consumability, the management company's drive for maximum exposure and profitability in a short span of time frequently leads to inhuman workload and performance schedule for the idols. TVXQ, for example, made three round trips (total of six flights) between Japan and Korea in a period of five days between December 27, 2008, and January 1, 2009, and thirty-five round trips between Japan and Korea in the year 2008 alone (Ha 2011). In June 2011, Girls' Generation flew to Korea, then to Taiwan, then to Paris, and then back to Japan during a four-day period, all in the midst of a grueling nationwide "Arena Tour" in Japan; exhaustion led Girls' Generation member Sunny to collapse during a concert in Saitama, Japan.[2] Thus, Lee Soo-man's reluctance to reduce the management system to the "merely contractual" dimension opens up a gray area within which clear cases of labor exploitation are glossed over as something else not only by the management companies but also the idols themselves, who know that both their place within the group act and the group's place within the highly competitive idol industry are far from permanent. And it is precisely this gray area that JYJ's lawsuit against S.M. brought into spotlight.

From TVXQ to JYJ

To date, TVXQ remains both the crowning achievement of the S.M. model—proof of concept for what Lee Soo-man termed CT, short for "culture technology," a technology "much more intricate and complicated than information technology"[3]—and its biggest threat. A five-member act that debuted in 2004, TVXQ was modeled after the Backstreet Boys and trained heavily in a cappella ballad singing, in addition to dance-pop choreography. The group was an almost instant success in Korea; their first album, *Tri-Angle*, reached the top of the charts. TVXQ's debut in Japan the very next year, however, was a disappointment. S.M. adopted a localization strategy of introducing TVXQ as a J-pop group rather than as a K-pop idol, collaborating with the Japanese agency Avex Trax, and working with Japanese producers and songwriters. With few exceptions, TVXQ's songs were originally written in Japanese, and not Japanese versions of songs already released in Korea. Despite rough early going, the localization strategy proved successful in the long run, paying big dividends by 2008. Three years after their disappointing debut, TVXQ's popularity had grown to such a degree that they were able to hold the coveted "Arena Tour."[4]

TVXQ's success marked the beginning of the second Hallyu in Japan. Before TVXQ, Hallyu was largely classified as an obasan phenomenon, with the Japanese media focusing on "frenzied" women in their forties or above who had suddenly turned into giddy teenagers before their beloved Korean drama stars like Bae Yong-joon (aka.Yon-sama or "Lord Yon"), Won Bin, Choi Ji Woo, and others (Kaori and Lee 2007, 202–4). Reports of the Korean Wave in the Japanese media routinely featured interviews of teenagers who confessed that they were ashamed about their mothers' devotion to Korean dramas. S.M.'s decision not to ride the wave of the Korean drama fever in Japan or turn to the already established fandom of primarily middle-aged women allowed TVXQ to break the existing generational barrier in Hallyu fandom in Japan.[5] TVXQ went onto break all manner of records on Oricon Chart for foreign performers. Its fourth album, *The Secret Code*, sold some 310,000 copies and attracted 300,000 fans to concerts, including two back-to-back events at Tokyo Dome, a feat that not even BoA had accomplished. BoA, in fact, had previously enjoyed considerable crossover popularity in Japan but had not succeeded in creating a sizable fandom. In contrast, TVXQ boasted a fandom of 200,000 members in its official Japanese fan club called "Bigeast" by 2009. By all indications, it was clear that S.M. had succeeded in establishing K-pop as an attractive brand of popular music that combines the singing and dancing skills associated with performers considered as "artists" in Japan, with the fan appeal and currency value of idols-as-commodities. TVXQ's tremendous success would open the door through which numerous other K-pop groups would subsequently walk, all the way to the bank, taking world's second largest music market by storm. Taking a page from the jimusho system's playbook and modifying it aggressively, Korea's largest kihoeksa had heralded Hallyu 2.0.

At the pinnacle of such success in Japan, however, came the news that three members of TVXQ were seeking to challenge the entire management system by filing a lawsuit to terminate their contract with S.M. The lawsuit shed light on the exact terms of the contract that had provided the basis for a relationship between the management company and the idol that was supposed to stretch beyond the "merely contractual." The terms of the contract, which TVXQ members had signed while they were still minors, was thirteen years from the date of release of the group's first album, excluding the years of military service. (South Korea enforces universal male conscription.) Considering that the average lifespan of idol groups was about five to six years, a thirteen-year contract essentially meant a lifetime contract. The contract stipulated that the group would receive a certain percentage of the net profit, but profit calculations were never transparent.[6] The group was obligated to make promotional appearances for the company without pay, and had no power to adjust its own schedule. In addition, members had to transfer over to the company all rights pertaining to the songs they themselves had composed. In the case of a breach of contract, the members had to compensate the company an astronomical sum: "three times the company's basic investment + two times the profit that artist would be expected to earn were the contract term to be observed + $ 100,000." According to this calculation, TVXQ would have had to pay S.M. $40 million to end the contract. The same contract, however, stipulated no obligations for S.M. If S.M. wanted to cancel the contract, it would be able to do so at will.

The Seoul Central District Court concluded that the contract was indeed unfair and issued the provisional injunction to void exclusive contract that Jaejoong, Yoochun, and Junsu had sought. (The other two members of TVXQ, Yunho and Changmin, had decided to stay with S.M.) The provisional injunction gave the three members the legal basis to continue on as performers under their initials, JYJ. The battle between JYJ and S.M., however, was only beginning. S.M. filed an appeal against the court's ruling, and began to move the entertainment industry to block JYJ's appearance on television, radio, magazines, and even in concerts. In this, the second round of the conflict when the weapon that S.M. wielded was not the law but its tremendous influence over the entire entertainment industry in Korea, JYJ was indeed the proverbial David to S.M.'s Goliath. No fellow entertainer and no organization expressed public support for JYJ against S.M. Public opinion remained uninterested for the most part in the human rights of the idols whose image and lifestyle they associated with wealth and glamor. Some even expressed sympathy for the management company's need to recoup their heavy investments. It seemed only a matter of time before JYJ would buckle under pressure, and it was precisely at this juncture that the JYJ fans sprang into action.

Youth Subculture as Sites of Resistance

Idol fandom occupies an interesting place in the history of music-mediated youth subculture in Korea. Until the 1990s, youth subculture was strongly associated with resistance, not only of the dominant culture but also of the state authority. From the late 1960s to the 1970s, jeans and the acoustic guitar became symbols of the folk music movement through which Korean youths expressed their desire for freedom from the oppressive regimentation of life under the military dictatorship. In the 1980s, resistance songs functioned as catalysts for mass protests and campus-wide democratization movement. According to Kim Ch'angnam, "The liberal youth subculture of the early 1970s turned to purism and romanticism in dreaming of an escape from the unjust society, and the 1980s' youth subculture, with its orientation toward people's struggle and basis in a powerful political ideology, sought liberation from the oppressive state power" (Kim 2004, 29). It was with the appearance of Seo Taiji and Boys in the 1990s that youth subculture moved to the very front of popular culture, shedding its close association with political resistance. The explosive popularity of Seo Taiji's marriage of hip-hop and dance-pop made the teenagers recognizable for the first time as active consumers.

S.M. was the first management company to take this generation seriously as consumers, and manufacture a product packaged specifically to appeal to its tastes. Speaking about his motivation for putting S.M.'s first idol group together—the five-member boy band H.O.T., short for High-five of Teenagers—Lee Soo-man acknowledged that the idol group was indeed created "carefully, cold-bloodedly," based on available research about adolescents' aspirations. Relying on the results of a survey that found that teenagers were most envious of good dancers and wanted to own a motorcycle the most, S.M. recruited good dancers for the act and put them on motorcycles for their first music video (Chŏng 2011). Thus the idol system was born in Korea, and with it an idol fandom. The idol business is a fandom business in the end, as the saying goes; because the idol-as-commodity depends absolutely on the existence of loyal consumers, the management companies have developed a fandom system concomitantly with the idol system. S.M., for example, launched an official fan club for H.O.T., created regional chapters, and instituted a pyramidal officer system in each. The fandom was mobilized systematically on the day of the album's release to make the album take the top spot on the charts.

Consumption thus becomes a measure of the fans' dedication and the primary vehicle of expressing their identity. Ahead of album signing, fans purchase multiple copies of the same album in order to increase their chances of being selected to attend the signing. The management company produces multiple versions of the same album to induce more consumption. For example, S.M. produces fourteen versions of the same album for Super Junior with a different cover for each of the thirteen members of the group, and one showing all thirteen on the cover. Dedicated fans purchase all of the different versions. If the idol stars in a show, the fandom "offers tribute" (chogong) by organizing support activities such as sending gifts or catering meals for the actors and staff. All these activities are recognized as exhibiting the "firepower" of the particular fandom, and fandoms compete with one another to prove their love. (In self-derision, several fans I talked to referred to themselves as "ATM machines" for the management companies.) While it may certainly be possible to see the everyday micropolitics of what John Fiske called "semiotic, enunciative, and textual productivity" at work within the idol fandom (Fiske 1992, 37–42), no one today would deny that the kind of macropolitical struggles that had defined the youth subcultures of the 1970s and 1980s have receded. Idol fandom, subordinate to the commercial logic and readily mobilizable for consumption, is part and parcel of the larger management system.

Though brief, the history of idol fandom presented above helps us see what is so remarkable about the kind of fan activism spawned by JYJ's litigation against S.M. Bridging the micropolitical and the macropolitical, JYJ fans foregrounded their rights as consumers and mobilized fan practices of information sharing, discussion, and organization, in order to embark upon a highly intricate, coordinated, and sustained campaign against the power of the entertainment industry. The next section details the major milestones in JYJ fandom's sustained and multifaceted struggle against S.M., the management system, and the entire entertainment industry in Korea.

The Fans against the Industry: Journey into JYJ Fandom

At the time of TVXQ's split, there were three main online fansites devoted to TVXQ in Korea—Ikadong, *DC Inside*'s TVXQ Gallery, and Dongne-

Bangne (tongne pangne, hereafter DNBN). DNBN quickly emerged as the locus of JYJ fan activism in the early days of the members' lawsuit.[7] After an initial period of confusion and some internal dissension, DNBN quickly rallied around JYJ and began to organize. In the first year of the lawsuit, fandom activities in support of JYJ fell into three different categories. The first was a publicity campaign. The campaign was felt to be particularly important since the media coverage tended to focus not on the contract dispute but on JYJ's "lucrative" side-deal with a cosmetics company, essentially taking S.M.'s side and painting the three young men as "selfish ingrates" who had turned against the company that had made them superstars in the first place. The fans were also angered by the way the media portrayed their petition drive as "crazed" and "fanatical." With spontaneous contributions from individual fans, DNBN took out a front-page ad in the liberal daily *Hankyoreh* (Han'gyŏre) with the main copy that read, "What do your work conditions look like?"

1. Contract period to last at least thirteen years
2. A seven-day work week, no monthly days off
3. Salary to be determined by the employer, no negotiation allowed
4. All scheduling and job-related decisions to be determined by the employer
5. In the case of early termination, several tens of millions of dollars to be paid to the employer as penalty
6. In the event of personal time off, the contract period to be extended

These, of course, were the exact terms of TVXQ's contract with S.M. The ad called upon the readers to reflect on whether they would accept such working conditions for themselves, thereby underscoring the fact that the essence of JYJ's lawsuit was a question of systematic labor exploitation. The creation of the ad also reflected a process of online consensus building within the fandom. The emotions were high in the early days of the lawsuit, and many fans wanted to include incendiary language in the ad itself. A lively online discussion followed regarding the most effective approach. Ultimately, the view that a more measured tone and a message highlighting the labor rights of the three members should be adopted held sway. DNBN followed up with a second ad twenty days later. The second ad featured three "See no evil, hear no evil, speak no evil" monkeys in bondage, with the accompanying lines, "Don't try to see anything, don't insist on anything, and don't expect to hear anything in response." If the focus of the first ad was the artists' labor rights, the second ad brought their human rights into sharp relief and pointed an accusatory finger at the industry practice that had robbed them of autonomy. The universal values to which the fans appealed in these ads combated the negative image of TVXQ fandom as consisting of motley, screaming teenagers, and helped consolidate a sense of purpose among the fans themselves. DNBN supplemented these ads with a number of press releases as well, and collected more than 120,000 signatures in support of JYJ.

The second type of activity concerned the fans' rights as consumers. The revelation of the terms of the contract, especially as it concerned the payment of profits to TVXQ, filled the fans with indignation. The realization that all of the different ways they had supported TVXQ over the years as consumer-fans had actually fattened S.M.'s pockets and not the idols' led fans to call for a boycott of all S.M. products. In addition, fans took S.M. to court in a class action suit for the postponed SM Town concert in the aftermath of the TVXQ split. S.M. had already refunded the full price of the concert ticket, but the fans succeeded in getting the court to decree that S.M. should pay an additional 10 percent of the full value of the ticket to everyone who had purchased a ticket for the concert (Chang 2010).

Finally, fans appealed to government agencies, submitting multiple petitions to the National Human Rights Commission and Seoul Central District Court, and also filing a complaint with the Fair Trade Commission. In these pleas they drew attention to the unfairness of the contract between JYJ and S.M. and called on the commission to provide a revised standard contract for the industry (Kim 2009). Due in no small part to the fans' continued activism, in October 2011, Fair Trade Commission finally issued a revised standard contract for management companies and singers. The specific terms of the recommendation touched upon every single point of grievance that JYJ had brought to light in regard to their old contract with S.M., suggesting that the group's demands were largely justified.

We can examine several of these provisions in detail. The first, of course, concerns the term of the exclusive contract. The revised standard contract limits the term to a maximum of seven years save in exceptional cases. The contract also provides for the protection of the idol's right to privacy and other human rights, making the relationship between the idol and the management company more symmetrical and giving the idol a legal basis for refusing unreasonable demands by the company. Another provision stipulates that the idol has the right to determine his activities in accordance with his physical and mental condition. In other words, the company cannot unilaterally determine the idol's schedule and force it upon him. In the case of TVXQ, the team's Japanese debut was a unilateral decision in which the members had no say. Such a practice would be prohibited under the terms of the new standard contract. In addition, companies now have to protect copyright and neighboring rights of idols over their own compositions. Nor can companies demand exorbitant penalties from idols for terminating the contract early.

JYJ's early victory in court, however, marked only the beginning, not the end, of their struggles. A few weeks before the Seoul Central District Court's ruling granting the group an injunction to void the exclusive contract with S.M. in October 2009, thereby clearing the way for the trio to resume their careers under a different management company called C-JeS, S.M. had come together with other major management and production companies in the entertainment industry to launch a powerful new private organization consisting of industry CEOs called the Korean Popular Cultural Industry Federation (KPCIF). KPCIF became an oligopolistic conduit for administering pressure on the industry and blocking media exposure for JYJ when the trio released their first English album, *The Beginning*, the following year. In fact, the album itself was a direct outcome of the way the industry had ostracized JYJ in the aftermath of their challenge to S.M. The trio could not get any support from their colleagues. No one would give them a song to sing and no recording company would produce their album. In Japan, too, Avex suspended JYJ's activities without releasing them from the contract; it would take another two years for JYJ to win a legal victory in Tokyo District Court.[8] Thus locked out of the music industry in both Korea and Japan, JYJ had to find producers and composers in the United States. Eventually, they worked with Kanye West and Rodney Jerkins, and released their album via Warner Brothers Music. Following the release of *The Beginning*, KPCIF circulated letters to all television networks, cable companies, radio stations, and online music stores "requesting" that they refrain from playing or selling JYJ's songs. The reason the letter gave for the necessity of such an extraordinarily repressive measure was that JYJ was in litigation with S.M., and would therefore dampen the momentum of Hallyu. KPCIF thus appealed to and reproduced the virulent nationalist discourse surrounding the Korean Wave phenomenon.

The actions of KPCIF and the response of the Korean entertainment industry opened a new chapter in JYJ fan activism. Within the South Korean media environment, television is the all-important hub that connects all the spokes of the entertainment wheel together. Therefore, preventing an entertainer from appearing on television is like delivering a death sentence. Acting like a cartel, the management companies brought their weight against JYJ to prevent it access to airwaves, public and private. JYJ could not promote its album at all in the media, let alone have its music be heard, and had it not been for the concerted efforts of the fans, *The Beginning* could very well have been dead on arrival. The fans' identity as consumers took the front seat again. Rallying their purchase power, fans catapulted album sales to the top, with preorder and presale requests for 99,999 limited-edition CDs numbering more than 400,000. Fans also deployed their identity as consumers to condemn the industry's violations of antitrust laws. In a thirteen-page petition filed with the Fair Trade Commission, fans meticulously detailed all the ways in which KPCIF and S.M. violated their rights as consumers. One concrete example concerned online music services like MelOn, JukeOn, and BugsMusic. These services charge monthly membership fees to allow the user to stream or download the latest songs. The fans argued that they were being barred from enjoying the very product they had purchased when the music service refused to carry JYJ's music despite its tremendous popularity. In addition, six thousand overseas fans from 118 countries submitted petitions to Seoul Central District Court demanding that JYJ be allowed to appear on music and variety shows on television, and fans also demanded explanations from the broadcast companies as to why they were barring JYJ from appearing on their programs.

Two other instances of self-organization on the part of the JYJ fandom deserve mention here in terms of their logistical creativity and sophistication. One was the advertising campaign that ran in early 2011. With contributions amounting to $160,000 collected in ten days, with overseas fans from Taiwan, Japan, and the United States joining the efforts as well, fans published ads supporting JYJ on 120 buses and twenty-one subway stations. The process of creating the ad itself was a collective affair: out of numerous suggestions made by fans, the copy "JYJ, we root for your youth!" was selected after numerous rounds of discussions and voting, all of which took place in cyberspace. While the first advertising campaign that DNBN had led in 2009 was primarily aimed at the urgent task of getting what the fans saw as the truth of the situation out to the public at a time when the major channels of communication were controlled by S.M., the second advertising campaign performed the additional function of drawing fans closely together and encouraging their own struggle as well. JYJ had become a cause, and its fight had become the fans' as well, not by proxy but in very real terms. In my interviews with several fans who took on leadership roles within the fandom, for example, I heard of several different ways that the fans themselves had been physically bullied and otherwise intimidated to drop the struggle. Thus, this advertising campaign was an act of both self-production and self-consumption. In rooting for JYJ's youth, a slogan that deliberately revived youth subculture's historical association with resistance in Korea, the fans were also rooting for their own youth and exhorting themselves to persevere. As advertisers, producers, and target consumers all at the same time, JYJ fandom consolidated both their sense of community and their identity as social activists.

Another notable event occurred in early 2012 when CGV, one of the largest multiplex chains in Korea, decided to cancel the screening of *The Day*, a documentary film about JYJ (Cho 2012). CGV is a subsidiary of CJ Group, a conglomerate with a thriving entertainment wing. CGV had agreed with C-JeS to premiere *The Day* around Valentine's Day. Fans had been eagerly awaiting the premiere because the limitations that the industry placed on JYJ's media exposure had severely curtailed the venues through which fans could consume their idol. When CGV thus reneged on the contract without an explanation and ignored both the fans' and C-JeS's vociferous protestations, the fandom sprang into action. Fans decided to boycott any and all products of the CJ Group, the parent company of CGV, and used social media to perform and publicize the boycott. They took a picture after breaking their CJ membership card in half, and posted the image of the destroyed card on Twitter. While the boycott and the publicity campaign on twitter did not lead CGV to reverse its decision, an earlier campaign surrounding what fans viewed as false reporting actually did lead to immediate, appreciable results. When September 2011 issues of *GQ* and *Allure* carried articles about JYJ in which the reason for JYJ's departure from S.M. was attributed to the trio's cosmetics business, fans tweeted the writers of the articles to explain that these were unfounded rumors (Chang 2011; Shin 2011). However, the writers treated them as if they were fanatics who could not accept any criticism of their idols. Angered by the patronizing suggestion that they were irrational and puerile, JYJ fans adopted a different tactic and started tweeting the CEO of the Doosan Group, the company that publishes *GQ* and *Allure*. They knew that Doosan Group's CEO was an avid user of Twitter. Fans from all over the world sent tweets to the CEO in which they explained the situation surrounding JYJ's contract dispute with S.M. The strategy worked. The CEO ordered the editors of the two magazines to publish an apology and a correction in the subsequent issue. It was a meaningful triumph for the fans. They had learned to use the existing hierarchy of power to resolve the given conflict in their favor.

Even though JYJ fans did not win all of the battles they engaged in, their macropolitical struggles did lead to real, appreciable changes to the industry. On July 24, 2013, three years after KPCIF had circulated its letter to the various media outlets, the Fair Trade Commission concluded that S.M. and KPCIF had indeed exercised undue influence on the industry to obstruct JYJ's career (Shin 2013). "Considering the nature of KPCIF as an organization consisting of entertainment-related businesses and S.M.'s influence as one of the three largest management companies, the document it circulated did have the effect of pressuring related companies," found the Fair Trade Commission. "The meaning of the current decision lies in prohibiting a large management company from working with an industry organization and using its influence in order to obstruct the activities of a group of entertainers with which it is undergoing a contract dispute." Even though JYJ has yet to make an appearance on a music or variety show on television, the Fair Trade Commission provided a clear warning against the oligopolistic practices of the entertainment management companies, puncturing the discourse of nationalism surrounding Hallyu to reveal the JYJ case as one of labor exploitation and influence peddling. It was fans who had played an instrumental role in bringing about this ruling. The lengthy and arduous process had made the JYJ fandom aware of itself as capable of constituting a power bloc that can influence the political economy of idol entertainment. No longer the ATM machines into which the management companies can expect to insert the card called "cultural contents" and draw cash instantaneously, JYJ fandom has managed translate participatory fan culture into highly visible forms of civic engagements.

The JYJ Republic

An enduring bone of contention within the former TVXQ fandom after the splitting of the group in 2009 concerned the question of proprietorship over the TVXQ name. For majority of the fans, the name TVXQ belonged to the idols themselves, the five members of the group whom they loved so dearly. For S.M., however, TVXQ was a commodity and the name belonged to the creator of the brand, the management company. Lee Sooman suggested as much when he stated during his Stanford Graduate School of Business talk that the culture technology of Hallyu inhered not in the contents themselves but belonged to the producer of those contents. As had been done with the Japanese idol group Morning Musume— members could "graduate" out of the group, be "lent" out to other acts, be reshuffled, or added altogether, all without damaging the group itself—S.M.

had the ambition to turn TVXQ into a brand that would not be attached to the vagaries associated with individual performers, like growing old, for example. With the biggest fandom in the world, the TVXQ brand was very valuable indeed.

Many JYJ fans also rooted for the two performers, Yunho and Changmin, who had decided to stay with S.M., and hoped for the day when the five members would be reunited as TVXQ. S.M.'s 2010 decision to release a comeback album for TVXQ with Yunho and Changmin only thus struck many fans as an act of betrayal. Fans had expected the two members to resume performing, but under a different name altogether. JYJ had done the same out of the respect for the TVXQ name, which they felt belonged to all five members. Moreover, the lead song of the new album, "Why? Keep Your Head Down," contained lyrics that many fans believed were meant to "disrespect" JYJ. The album killed the hope that the five-member TVXQ could one day return. Now fans had to decide whom they would support: the two-member TVXQ or JYJ. The JYJ Republic was born precisely from this choice. Despite some heated disputes, all three major fansites decided to support JYJ exclusively in the end. The sites still used the name TVXQ, but identifying themselves as supporters of JYJ, the fans conveyed their belief that the legacy and tradition of TVXQ rests with JYJ.

While fandom has more frequently been imagined as a "nation"—for example, Celtic Nation for Boston Celtics and A-Nation for the idols belonging to Avex Trax label in Japan—I use the metaphor of the republic in order to highlight the horizontal organization and emphasis on autonomy that characterize the JYJ fandom. Indeed, there is a strong sense of citizenship among the fans, born of the experience of sustaining an organized and multifaceted struggle against S.M. and the Korean entertainment industry over several years. Anyone who has spent even a short period of time within these JYJ online communities readily discerns a sense of pride that permeates the fansites for having defended not only the artists they love but their own conscience and indeed the cause of justice. The culture is very much participatory and the collective good is highlighted. Not surprisingly, the fandom's motto invokes the word justice: "Justice is helping the weak." Citizenship is open all, though most members are women. (About 90 percent of JYJ fans in Korea are women, of which about 70 percent are in their twenties and thirties.)

Moreover, the fandom is highly effective in self-policing. As with any idol fandom, JYJ fandom has its share of ugly fans, and yet, possibly because of the fandom's high moral tone and remarkable vigilance in protecting the artists, the ugly fans are systematically marginalized as illegal immigrants to the republic. In addition to the well-studied phenomenon of antifans,[10] there are two other notable types of such illegal immigrants: stalker fans (sasaeng) and vicious individual fans (akkae). Sasaeng fans are those who go to criminal extremes to stalk JYJ. Some JYJ sasaeng fans in the past have duplicated the members' cellular phones, installed video cameras in their garages, or snuck into their homes to take candid photos. Akkae fans favor one member of the group to the detriment of the other two. Such fans routinely sabotage other members in vicious ways in the process of putting their favorite forward. Within the JYJ Republic, citizens restrict sasaeng and akkae activities by refusing them interaction and blocking their posts.

If, as Henry Jenkins has argued, "fandom may represent a particularly powerful training ground for future activists and community organizers," then the JYJ Republic should provide an extremely fertile ground indeed. Starting with a simple but urgent desire to protect their beloved idol group from being destroyed by a powerful entertainment machine to which the members had pledged their lives in their youthful ignorance, the fans embraced the cause of labor rights, human rights, and antitrust laws. The universalist orientation of these causes expanded the horizon of civic engagement. For many fans, moreover, activism in the wake of JYJ's litigation was a politicizing process in a very literal sense. During the National Assembly elections of April 2012, for example, JYJ fans turned out in large numbers to cast their vote. Following Jaejoong's tweet encouraging the fans to get out and vote, and then post their selfies for proof, fans turned the act of voting itself into an occasion for fan activism. They took selfies holding up messages ranging from "Go JYJ, Fuck S.M." to "JYJ to the Television Station, Us to the Polling Station." Hundreds of selfies were collected, and the montage thus created was shared on the fansites and through social media. Newspapers covered the phenomenon under headline such as "JYJ—fan devotion with a conscience" (kaenyŏm p'aensim), and even the mayor of Seoul, Park Won-soon, took notice. Continuing this pattern of political participation, JYJ fans voted in large numbers in the 2012 presidential election as well. Within the most politically disinterested demographic in Korea—women in their twenties have historically shown the lowest voting rate—the JYJ Republic had made its mark.

Conclusion

On November 28, 2012, the forty months of dispute between Kim Jaejoong, Park Yoochun, and Kim Junsu of JYJ and S.M. came to an official end.[11] The parties agreed to go their separate ways, without interfering in each other's business and without seeking damages from each other. While fans celebrated the occasion by calling it "The JYJ Independence Day," the compromise that concluded the lawsuit left many dissatisfied. Despite the public recognition of the ways in which S.M. and KPCIF had exercised undue influence to keep JYJ off the air, no fines were assessed and no specific actions prescribed as compulsory. As this article is being written, JYJ has been free for over a year, but the trio has yet to appear on music and variety television programs in Korea. The link between the S.M. brand and the Korean national brand has grown even stronger, thanks to the global popularity of S.M. idols such as SNSD and EXO, and to the promotional genius of Lee Soo-man in couching his company's phenomenal success in terms of Korea's triumph in the world. What this means for the JYJ Republic is that the fight continues.

If the JYJ Republic had remained within the consumerist play culture of the idol fandom, buying tickets, albums, and idol goods, engaging in pseudo-romance and writing fan fiction, and producing and circulating secondary texts, this chapter would not have been written. This is not to deny the tremendous importance of social meaning-making and everyday empowerment that occur within this play culture, an aspect of fandom highlighted in works of popular culture theorists ranging from Fiske to Jenkins who have sought to combat the reification of fandom as the pathological Other (Gray, Sandvoss, and Harrington 2007, 2–5). But it is precisely the way fans of JYJ managed to bridge the micropolitical and the macropolitical that drew me to the phenomenon. Women and teenage fans took on S.M., perceiving JYJ indeed as a boy with a slingshot pitted against a giant and identifying with such a figure from the place of the socially weak. In the process, they underwent political empowerment as a collective. Expanding outward from a specific grievance against one company, the fans grew to share a pointed sense of concern about the entertainment industry at large and embrace the cause of social justice more broadly. In addition, at a time when the fans saw themselves as engaging in a publicity battle with S.M. over the image of JYJ, the belief that their actions could reflect positively or negatively on the idol served as a powerful incentive to engage in actions that would further the common good. The culture of donation, not only of money and material goods toward the society's most marginalized, but of skilled labor ranging from translation to copywriting to video editing, thrived within the JYJ Republic during the lawsuit. It thrives still and combines with an emphasis on political activism to confer a powerful sense of collective identity on the fandom. It remains to be seen what the future holds for the JYJ Republic, but as an "aca-fan" who first went to visit and ended up staying,[12] I hope that the inside story we have examined here will remain an importance case study for both historians of youth subculture in South Korea and scholars of fan activism in the late capitalist world.

NOTES

1. Another frequently used word for the management company is *sosoksa. Sosok* means "to belong." The word suggests that the individual idol's identity is closely tied to the management company.

2. Other female idols who lost consciousness during a performance include Crystal of f(x), Jeeyeon of T-ara, and Hyeri of Girls' Day.

3. Speaking in 2011 before a crowd of aspiring entrepreneurs gathered at Stanford Graduate School of Business, Lee Soo Man elaborated his concept of culture technology, dividing the Korean Wave into three stages depending on the degree of transnational collaboration and localization. See https://www.youtube.com/watch?v=bGP5mNh9zo8.

4. An arena in Japan holds up to ten thousand people.

5. The fact was brought personally home to me in 2009 when I watched a Japanese TV show called *Sanma* (Dream Special). The popular variety show centers on making the viewers' wishes come true. On this particular episode, a reporter went out to the streets, approached three high school girls, and asked them about their wish. The girls, all members of a dance club at a local high school, responded that their dream was to dance with TVXQ. Their dream was granted, and when TVXQ showed up at their school, 1,500 teenage boys and girls gathered in the auditorium went wild. The scene impressed upon me the extent to which TVXQ's music and dance had become cool to consume among Japanese teenagers.

6. Yoochun's "A Song Without a Name" (2011), in which he exposes working conditions for an idol at S.M., suggests that S.M.'s net profit calculations left the members of TVXQ mysteriously in the red even after their album had become a chart-topper in Japan. The members' demands to see how S.M. was tabulating itemized expenses to be subtracted from the members' pay were routinely ignored by the company.

7. Even before JYJ's litigation against S.M. became public, rumors that TVXQ might disband had circulated within the fandom. On DNBN, the site's manager, who sided with S.M., posted an announcement that accused Jaejoong, Yoochun, and Junsu of trying to leave TVXQ because of their private business interests, and urged the fans to try to stop the members from leaving. The majority of fans, however, did not follow the manager's call, arguing instead that the decision should be left to the three members. The manager then decided to step down since she had lost her credibility among the members of DNBN, and announced that the site would be closed down in three days' time. If DNBN were closed, an entire archive of pictures, articles, exchanged messages, and memories that had been built up over the five years since TVXQ's debut would be lost. One person stepped forward to take charge of moving the archive to a new domain. But the fans did not know her since most fan activities had been conducted under nicknames and there had been limited offline opportunities to meet one another. Further-

more, a level of distrust was high in the fandom at the time surrounding TVXQ's split. In order to gain the fans' trust, the new manager disclosed her residence registration and student identification. She incurred considerable risk in thus exposing her identity on the Internet, but she felt that there was no other way to gain the fans' trust. DNBN successfully settled under a new web address.

8. Avex had been supportive of JYJ's split from S.M. at first, but likely reconsidered the decision when its support of JYJ hindered its access to a pipeline of other K-pop acts. In early 2010, for example, S.M. signed its hugely profitable girl group SNSD with Universal rather than Avex for its Japanese release. On January 18, 2013, the Tokyo District Court ordered Avex to release JYJ from the exclusive contract and pay the group 660 million yen in damages.

9. See, for example, the study by Gray, Sandvoss, and Harrington (2007).

10. It is in the report from *KBS TV News*, November 19, 2012. http://news.kbs.co.kr/news/NewsView.do?SEARCH_NEWS_CODE=2575180.

11. For an informative debate surrounding the term, coined by Henry Jenkins, see the transcript of the conversation between Henry Jenkins and Suzanne Scott in Jenkins 2013, viii–xiv.

WORKS CITED

Aoyagi, Hiroshi. 2005. *Islands of Eight Million Smiles: Idol Performance and Symbolic Production in Contemporary Japan*. Cambridge: Harvard East Asia Center.

Basinger, Janine. 2009. *The Star Machine*. New York: Vintage.

Chang, Ik-ch'ang. 2010. "SM Entertainment, Indefinite Postponement of Concert." *Economy Today*, April 30. http://www.eto.co.kr/news/outview.asp?Code=20100430113611003&ts=70139.

Chang, U-chŏl and In-yŏng Hwang. 2011. "Who is the Best?" *Allure*. October.

Cho, Yŏn-gyŏng. 2012. "Cancellation of JYJ documentary, 'we'll confront it squarely.'" In *Newsen*. January 30. http://www.newsen.com/news_view.php?uid=201201301024371001.

Ch'oe, Chŏng-ju. 2009. "3 members of TVXQ, 'it's not disbanding.'" In *Seoul News*. August 3. http://nownews.seoul.co.kr/news/newsView.php?id=20090803603023

Chŏng, Hyŏng-mo. 2011. "Audition in Kazakhstan" In *JoongAng Daily*. July 17. http://article.joins.com/news/article/article.asp?total_id=5802056&ctg=1200&cloc=joongang|home|newslist1.

Fiske, John. 1992. "The Cultural Economy of Fandom." In *The Adoring Audience: Fan Culture and Popular Media*, edited by Lisa A. Lewis, 37–42. New York: Routledge.

Galbraith, Patrick, and Jason Karlin, eds. 2012. *Idols and Celebrity in Japanese Media Culture*. New York: Palgrave MacMillan.

Gray, Jonathan, Cornel Sandvoss, and C. Lee Harrington, eds. 2007. *Fandom: Identities and Communities in a Mediated World*. New York University Press.

Ha, Yu-jin. 2011. "Deadly Schedule of TVXQ." *JoongAng Daily*, June 8. http://article.joins.com/news/article/article.asp?total_id=5609955&ctg=1502.

Jenkins, Henry. 2012. "Cultural Acupuncture: Fan Activism and the Harry Potter Alliance." *Transformative Works and Cultures* 10. http://journal.transformativeworks.org/index.php/twc/article/view/305/259.

Jenkins, Henry. 2013. *Textual Poachers: Television Fans and Participatory Culture.* New York: Routledge.

Joo, Jeongsuk. 2011. "Transnationalization of Korean Popular Culture and the Rise of 'Pop Nationalism' in Korea." *Journal of Popular Culture* 44 (3): 489–504.

Kaori, Hayashi, and Eun-Jeung Lee. 2007. "The Potential of Fandom and the Limits of Soft Power: Media Representations on the Popularity of a Korean Melodrama in Japan." *Social Science Japan Journal* 10 (2) 202–4.

Kim, Ch'ang-nam. 2004. "Kim Min-gi kŭrigo saeroun chŏngnyŏn munhwa." In *Taejung ŭmak kwa norae undong, kŭrigo chŏngnyŏn munhwa,* ed. Kim Ch'ang-nam, 15–36. Seoul: Hanul Akademi.

Kim Pomt'ae. 2009. "120,000 Signed Requesting Correction of TVXQ Unfair Contract." *Ohmy News,* modified August 20, 2009. http://www.ohmynews.com/NWS_Web/view/at_pg.aspx?CNTN_CD=A0001200486.

Lee, Dong Yeon (Yi, Tong-yŏn). 2011. "Aidol p'ap iran muŏt in'ga" (What Is an Idol?) In *Aidol* (Idol), ed. Dong Yeon Lee, 14–48. Seoul: Imaejin.

Marx, W. David. 2012. "The *Jimusho* System: Understanding the Production Logic of the Japanese Entertainment Industry." In *Idols and Celebrity in Japanese Media Culture,* ed. Patrick Galbraith and Jason Karlin, 35–55. New York: Palgrave Macmillan.

Shin, Hyunjoon. 2009. "Have You Ever Seen the Rain? And Who'll Stop the Rain? The Globalizing Project of Korean Pop (K-pop)." *Inter-Asia Cultural Studies* 10 (4): 507–23.

Shin, Kiju. 2011. "Idol Patriarchy." *GQ,* October.

Shin, Sŏng-a 2013. "Fair Trade Commission Issues Correction Order against SM to Stop Disturbance of JYJ Activities." *New Daily,* July 24. http://www.newdaily.co.kr/news/article.html?no=163962.

PART 3.

Korean TV Drama and Social Media

6

The Interactive Nature of Korean TV Dramas

Flexible Texts, Discursive Consumption, and Social Media

Youjeong Oh

This chapter explores the production and consumption of Korean TV dramas[1] and their interactive nature. Korean TV dramas, one of the leading cultural commodities in the phenomenon of Hallyu, have generated various scholarly discourses, mainly concerning the driving force of their popularity and their reception to foreign audiences (Kim 2005; Cho 2005; KOFICE 2008; Chua and Iwabuchi 2008; Lee 2012). Extending the cultural discourses toward the industrial and social arenas, this chapter presents details about the ways in which Korean TV dramas are produced and consumed from the ethnography of the drama industry and the virtual ethnography of online drama discussion boards. First, the chapter begins with a brief overview of the political economy of *live production* in which two episodes are produced weekly for the following week's broadcasting. The live production entails interesting twists: while the last-minute production imposes an immense workload upon workers, and thus rests on labor exploitation, it also carries rooms for audience participation in making of dramas. Second, the chapter examines the *discursive consumption* of television dramas in which viewers actively share the experiences of drama watching, discuss stories and characters, collaboratively create parody texts for amusement, collectively provide meals and presents to the production staff, and suggest hoped-for plots and endings. Third, focusing on the ways in which producers capitalize on the discursive consumption of audience groups, it discusses how interactions between production and consumption take place. Through the practices of *live production*, Korean drama producers actually change ongoing narratives in response to viewer ratings and reactions to previous episodes.

As the discursive consumption suggests, television dramas become a source of collective discussion, collaborative production of secondary texts, and interactions among people. As audience groups virtually gather and create, share, and exchange ideas and pleasures from talking about television dramas, the online drama discussion boards become a form of social media (Kaplan and Haenlein 2010). The production side not only pays sharp attention to what happens in the drama discussion boards, but also adopts audience suggestions via social media to the cultural production. In sum, both the production and consumption of Korean TV dramas engage with and tap social media; and, social media facilitates active interactions between producers and consumers, from which Korean TV dramas are being made.

Live Production

The process of "last-minute live filming" (saengbang ch'waryŏng) is a standard practice in the Korean drama industry. Apart from the first few episodes, filming is usually done only a few days in advance of (or on the same day as) the airdate. Script changes are often made last minute, while the final editing of the film is just as rushed, with little time to review the episode before it is released. The closer to the final episode, the more tense the shooting because the demands of production mount. Drawing on the industrial conventions to refer to last-minute production, this chapter calls these practices "live production." Many hit dramas have suffered from poor endings because of hasty scriptwriting and rushed shooting. For the last episode of *Sign* (SSain, 2011), the entire shooting was completed only fifty minutes before broadcasting. It is reported that four staff members raced against time to bring the video to the editing room.[2] As a result, the protagonist lost his voice (because of lack of sound) for twenty minutes during the broadcast. In the middle of episode 19 in *Man from the Equator* (Chŏkto ŭi namja, 2012), the screen suddenly reproduced scenes from the beginning and then the screen went black. Subsequently, a caption was displayed on the screen stating that because of unforeseen circumstances, episode 19 had ended and the final episode would be aired on the next day. News articles reported that the edited version of a film that was shot on the airdate was not delivered to a master control room of the network in time.[3] In *Athena: Goddess of War* (Atena: chŏnjaeng ŭi yŏsin, 2010) and *Painter of the Wind* (Param ŭi hwawŏn, 2008), injuries to the lead actors led to one episode of each drama being canceled. Both incidents were due to the tight shooting schedule.

What and who are driving these "crazy" but repeated processes? Three factors cause this practice: (1) uncertainty over channels, (2) an emphasis on raising viewer ratings, and (3) cutting production costs. First, independent producers[4] cannot produce more than two or three episodes before broadcasting without the guarantee of a channel. There are more than one thousand independent production firms in South Korea, while only three terrestrial broadcasting stations exist.[5] The disparity in numbers[6] indicates the fierce competition among producers to win a channel, and this ambiguity has established "precontract and postproduction system." Independent producers circulate drama proposals (usually consisting of a show synopsis and a script of the first episode) among three broadcasting stations to win a channel that can broadcast their drama. Only after a channel is affirmed do their proposals become tangible and a substantial production team is established. Broadcasters usually narrow down the possibilities to two or three drama candidates before choosing a winner only a few months before the actual airdate. Given the uncertainty of channels, the preproduction of whole drama series is extremely risky; a completely filmed drama series may not be able to find a distribution channel.

Second, "last-minute filming" is a business practice intended to realize high viewer ratings. Broadcasting firms and drama producers share the interests in viewer ratings; higher ratings not only generate more sales of commercials, but also raise the unit price of commercials. In addition, ratings are the basis not only for whether a drama will be sold in overseas and additional markets, but also for its price in those markets. This critical commercial logic has created a system of what is called *jjokdaebon* (a slice of script) or "hasty script" in the Korean drama industry. Under this system, extremely short sections of scripts arrive on set, barely meeting the live-shoot schedule. Without having the whole plot of an episode and the time to study the script, actors shoot the short scene that the one-page script describes. The business rationale for the last-minute script writing and revisions is to listen to the voices of the audience. After airing the first few episodes and observing the viewers' response, directors and writers collaboratively rework the direction of a drama by changing plotlines, introducing new figures, or adding some provocative scenes. A drama producer remarked that "television series have to change according to audience's reaction. Thus the script must be carefully polished, and a lot of time has to be invested in it. Dramas that are shot in advance cannot gauge the viewers' reaction, so they are often not accepted by them."[7] Stories of dramas are being adjusted all the time, and the translation of scripts into actual filming is a last-minute occurrence.

Third, as a measure to cut production costs, the filming process is made as short as possible, also contributing to "last-minute" shooting. Drama production costs are two-tiered: costs for creative workers and actual production costs. Above the line is invested to pay for star actors, ace writers, and sometimes high-profile directors who are paid on a per-episode basis. Below the line, usually less than half of the budget, is paid for several supporting and extra cast members, on-the-spot crew members, camera shooting, sets and special equipment, visual effects, and on-location shooting. Given that those crews and supporting roles are paid per day, the best way to cut actual production costs is to reduce the number of filming days.[8] In *On Air* (On eŏ, 2008), a drama that depicts the inside of the Korean drama industry, one dialogue between a producer and a staff at an independent production firm is particularly instructive: "Once cameras roll, the minimum cost is no less than $20,000. . . . Thus, we will take a day off." To produce a drama with minimum cost and maximum efficiency, most episodes must be shot only a few days before (or on the same day of) the airdate.

Live production embodies intriguing twists. First, the mechanisms to maintain eleventh-hour production has led to labor exploitation, as the intensive workloads against tight deadlines are shifted onto workers. Korea is a unique place where prime-time dramas air two episodes a week. The last-minute production of Korean dramas, producing two episodes totaling 140 minutes a week, entails seriously excessive and intensive labor, forcing workers into a condition where they suffer from constant sleep deprivation, and alternating periods of stand-by waiting and multitasking during a three- to six-month period when a drama is being aired. As discussed above, actors and workers are contracted on per-episode or per-day basis, which means no contract terms specify how many hours compose a day. Drama producers take full advantage of such vague terms and extract overwork from workers. Scholarly discussions on labor in the television industry have concerned the "affective nature" of work: the pleasures of acclaim, rewards, self-realization, and creativity do matter and become the basis for self-exploitation in creative work (Hesmondhalgh and Baker 2008). The pleasures of being a freelancer and creative worker also apply to workers in the drama industry in Korea. The more critical and practical factor, however, in coping with the live filming and excessive labor resides in the public nature of TV dramas. A filming staff member remarked, "Not sleeping is required practice in this field. We are so used to it. Nevertheless, drama should be broadcast. It is a promise with the public."[9] Given this understanding with the public, there is an implicit consensus among all participants that broadcasting cancellation should be prevented.

The improvised production environment, however, has nurtured an atmosphere in which producers actively listen to voices of audiences and actually accept and apply them in ongoing production. Cultural industries are risky because they center on the production of "texts" to be bought and sold (Hesmondhalgh 2002). For Garnham (1990), risk derives from the fact that audiences use cultural commodities in highly volatile and unpredictable ways. Bilton (1999) addresses the unpredictable characteristic with the value of "symbolic goods": the product's value depends upon a subjective judgment at the point of consumption. Live production functions to manage the unpredictable nature of audience tastes in almost real time, making more consumer-tailored and commercially profitable television dramas. Scholarly discussions on industrialized cultural production have shown the contrast between "cultural determinism" (Horkheimer and Adorno 1979) and "individual agency in consumption" (Fiske 1989a; de Certeau 1984; du Gay 1997). Beyond this opposition, live production practices manifest the ways in which the measures for material profits also engage with the consumption practices of audiences, connecting them to cultural production.

Discursive Consumption of Korean Dramas in DC Inside

Reception of television drama refers to much more than passive watching; reception includes talking about viewing experiences, recapping plots and discussing them, admiring characters and actors, capturing and modifying drama images, generating one's own movies, suggesting future plotlines, advertising dramas to acquaintances, creating review books (described below), producing drama-themed souvenirs, and supporting the production. Because all these activities take place in the course of *talking* about dramas among anonymous publics, I call them the "discursive consumption" of television dramas.

The development of Web 2.0 has particularly enabled the collective and collaborative discursive consumption of television dramas. There are various online venues to facilitate the discursive consumption of TV dramas in

South Korea: official drama websites, discussion boards in portal sites,[10] and DC Inside (www.dcinside.com).[11] Although any form of online public space may serve as a medium for the socialization of drama viewers, DC Inside, because of its unique cultures of users, has enormously contributed to the spectacular reception of popular culture in general. As the website becomes the most vibrant space where the discursive consumption of TV dramas is carried out, DC Inside has also become critical to producers.[12] This section briefly introduces DC Inside and discusses the features that constitute consumption practices and their influence on production.

DC Inside is one of the biggest online communities in South Korea.[13] Started in 1999 as an online venue in which early adopters of electronic devices shared information about digital cameras and other gadgets, DC Inside has now grown into a mega community that is influential across all arenas of popular culture and social discourse. The main category of the site is known as the gallery, a bulletin board designated for specific topics such as "Domestic Baseball," "Social Issues," and "StarCraft"; and users of each gallery are called *gallers* (kaellŏ).[14] As of January 2014, there were about 1,600 individual galleries covering diverse topics including politics, society, military, games, shopping, foods, sports, entertainment, academics, music, travel, and others. While the extraordinary numbers of galleries shows the size of the community, DC gallers have developed unique operational practices that also shape the consumption and reproduction practices of television drama, as well as the interactions between consumption and production.

First, DC users deny the formation and exercises of authority in virtual public space. The site offers to anybody full admission and rights to write and read any content without membership. Yet site operators are thoroughly separated from gallers; the only role of operators in galleries is to announce this instruction: "Please post images and texts relevant to a topic of a gallery," and operators never engage with what occurs within galleries. This thorough detachment of operators from gallers functions to block the possibility that vertical or hierarchical relations are formed. In addition, DC gallers use everyday language (banmal), as opposed to honorifics (jondaenmal), among them.[15] The erasure of honorifics in discussion has had a tremendous impact in leveling the socioeconomic and generational backgrounds of users, dismantling any form of authority.

Second, DC gallers have developed what they call *image communication*. As DC Inside began as a community for digital camera users, it boasts enormous number of "cool" and "funny" images that users post. Gallers also produce *captured images* from scenes of TV programs and films. The inundation of images kindles users' voluntary modification of the posted images in innovative ways by drawing on other technologies such as Photoshop. In addition, short movies are created from collections of posted images. In such ways, images are continuously produced, consumed, circulated, and reproduced. What is notable is users' creativity in making the images strong enough to be delivered as messages without (long) texts. Images have become a powerful and instant communication medium, especially among younger generations who are more familiar with images than texts. With image communication, DC galleries constitute a web environment in which boundaries between production and reproduction become blurred, as well as serving as a form of entertainment.

Third, despite image-dominant communication, DC gallers are famous for their creative *language games*. They deconstruct and reconstruct the Korean language in the following ways; gallers grant unconventional meanings to words; transform nouns into verbs and adjectives; play pronunciation games; and create totally new words, adopting inspiring and humorous metaphoric terms. Because of its surprising twists and reversals, the DC language is unfamiliar to novice visitors, often making them puzzled about what is happening on the site. When new visitors ask about the meaning and use of DC languages, other skillful users explain them, but invariably mock the newcomer at the same time. Eventually the operators added the "DC Dictionary" section to facilitate users' mutual understanding. Language games happen in unexpected and spontaneous ways; one user accidentally or intentionally attempts a new language form; and when it is fresh enough to entertain other gallers, they voluntarily use the new term, spreading it across other galleries and eventually listing the new language form in the DC Dictionary. Like image communications, language games constitute a significant part of entertainment in DC Inside.

The distinct operational, cultural, and verbal practices developed in DC galleries have brought about innovative and proactive user participation that has also nurtured the spectacular consumption practices of popular cultural content.[16] As the number of galleries (273 as of January 2014) about Korean drama indicates,[17] dramas, and TV programs in general, are excellent sources from which DC users consume content they can reproduce. Because of their critical influences not only on the consumption but also on the production of Korean TV dramas, I explore DC drama galleries and observe how the unique "DC cultures" have boosted the collaborative discursive consumption of serial dramas. Particularly, I conducted in-depth research of the DC Inside "*Sungkyunkwan Scandal* (Sŏnggyun'gwan sŭk'aendŭl) Gallery," which boasts the most vibrant user discussions. *Sungkyunkwan Scandal* is a drama series broadcast in 2010 on KBS.[18] Although it did not record high ratings, *Sungkyunkwan Scandal* triggered a national response and gained extensive and enthusiastic viewer comments. So far, the official drama website[19] has received more than half a million viewer postings; and in the *Sungkyunkwan Scandal* Gallery, more than 280,000 postings have accumulated (given that the drama series has twenty episodes, that number amounts to more than 14,000 postings per episode). [20] Through an in-depth ethnography of the gallery, this section analyzes the discursive consumption practice of TV drama from the following three perspectives: appreciation/suggestion, entertainment, and information sharing and support.

1) Appreciation/Suggestion

Audience groups engage in what Nancy Baym (2000) calls *interpretive practice*, multiple forms of appreciation/suggestion in response to television dramas: character analyses, reviews/critiques about episodes, analyses of plot development, descriptions of memorable scenes, and parody images or short movies. While the interpretive practices mediate the drama itself—its plots, scenes, and directing, most audience conversations revolve around characters, as viewers develop an adoration of and attachment to them. From psychological research, Zillmann (1994) points out that the most critical factor in grabbing audience attention is character, arguing that emotional involvement with drama happens through the development of affective dispositions about characters, either in a positive or in a negative way.

The discursive appreciation of characters is about displaying and sharing personal emotions such as romance, love, joy, excitement, longing, yearning, disappointment, and frustration.

Some examples of character appreciation in response to *Sungkyunkwan Scandal* are the following: "Isn't Sun-joon cute and sexy? He is not only handsome, but has an appearance with which he can perform various characters."[21] "Geol-oh (Jae-shin) looks so masculine. I am amused by his wild sexy looks." "I am jealous about Park Min-young who works together with three beautiful men." One galler made a short movie made up of captured images of Sun-joon, saying, with plaintive piano music in the background, "Sun-joon, Yoo-chun, you were the best. I hope to see you in other dramas." Within these postings, other gallers added replies about feelings of tenderness of warmth, or their doleful thoughts about Sun-joon.[22] Many gallers wrote about Jae-shin, who carries the torch for Yoon-hee, conveying delicate personal emotions as if they experienced one-sided love, they express in detail how painful this unrequited love is.[23] The appreciation practices of Korean TV drama involve publicly talking about such personal and private emotions as love, a fluttering heart, and heartbreak.

Previous studies show that "fairytale-like romance" in Korean TV dramas has grabbed the interests of Asian audiences (Chan and Xueli 2011; Kim 2005), and it is "sensitive" male characters—often characterized as a devoted Prince Charming who is willing to sacrifice everything for love— that are central in making the fantasy. Empirical studies confirm that the "soft masculinity" of male characters in Korean dramas is formed more by the moral maturity of characters than their masculine and sexual body; interviewees often emphasize the male characters' sensitive, soft, noble, and gentle personality more than their bodily attractiveness (Jung 2011). In online discussions, however, which can be more open, informal, and personal than interview settings, it is male actors' appearance, as much as their characterization in the drama, that viewers comment on without hesitation. Given these blunt expressions and discussions of desires in response to male actors' appearance, body, and sexuality, we can easily imagine gendered audience groups participating in the *Sungkyunkwan Scandal* Gallery. This character appreciation oriented around male characters distinguishes Korean audiences, to some extent, from viewers of U.S. soap operas, whose female audience members admire powerful female characters and their transgressive femininity (Modleski 1982; Brown 1992; Ang 1990).

Collaborative interpretation practices are also historical. As mentioned, around 14,000 reviews per episode are posted in the *Sungkyunkwan Scandal* Gallery. Thus, even passionate fans cannot check every single posting. The DC Inside drama galleries have developed two unique measures to help others quickly catch what is going on in a gallery: "concept postings" and "review collections." When a posting obtains more than ten recommendations, it is automatically shown in the "concept postings" section, which therefore becomes a collection of recommended postings. Thus, even though hundreds of comments are poured out hourly in a drama gallery, in order to quickly review the history of a gallery one does not need to review all postings; instead one can go to the concept postings, thoroughly examine them, and grip the *essences* of the gallery. Some good comments, however, are unfortunately not listed in the *concept postings*, because they might be posted in the early morning and not viewed enough. In such cases, some gallers post a review collection that contains direct links to readable reviews. For example, one review collection[24] has as many as 259 absorbing reviews. The review collections usually garner enough recommendations to be moved into concept postings that are easily accessed by more people. Concept postings and review collections, therefore, are a condensed history of a gallery shaped by users' voluntary recommendations.[25]

These diverse appreciation practices naturally lead to active suggestions. Comments and suggestions are very specific, covering storylines, character development, the number of appearances of characters, love lines, background music, filming techniques, and styles of acting. When the story development seems to "go to *Andromeda*,"[26] that is, stories become far-fetched, active users generate comments and suggestions to the production team. In the case of *Sungkyunkwan Scandal*, suggestions about music dominated the gallery. KBS acknowledges copyright of original sound tracks by drama producers;[27] thus, KBS dramas are well known for their frequent employment of sound tracks. *Sungkyunkwan Scandal* is particularly notorious for its excessive use of background music. Among the drama gallers, episode 12 has been called a "BGM crisis" because background music plays during sixty-seven minutes of a seventy-minute show.[28] After the broadcast, hundreds of gallers complained that they could not concentrate on the episode because of the intrusive music. Later episodes featured less background music, especially music with lyrics, leading gallers to believe that the production team must have listened to their complaints.

2) Entertainment

Entertainment is the most dynamic part of discursive consumption, generating additional pleasures beside the original television shows among users who inhabit the drama galleries. I categorize the entertainment practices of drama galleries into three types: producing secondary texts, an attendance check (ch'ulch'ek, a shortened version of *ch'ulsŏk ch'ek'ŭ*, explained below), and watching together. All three forms of entertainment practices are based on their *social* features; pleasures are engendered by sharing something with others through social media.

The production of secondary texts includes modifying drama scenes in playful ways, producing funny parody images and comic personal drawings about drama characters, creating collages of political and social satire using images and characters from dramas, and making short movies and fan fictions employing characters from the drama. These activities become more animated and entertaining if there are immediate responses from other gallers. When entertaining texts are ingenious enough to shock gallers, there follows a *reply game*, a voluntary game to add endless replies to a posting in rhythmic (via rhyme schemes) and innovative ways that create new stories. The entertainment practices through image communication and reply games are collective and incremental production processes, as all images and movies posted are subject to further development by others.

Second, surprisingly, an attendance check is a significant part of entertainment not only for drama gallers but for the entire community of DC Inside. The practice begins with a galler's spontaneous call of "Let's do attendance check! Who is in the gallery now?" Other gallers voluntarily respond with "I am!" and dozens of replies constitute the check in each instance. After the spontaneous check, the initiator usually posts an image in which the names (either fixed or temporary nicknames) of respondents are collected, with words to the effect that "this is the attendance at 7 p.m." An attendance check in DC Inside is not designed to identify individuals; rather, gallers want to confirm that they have accessed the same space (gallery) at the same time. The check establishes senses of belonging, similarity, simultaneity, and thus attachment to each other among users. Therefore, the spontaneous check temporarily forms a *community*, a group of people who are dedicated to a similar interest at the same time.

Third, "watching together" is another form of entertainment. Even waiting for a broadcast together is a sort of excitement for drama gallers. When the airtime approaches, gallers circulate messages such as "One hour away," "Thirty minutes left!," "On-air discussion room will be open, please join," and "Now, it starts!!" During the on-air broadcast of a drama, many gallers watch and talk together, not with their family members in their living room, but with anonymous others in drama galleries. "Did you see it?" "What do you guys think about the last scene?" As the broadcast approaches its end, the traffic in discussion boards becomes busy and reaches a peak right after the airing. Not only gallers who have been in the gallery during the airing, but others who enjoyed watching on their own flock to the gallery and begin heated discussions.

3) Information Sharing and Support

Active audience groups do extensive information sharing about their favorite dramas. Here, information refers to any material, other than the original drama text, related to a drama series or its actors, such as press articles or online messages. Specific examples of these texts and the ways of sharing them include the following: "The Original Sound Track has been released! Let's download it, let's do streaming" (downloading and streaming statistics determines a song's chart rank); "Preview of the next episode is now up on the drama official site! For your convenience, here's a direct link to it (Or I uploaded the preview here!); "News articles are out today! Let's go to 'recommend' it!"[29]; "New images or messages from the production team are now released on the official site. Go and check them out!"; "A new message from a director is on the *Sungkyunkwan Scandal* Twitter, saying 'We just finished the final editing of episode 2. Look forward to today's broadcasting.' Wow, did they JUST finish? I wonder if they're already in the 'live production' stage of episode 2 and worry about the quality of future episodes."

Information-sharing practices reveal the viewers' affection for a drama series; adoring fans do not stop at appreciating the original dramas, but voluntarily search any information relevant to them and spread that information to the public. Such affection also has the effect of supporting the show. Because the commercial standard of television dramas is viewer ratings, fans of a drama do their part to promote their favorite drama by introducing the drama to their acquaintances or leaving complimentary comments on drama-related news articles. Yet drama fans carry out more specific material and emotional forms of support. Types of support can be as creative as providing flu shots to the entire production team of *Beethoven Virus* (Pet'oben pairŏsŭ, 2008), but generally include the following two types: (1) delivering snacks and presents to the production team and (2) producing review books.

The most pervasive form of support is snack delivery. Usually, one person spontaneously opens a discussion about the snack support, saying, "How about offering some snacks and presents in the name of our gallery (or fan cafés)? I will open a bank account right now; if any of you would like to join, please transfer money to the account." Hundreds of replies often follow, such as "Great idea! I wanna join"; discussions about what types of food and presents to be delivered ensue. Because participants do not have any idea about the initiators' personal information, other than a name on the bank account, the whole process from money-raising to delivery must be transparent; volunteers (usually the initiator and some recruited helpers) post all nicknames of those who transferred money, the screenshot of the bank account, the total amount of money raised, photos of presents and snacks that were bought and packed, all receipts, and images that confirm delivery of the gifts.[30] What is notable is participants' voluntary devotion to preparing hundreds of snack-boxes and posting dramatic images of every single item.[31] Usually, the snack support event ends with verification postings by actors and staff members; they usually post photos showing they are actually eating the snacks received from the gallers, often saying, "We really enjoyed them. Thank you. We will present a better-quality drama in return for your favors" (for more details, see the "verification" section below).

Drama gallers also voluntarily produce *review books* or *photo books*, selecting fan-produced images and impressive reviews from gallery postings and collating them into a book.[32] Those books are professional in terms of design and editing, supported by voluntary workers who are specialized in magazine design and photography. Review books represent gallers' affection for a drama itself, rather than for a few celebrities, and are thereby delivered to all actors and staff members of the production team. Besides signifying fans' support, review books entail broader implications; they are a printed form of television dramas, published forms of the discursive consumption of television dramas, and a history of drama galleries.

These practices of discursive consumption provide empirical evidence of viewers' use of the media text (Jenkins 1992a; 1992b). Audience groups engage in production, not merely reception, and the production of secondary texts enables audience groups to produce their own meanings and pleasures (Fiske 1989a; Morley 1992; de Certeau 1984; du Gay 1997). These discursive consumption practices indicate the ways in which television dramas become a source of collective discussion, cultivation of additional pleasures, and interactions among people via social media.

Interactions between Production and Consumption

While discursive consumption itself enhances audience enjoyment, it also prepares a field in which the interaction between production and consumption become tangible, all the more so given the live production of Korean TV dramas. Benefiting from practices of live filming, drama producers immediately reflect audience responses and improvise storylines. I analyze the interaction between production and the discursive consumption with respect to the following three modes: verification, revaluation, and plot change.

1) Verification

Verification refers to the practices that production teams and actors post as writings or photos in online discussion boards to express their gratitude for fan support. In the *Sungkyunkwan Scandal* Gallery, eleven actors of the drama and two actors' managers left as many as thirty-one verification postings with photos of gifts they received from gallers and thank-you notes.[33] Actor Cho Seong-ha, who performed the role of King Jeongjo in the drama, expressed gratitude to the gallers: "I am particularly grateful for the review book in which hundreds of gallery postings and images were collected. Every single page of the book moves me. All of the contents of the book and your encouraging words have given enormous energy to the producers, writers, actors, and crew members."[34]

The general producer of the drama, Lee Hyun-wook of the production firm Raemongrain, posted three messages, and one of them contained the following: "Can I participate in the gallery as a drama producer? I have visited this site each time our drama begins, when our drama is being aired on Mondays and Tuesdays, when the broadcast is almost finished, and when I want to know about viewer responses to our drama. Reading the ever-increasing postings in the gallery, we have monitored what we missed, what we lacked, what we did well, and what we should modify in the production."[35] Verification practices are an indirect form of interaction between producers and viewers, a message from the production side to confirm, "We are listening to what you are saying." Reversing the conventional reactions from the consumption side, audience groups also have reactions from the production side via verification postings.

2) Revaluation

Energetic discursive consumption has created so-called *mania dramas* and shed new light on them. Mania dramas are those that recorded lower viewer ratings, and are thus not successful by commercial criteria, but which garner extensive audience support because they are perceived to be of good quality. Not all dramas with lower viewer ratings are evaluated as mania drama; they should touch the subcultural sensibilities of viewers with newly attempted subject matter, unconventional story development, and well-rounded characters. Although they did not achieve commercial success because of their experimental status, which usually does not appeal to a broader audience, *mania fans* are enthusiastic about these dramas' freshness and innovation. Two dramas written by scriptwriter Noh Hee-kyung in the 1990s, *Lies* (Kŏjinmal, 1998) and *Did We Really Love?* (Uri ka chŏngmal sarang haessŭlkka, 1999), produced mania fans who repeatedly watched these dramas and extensively interpreted and appreciated them, virtually initiating the history of discursive consumption of television dramas via PC communications. Since then, *Ruler of Your Own World* (Ne mŏttaero haera, 2002), *The Legendary Police Woman Damo* (Chosŏn yŏhyŏngsa Tamo, 2003), *Me Ri, Dae Gu's Attack and Defense Battle* (Meri Taegu kongbangjŏn, 2007), and *The Devil* (Mawang, 2007) have also been called mania dramas, continuing the tradition. If not at the mania level, *You're Beautiful* (Minam isineyo, 2008) and *Sungkyunkwan Scandal* (2010) provoked greater audience discussions and praise despite their lower viewer ratings. A director of *You're Beautiful* remarked, "Active fans are distinctive from the general audience in that they voluntarily promote our drama, driven by their affection for it. Although our drama did not record higher ratings, because it competed with popular drama *IRIS* (*Airisŭ*), thanks to those fans' support, we are proud to have produced a well-loved drama."[36]

Revaluation is also an indirect form of interaction between production and consumption. Although it does not contribute to making changes in the actual production process, revaluation enormously affects the sale of VOD (video on demand) via the official drama website. Through extensive discussions and praises by passionate fans, mania dramas may go viral belatedly among the public and earn subsequent repeats through the Internet. Although such dramas do not achieve commercial success represented in viewer ratings, the sale of VOD, which has turned out to be unexpectedly lucrative, brings profits to broadcasters. By raising popularity, revaluation also enhances credits for actors, writers, and directors of a drama series, influencing their future production.

3) Plot Change

Plot change is a direct form of interaction through which audience voices can be adopted in drama production. Plot changes occur mainly in two ways. The first involves modifying the planned endings of dramas. More than a few dramas revised their proposed endings because of viewers' requests. Scriptwriters of *Love Story in Harvard* (Lobŭ sŭťori in Habŏdŭ, 2004) originally intended to include the death of a female protagonist. Replying to frantic viewer requests, however, the drama concluded with a happy ending. Audience groups also changed the direction of the drama *Wonderful Life* (Wŏndŏp'ul laip'ŭ, 2005), which initially intended to feature the death of a girl, Shin-bi, who failed to get a bone-marrow transplant. Meddling viewers reacted to the original storyline, saying, "How could the drama be a 'wonderful life' if it ends with the death of Shin-bi?" Writers accepted viewer requests, and the conclusion of the drama was converted to a happy ending.[37] Recently, passionate viewers overwhelmed the website of the drama *Secret Garden* (Sik'ŭrit kadŭn, 2010), calling for a happy ending without anybody's death. The drama website was virtually paralyzed by floods of viewer comments. Responsive to these requests, a writer of the drama posted a message on her Twitter account, assuring adoring fans that both couples in the drama will have happy endings.

The second type of plot change is adjusting the appearances of characters. Korean TV dramas have developed stereotyped character relations in that four main characters (two male and two female) form a love rectangle. Here, top male and female protagonists make a lead couple and the other pair acts as subcharacters. However, "Sometimes totally unexpected character couples emerge into the spotlight. In such cases, we have to modify the love lines."[38] In *Giant* (Chaiŏnt'ŭ, 2010), the Min-woo and Mi-joo couple garnered widespread support from viewers who called for their more frequent appearances. In *How to Meet a Perfect Neighbor* (Wanbyŏkhan iut ŭl mannanŭn pŏp, 2007), the appearances of Jun-suk (performed by Park Si-hoo), originally a supporting role, grew significantly in the later episodes, backed by the character's popularity. Sometimes groups of fans have heated online discussions about the acting and quantity of screen time of their favored actors. In *Dream High* (Tŭrim hai, 2011), fans of Sam-dong and Jin-guk competitively requested writers to describe their stars as fabulously as possible and to allocate more screen time to them. Plot change indicates the flexible, adjustable, and improvised features of Korean television dramas, being ready to be modified to cater to sensitive audience groups.

Interactive production capitalizes on the nature of the *serial*—defined by Allen as "a form of narrative organized around institutionally-imposed gaps in the text. . . . These gaps leave plenty of time for viewers to discuss with each other both the possible meanings of what has happened thus far as well as what might happen next" (Allen 1995, 17). Taking advantage of live filming, the gaps between texts not only allow viewers to reflect and discuss among themselves, but also provide producers time to listen to viewers and take action. Although Fiske (1989a) claims that meanings and pleasures produced by consumers are not engaged in exchange for material profits, Korean drama producers capitalize on discursive consumption, drawing in audience groups as free laborers to provide feedback and suggestions. Riding on the practices of "last-minute filming" and the benefits of social media, the commercial utilization of audiences' discursive consumption takes place every week, almost in real time. In turn, the audience is rewarded with flexible texts that favor and better serve its tastes.

Conclusion

TV drama-driven Hallyu in just after the turn of the century, represented by *Winter Sonata* (Kyŏul yŏn'ga, 2002) and *Jewel in the Palace* (Tae Changgŭm, 2003), has shaped the Korean drama industry into a speculative field with independent producers and fierce competition among vested interests over exports. Korean drama producers may have had exaggerated expectations about the success of Korean dramas in overseas markets, riding on the Korean Wave, while lacking solid financial and production capabilities. This speculation has configured the *live production* practices of Korean TV dramas. On the other hand, the rise of social media has fostered practices of *discursive consumption* in which collective and collaborative discussions heighten the pleasures of drama watching. Based on in-depth ethnography of DC Inside, this chapter has discussed the operational and cultural features of social media and provided empirical details about how such features define discursive consumption. The role or social media, however, goes beyond the consumption level and facilitates interactions between producers and consumers. Korean TV dramas in the age of social media, which mediate the interplay between the political economy of live production and the cultural economy of discursive consumption, have been developed into highly flexible and interactive texts.

NOTES

1. In this chapter, I focus on Korean primetime serials, aired via terrestrial channels in 10:00 p.m. to 11:00 p.m. time slot.

2. http://news.chosun.com/site/data/html_dir/2011/03/12/2011031200059.html. Last modified March 12, 2011.

3. http://www.mediatoday.co.kr/news/articleView.html?idxno=102726. Last modified May 25, 2012.

4. "Independent drama producers" refers to individual production firms that are not associated with broadcasting networks. What matters is the independence from broadcasters; the size of firms and the features of products they make are not relevant to defining independent drama producers. As of 2010, a total of 1,514 independent drama production houses were registered at the Ministry of Culture, Sports, and Tourism.

5. There are four terrestrial broadcasting stations in South Korea: KBS, MBC, SBS, and EBS. Since EBS (Educational Broadcasting System) focuses on educational content, the other three compete against one another for drama content.

6. The disparity between demand and supply has given broadcasters monopolistic power over channels, on the one hand, and independent producers have less autonomy and power vis-à-vis broadcasters, on the other.

7. Personal interview, spring 2011.

8. " Mo p'idi ŭi kŭge mo!" Last modified August 23, 2011. http://www.pressian.com/article/serial_article_list.asp?series_idx=460.html.

9. Personal interview, spring 2011.

10. There are three large-scale locally grown portal sites in South Korea: Naver (www.naver.com), Daum (www.daum.net), and NATE (www.nate.com).

11. DC Inside is a huge online community that requires further discussion. To explore the web space from an sociocultural anthropological perspective, see G. Lee 2012, which examines DC Inside from the perspectives of gift, war, and power.

12. An interview of a manager of the news team in DC Inside is indicative: "We have had many requests from drama producers and entertainment agencies to create a drama gallery, which is an indication of the influences of, and stakes in, a DC gallery. But the creation and operation of a gallery totally depend on users; there must be bottom-up booms and requests." Source: http://news.khan.co.kr/kh_news/khan_art_view.html?art id=201005021734275&code=960801, last modified May 3, 2010.

13. As of January 2013, the average daily visitors to the site exceeded two million and the daily page-view 40 million (see http://www.dcnews.in/etc_list.php?code=you&id=25941).

14. Users of DC Inside may gravitate toward several different galleries, but usually have a main gallery in which they reside and with which they identify. For example, when one's main daily destination is the "Star Craft Gallery," one is called a Star Craft galler, i.e., gallery user.

15. The relationship between a speaker or writer and his or her subject and audience is paramount in Korean. When talking about or addressing someone of superior status, a speaker or writer usually uses special nouns and verb endings. Speaking/writing to the general public, such as an online community. also involves honorifics to show respect toward the audience and to indicate the level of formality of a situation. In the early 2000s, DC gallers also used honorifics, but gradually changed their habits to use everyday language, and these days none of the gallers use honorifics. If someone happens to use honorifics, she or he would become an object of ridicule as a novice in the DC culture.

16. On the other hand, there are unresolved issues such as copyright infringement and cyber vigilantism. The latter refers to practices known as *singsang teolgi* (singsang t'ŏlgi, personal information theft), discovering and publicizing personal information online. See Jung 2012.

17. The number of drama galleries continues to increase as new drama series come out. Yet not all newly launched dramas are honored with a DC gallery; there must more than 70,000 user requests to generate a new gallery.

18. It is often called a *campus historical romance*, as the drama centers on Sungkyunk-wan, the nation's highest academic institution, set in the time of the Chosun dynasty (1392–1897), when the sons of noblemen attended it. Here one young woman (Kim Yun-hee), disguised as a male, sneaks into the institution (virtually closed to women) posing as her brother and subsequently finds herself in romantic entanglements with her fellow students. The drama series deals with the issues of gender, class, and party politics through the experiences of friendship, competition, love, and inner growth of four lead characters: Sun-jun (played by Park Yoochun), Jae-shin (played by Yoo Ah-in), Yong-ha (played by Song Joong-ki), and Yun-hee (played by Park Min-young).

19. http://www.kbs.co.kr/drama/scandal/index.html.

20. Other public bulletin boards for drama discussion include Daum TV Zone (http://telzone.daum.net) and the drama space on Bestiz (http://www.bestiz.net). Some overseas websites such as http://www.missyusa.com and http://www.dramabeans.com also held active discussions about the drama series both in Korean and English.

21. http://gall.dcinside.com/list.php?id=scandal&no=209341&page=24&recommend=1&recommend=1&bbs=.

22. http://gall.dcinside.com/list.php?id=scandal&no=232068&page=23&recommend=1&recommend=1&bbs=.

23. http://gall.dcinside.com/list.php?id=scandal&no=302018&page=10&recommend=1&recommend=1&bbs=.

24. http://gall.dcinside.com/list.php?id=scandal&no=247434.

25. Jenkins (1992a; 1992b) argues that watching a show regularly is not the same as being a member of a fan community; being a member of a fan community entails knowledge of the interpretive convention and metatext (detailed collaborative analysis of past episodes produced by fans).

26. This is also a part of the language games DC users enjoy.

27. Broadcasters and independent drama producers have asymmetrical power in holding copyright for a drama; taking advantage of their monopoly on television channels, broadcasting firms usually retain all copyrights and distribution rights of a drama after the first airing. Given this profit-redistribution structure, music rights are one of few rights from which independent producers can generate profits.

28. http://gall.dcinside.com/list.php?id=scandal&no=111042.

29. On portal sites that host numerous daily news articles, the number of user recommendations pushes articles to the front so that more people can read them. Fans of certain dramas circulate the news articles about their favorite drama to the wider public.

30. http://gall.dcinside.com/list.php?id=scandal&no=70352, http://gall.dcinside.com/list.php?id=scandal&no=126634.

31. http://gall.dcinside.com/list.php?id=scandal&no=126644.

32. http://gall.dcinside.com/list.php?id=scandal&no=126640.

33. A collection of verification postings can be seen here: http://gall.dcinside.com/list.php?id=scandal&no=65500.

34. http://gall.dcinside.com/list.php?id=scandal&no=136503.

35. http://gall.dcinside.com/list.php?id=scandal&no=39633.

36. http://news.khan.co.kr/kh_news/khan_art_view.html?artid=201005021734275&code= 960801. Last modified May 3, 2010.

37. http://sports.hankooki.com/ArticleView/ArticleView.php?url=entv/201101/sp2011011 006033394350.htm&ver=v002.html. Last modified January 10, 2010.

38. Personal interview with a scriptwriter, spring 2011.

WORKS CITED

Allen, Robert C. 1995. *To Be Continued . . . : Soap Operas around the World*. London: Routledge.

Ang, Ien. 1990. "Melodramatic Identifications: Television Fiction and Women's Fantasy." In *Television and Women's Culture: The Politics of the Popular*, ed. Mary Ellen Brown, 75–88. London: Sage.

Baym, Nancy K. 2000. *Tune In, Log On: Soaps, Fandom, and Online Community*. Sage Publications.

Bilton, Chris. 1999. "Risky Business: The Independent Production Sector in Britain's Creative Industries." *International Journal of Cultural Policy* 6 (1): 17–39.

Brown, Mary Ellen. 1992. *Soap Opera and Women's Talk: The Pleasure of Resistance*. Sage Publications.

Chan, Brenda, and Wang Xueli. 2011. "Of Prince Charming and Male Chauvinist Pigs: Singaporean Female Viewers and the Dream-World of Korean Television Dramas." *International Journal of Cultural Studies* 14 (3): 291–305.

Cho, Hae-Joang. 2005. "Reading the 'Korean Wave' as a Sign of Global Shift." *Korea Journal* 45 (4): 147–82.

Chua, Beng Huat, and Koichi Iwabuchi, eds. 2008. *East Asian Pop Culture: Analysing the Korean Wave*. Hong Kong University Press.

de Certeau, Michel. 1984. *The Practice of Everyday Life*. Berkeley: University of California Press

du Gay, Paul. 1997. *Doing Cultural Studies: The Story of the Sony Walkman*. Thousand Oaks, CA: Sage.

du Gay, Paul, ed. 1998. *Production of Culture / Cultures of Production*. Thousand Oaks, CA: Sage.

Fiske, John. 1989a. *Understanding Popular Culture*. Boston: Unwin Hyman.

Fiske, John. 1989b. *Reading the Popular*. Boston: Unwin Hyman.

Garnham, Nicholas. 1990. *Capitalism and Communication: Global Culture and the Economics of Information*. London: Sage.

Hesmondhalgh, David. 2002. *The Cultural Industries*. Thousand Oaks, CA: Sage.

Hesmondhalgh, David, and Sarah Baker. 2008. "Creative Work and Emotional Labour in the Television Industry." *Theory, Culture and Society* 25: 97–118.

Horkheimer, Max, and Theodor Adorno. 1972. "The Culture Industry: Enlightenment as Mass Deception." In *Dialectic of Enlightenment*, trans. John Cumming. New York: Continuum.

Jenkins, Henry. 1992a. *Textual Poachers: Television Fans and Participatory Culture*. New York: Routledge.

Jenkins, Henry. 1992b. "'Strangers No More, We Sing': Filking and the Social Construction of the Science Fiction Fan Community." In *The Adoring Audience: Fan Culture and Popular Media*, ed. Lisa A. Lewis, 208–35. New York: Routledge.

Jung, Sun. 2011. *Korean Masculinities and Transcultural Consumption: Yonsama, Rain, Oldboy, K-Pop Idols*. Hong Kong: Hong Kong University Press.

Jung, Sun. 2012. "Fan Activism, Cyber Vigilantism, and Othering Mechanisms in K-pop Fandom." In *Transformative Works and Fan Activism*, ed. Henry Jenkins and Sangita Shresthova, special issue, *Transformative Works and Cultures* 10. doi:10.3983/twc.2012.0300.

Kaplan, Andreas, and Michael Haenlein. 2010. "Users of the World, Unite! The Challenges and Opportunities of Social Media." *Business Horizons* 53 (1): 59–68.

Kim, Hyun-mi. 2005. *Kŭllobŏl sidae ŭi munhwa pŏnyŏk: chendŏ, injong, kyech'ŭng ŭi kyŏnggye rŭl nŏmŏ* (Cultural Translation in the Global Age: Beyond the Barriers of Gender, Race, and Class). Seoul: Tto Hana ŭi Munhwa.

KOFICE (Korea Foundation for International Cultural Exchange). 2008. "Hallyu p'oebŏ:

Hallyu ŭi hyŏnjuso wa kyŏngjejŏkhyokwa punsŏk" (Hallyu Forever: The Current Situation of Hallyu and Its Economic Effects).

Lee, Gilho. 2012. *Woorineun Dissi: DC, Ingyeo, geurigo Saibeospeiseui Inryu* (We, the DC: DC Inside, Surplus, and Humans in Cyberspace). Seoul: Imagine.

Lee, Sooyeon. 2012. "The Structure of the Appeal of Korean Wave Texts." *Korea Observer* 43 (3): 447–69.

Modleski, Tania. 1982. *Loving with a Vengeance: Mass Produced Fantasies for Women.* New York: Routledge.

Morley, David 1992. *Television, Audiences, and Cultural Studies.* London: Routledge.

Negus, Keith. 1999. *Music Genres and Corporate Cultures.* New York: Routledge.

Radway, Janice. 1984, 1991. *Reading the Romance: Women, Patriarchy and Popular Culture.* Chapel Hill: University of North Carolina Press.

Zillmann, Dolph. 1994. "Mechanisms of Emotional Involvement with Drama." *Poetics* 23: 33–51.

7

Meta-Hallyu TV

Global Publicity, Social Media, and the Citizen Celebrity

Michelle Cho

Viewers with even the least bit of familiarity with Korean film and television can attest to the growing prevalence of narratives about the mass media, culture industries, celebrity-construction, pop idols, and publicity in recent productions.[1] Ha Gi-ho's period comedy *Radio Dayz* (Radŭio teijŭ, 2008), with its staging of the mysterious relationship between media, the state, capital, and the public, is but one example. Ha's film situates the inception of the serial-melodrama form in Korean broadcast media of colonial Gyeongseong (Kyŏngsŏng, present-day Seoul), envisioning a sort of origin myth, albeit anachronistic, of Korea as a nation of participatory media consumers. Against a stylized, colonial-modern backdrop, *Radio Dayz* imagines a direct relay between performers, producers, and audience, each a node in the production of an affectively constituted public sphere made manifest in the fledgling technologies of radio transmission. Linking the melodramatic excess of serial narrative with the ad hoc and advertisement-driven mode of production of the radio play, the film is both a metacommentary on the structures of mass entertainment in general and a thinly veiled allegory of the cultural economy of contemporary television dramas, a key sector of the culture industries in Korea and a constitutive component of the media convergence phenomena reified in the term *Hallyu*.

A cheeky industry parody calling out the relationship between sentimentality and commercialism, *Radio Dayz* nonetheless fantasizes an ideally responsive and participatory media landscape, especially in the *immediacy* of audience reaction in shaping the content of each successive installment of the radio serial. For the producers, performers, sponsors, and censors of *Flames of Love*, the maudlin and nonsensical radio production depicted in the film, the public embodies both master and slave—in dialectical fashion, the mass media alternately obey the commands and manipulate the desires of the general public, while also stimulating in this disembodied yet concrete entity the appetite for the various products advertised, stereotypes reinforced, and celebrity images constructed. In *Radio Dayz*'s vision of participatory reception, the public is both explicitly *national* and impossibly diffused, depicted both by rapt crowds huddling close to scarce radio receivers in the public commons and by far-off, disembodied listeners in the ether. *Flames of Love* must appeal to both the colonized and the colonizing populations, as well as technophilic audiences from such distant locales as the United States, whose infatuation with the futurism of broadcast transmission brings them into the fold of the radio drama's audience. As an implicit dramatization of the juggling act performed by popular culture content in conditions of increasing media convergence, *Radio Dayz* helps to indicate the extent to which metatextuality has become a fixture in Korean popular culture, advancing its appeal to both national and transnational audiences. One major implication of the film's metacommentary is the centrality of *projected desire* in the complex relay between media producers and consumers, in other words, the ways in which the media product always addresses an *imagined public*, a public that does not preexist media commodities in discrete forms but rather coalesces in the process of the latter's reception.

Focusing on the reflexive strategy of *fictionalizing* this production of publicity, this essay examines social media's disciplinary power and regimes of self-representation in two recent Korean TV dramas that dramatize Hallyu idol celebrity culture: *Oh! My Lady* (O! mai leidi, 2010) and *The Greatest Love* (Ch'oego ŭi Sarang, 2011). As Korean TV dramas increasingly turn to metaindustry, social-media-centered narratives, they offer a unique site in which to track the development of Hallyu 2.0. While, as Sangjoon Lee writes in this volume's introduction, Korean TV dramas have been the focus of much Hallyu research in the context of regional and transnational pop cultural flows, this chapter seeks to draw attention to a little discussed but crucial dimension of Korean TV dramas' structural conditions of production: Korean TV dramas, as products of Korea's national television broadcast system, embed the concerns of a national public in a transnational cultural export.[2] Following Irina Lyan and Alon

Levkowitz's suggestion in their essay on Israeli reception of Korean TV dramas, the focus on traditional values, including familial nationalism, adds to their appeal to transnational audiences who seek an alternative to the comparatively sexualized pop culture content on offer from Europe or the United States. Further, the performance of an affective, intimate public through the representation of participatory media helps both despecify Korean TV dramas' "national values," yet also maintain Hallyu 2.0's national brandedness as a sector of managed culture industries (see Jung-Bong Choi's essay in this volume for a fuller analysis of Hallyu as a national cultural export). Finally, the embedding of an imagined intimate public within a global cultural export serves a pedagogical function, portraying a cosmopolitan subjectivity made possible by technological infrastructure and social media, with its reorganization of concepts of identity, civic participation, and social legibility.

The dramas' fictionalized portrayal of the agency of publics and consumers reinforces the fantasy of their narrative's verisimilitude, which they maintain by association with normative categories of social life, especially family and work. In addition, the shows' entertainment industry setting accords with a common perception of celebrity culture: a carnivalesque, transmedial realm that upends stable values (authenticity, unmediated self-presentation) such that the very fact of mediation and artifice—the best acting and performance—signifies authenticity and sincerity. In the context of these shows, mass-mediated identity is posited as the site of not just cultural citizenship but subjectivity as such. My essay explores the ambivalence of this gambit in the dramas I address, to explore the implications of Korean popular culture's incorporation of the realm of critique that would seem to constitute its external limits.

In the analysis to follow, I bring assessments of media convergence, theorized most notably by media scholar Henry Jenkins, into dialogue with insights on the shifting categories of publicity, performance, theatricality, and subject formation, which arise from discussions in cultural studies, social theory, and performance studies. The ways in which performance and theatricality are interposed, together with accounts of how media convergence reorients our understanding of the public, will provide the critical vocabulary for reading these Korean TV dramas as mass cultural texts that dramatize their own public relations. I offer here an attempt to think through what the varied and shifting modes of *representing* the potency and perils of social media indicate about publicity as a paradigm of social relations, and further, what Korean television's ubiquitous use of social media as a *trope* has to say about the dialectic of corporate and consumer-driven processes of convergence in global media today. This inquiry contributes to ongoing analyses of Hallyu's significance to questions of national and transnational identity and, in particular, investigates the ways in which social media's constitutive role in Korean TV dramas requires us to rethink conceptions of publicity, the mediated public sphere, and the subjects produced therein.

Babes in Dramaland: K-Pop Idols and "Utopias of Self-Abstraction"

Oh! My Lady (2010) and *The Greatest Love* (2011) are Korean TV dramas that incorporate fan dynamics and the demands on the star as a commodified body into their narratives. The purpose of this treatment seems twofold. On one hand, the shows' multilayered reflexivity develops in the viewer a metaconsciousness that paradoxically facilitates further involvement in the wish fulfillment narrative; meta-awareness provides a semblance of critical distance, which compensates for the emotional intensities of love for fantastic objects (another way of thinking of fandom). On the other hand, these shows envision a media ecology that discounts utopian claims of convergence cultures, not least of which is Henry Jenkins's assessment that "collective intelligence can be seen as an alternative source of media power" (2006, 4). Though indeed "consumption has become a collective process" (4), the dramas convert the communitarian valence of Jenkins's theory of participatory culture into the oppressive force of public opinion as mob rule.[3] Within the diegetic space of the dramas, the public's aggressive and capricious judgments of its star commodities in no way realize the emancipatory potential of participatory reception—the public *wants* to be duped more thoroughly, and it is the stars' failure in this endeavor that causes public outcry. The obstructionism of the public becomes resolved as the sacrifice that the celebrity must make to public ownership of his or her image.[4] The question both shows raise is how to make sense of the duality of metatextuality's narrative function and its critical dimension.

Oh! My Lady revisits a now familiar scenario of a contract relationship between an "ordinary" citizen and a popular celebrity, most famously depicted by *Full House* (P'ul Hausŭ, 2004), a drama that starred K-pop phenom Rain (Bi) as a pop idol celebrity who falls in love with a woman whom he first employs as his housekeeper.[5] In *Oh! My Lady*, Choi Si-won, of the popular S.M. Entertainment (hereafter S.M.) idol group Super Junior, plays a fictional "flower boy" actor named Sŏng Min-u, who enlists the aid of a divorced housewife to look after the love child born of a previous tryst who has been unceremoniously dumped at his doorstep. The narrative impetus for the star's relation to the woman, Yun Kae-hwa (played by actress Chae Rim), is the concern he has for the negative effects on his image and career that the public revelation of his paternity will cause. While the dynamic between the celebrity and the hired parental surrogate/housekeeper begins antagonistically, as is typical in the "contract romance" genre, it eventually reverses into love, and the couple transforms their pseudofamilial relationship into a "real" family.[6] In this story, the star is punished by the public through near constant harassment by entertainment reporters and is exploited by his manager, who blackmails him by threatening to reveal his improprieties. The threat of "scandal" keeps the star a prisoner in his (admittedly lavish) company-controlled quarters; thus, the relationship between the star and the "ordinary" heroine offers the promise of a genuine relationship of care, in a context in which all of his other interactions are premised on the desire to exploit his monetized public image.

As an example of and a commentary on media convergence, *Oh! My Lady* stages its romance as the star's coming-of-age narrative—he begins as a petulant pretty-boy who tacitly accepts his status as a body evacuated of will. He obediently follows a regime of exercise and grooming, since he has no motivation to be anything but decorative. In the beginning of the series, the star's vanity conveniently serves his handlers' profit motives, in elevating appearance over all else. The star thus facilitates the media industry's consolidation of image and object. As the series progresses, the star becomes aware of his manipulation by his manager and, through his budding affection for his daughter and Yun Kae-hwa, "matures" by recognizing his star image as only one role among others he must also assume, including father, husband, and provider. The drama concludes with the idol star's sage recognition that damage to his public image might benefit his personal life, when he goes public with his daughter's existence and his love for Kae-hwa. In redeeming celebrity by tracking the star's realization of his own star text's superficiality, *Oh! My Lady* establishes a complex authorization of celebrity as self-fracturing. Those stars who master which roles are to be taken up in which contexts become celebrated as normative exemplars of public identity.

Besides depicting the dynamics of celebrity, *Oh! My Lady*'s primary metatextual device is the body of Choi Si-won, purportedly the most valuable member of boy band, Super Junior, if measured in advertising revenue. Super Junior is an idol group that exemplifies the K-pop industry's transnational strategies. As elaborated in this volume by Eun-Young Jung, S.M.'s pioneering "cultural technologies" center on transnational marketing and the localization of K-pop for particular markets.[7] When the narrative develops the character's "talents" through diversification—having the character star in a stage musical in order to prove his acting chops—the series fictionalizes its own act of content delivery (of the star image) across multiple platforms. The star's singing and dancing abilities feature centrally in a middle section of the drama, offering the audience the pleasures of metatextual awareness of Choi Si-won's status as a pop idol who must master a trifecta of performance skills: singing, acting, and dancing. In a winking reference to the common view that pop idols are bad actors, Sŏng Min-u is a heartthrob whose acting abilities are widely ridiculed.

One might expect a conflict to arise in the consumption of Choi Si-won, actual pop idol, and Choi Si-won acting in the role of a self-absorbed, immature pop icon in *Oh! My Lady*, because of the way that fans of Choi Si-won are interpellated by the drama's depiction of fandom as a denigrated identity. As Laura Lewis explains in the introduction to the essay collection *The Adoring Audience*, fandom is stigmatized "by emphasizing danger, abnormality, and silliness," in no small part because of the passions that characterize fandom as "a contradictory site of love and hate" (1992, xiv). Both *Oh! My Lady* and *The Greatest Love* villainize the ambivalent libidinal economy of fandom, raising the question of how the viewer reconciles her own status as fan with the fictional depiction of fandom as a form of mass hysteria.

However, I argue that the structures of identification intrinsic to media consumption prevent the viewer from identifying with the diegetic public's visible behavior, even as she might engage in some of the same activities as those depicted by the drama's fictional fans. Michael Warner's study of the ideals of anonymity, disembodiment, and abstraction in classic conceptions of the democratic public sphere help to elucidate this complex structure of identification and disidentification. In *Publics and Counterpublics*, Michael Warner theorizes "public discourse as a routine form of self-abstraction," explaining the logic by which consuming a representation of bad fan behavior immunizes the viewer from identifying with the fictionalized consumers, who represent the public at large. Warner writes, "No one really inhabits the general public. This is true not only because it is by definition general but also because everyone brings to such a category the particularities from which she has to abstract herself in consuming this discourse" (2002, 182). This paradox of exclusion by identification with "the general public" is particularly acute in an image economy, in which publicity also entails a mode of relentless visibility and continual self-mediation via social media platforms. Warner's incisive analysis stresses the dialectical relationship between the disembodiment of public subjectivity as a "utopia of self abstraction" and the centrality of the display of bodies as icons in a public sphere dominated by visual media. The transformation of the form and meaning of publicity in the increasingly technologized and commodified mass culture of images renders the identificatory mechanisms of publicity as dependent on visibility as abstraction. Moreover, in the context of transnational media publics, the suturing of variously identified national publics by Hallyu commodities relies on fractured sites of reception, which are made possible by social media.

According to Warner, the contradictions between "utopian self-abstraction" and "unrecuperated particularity" (2002, 168) for subjects of mass culture leads to the privileging of commodity consumption as a kind of abstractable particularity; consumption's transitive pleasures, accessed through a fantasy of absent witnessing and a conflation of consumer and public identity, translate the particularity of consumer choice into self-abstraction. The ascendance of social relations based on consumption as a strategy for identity formation transforms the function of public recognition, such that one's embodied specificity signals both particular identity categories (e.g., race, class, gender, culture, etc.) and the register of commodity consumption as a vehicle for self-expression. I extend Warner's identification of the commodity form as a crucial link to public subjectivity, in which the particularity of consumer choice provides access to a certain kind of abstract publicness, to suggest that thinking of oneself as a commodity—a mentality made inevitable, one might argue, by the entrepreneurialism of neoliberal ideology—fundamentally binds the desire for public identity with the commodity form of reification. In other words, to be public, one thinks of oneself as an object of others' consumption, rendering oneself both subject and social fact. This transformation of publicity's "utopias of self-abstraction" transfers the desire for access to an abstracted group identity ("the public") to identification with the publicity of the commodity form.

Thus, rather than identifying with the representation of the public on-screen, the viewer instead identifies with *the commodified body*—the celebrity—who serves as a model of public identity in general. In this sense, every fan is a potential celebrity, especially given the norms of mediated public existence via social media platforms like Twitter and Facebook, which are available to citizen and celebrity alike. Fans celebrate in the idol figure both the idol's public image and the self-abstraction they share in common. Warner's analysis points to this identification with the celebrity in the popularity of popularity itself—the fact that "individuals encounter in publicity the erotics of a powerful identification not just with public icons but also with their popularity" (2002, 181). Concomitant with this desire to be desired, however, is an identification with the vulnerability of the public body, because, as an embodied form, it cannot sufficiently satisfy the limitless desires of an abstract public. In Choi Si-won's casting in *Oh! My Lady*, the affective force of this dual identification operates on multiple registers and is magnified by Choi's status as an *actual* pop idol who must negotiate the desires and projections of fans and antifans across the globe. Moreover, the relationship of care developed between the celebrity and the character Yun Kae-hwa naturalizes self-presentation as commodity by portraying it as a developmental process and, therefore, both normative *and* organic.

In addition to identifying with the celebrity, the viewer also identifies with the heroine, who represents the "fan" who comes to know and love the disparity between the star's private and public selves, casting the act of consumption into an edifying, caretaking gesture (as is often the alibi for the intense possessiveness of the fan toward the celebrity). *Oh! My Lady* thus depicts the commodification of the star persona as a form of social reproduction, by constructing a parental relation between the "noncelebrity" heroine and the celebrity love object. In addition to naturalizing performance and split identity, the narrative arc of the drama reconciles the viewer's dual identification with the heroine as ideal fan and the hero as commodified body, culminating in the eventual nuclear family that results from their union. Yun Kae-hwa is depicted as caring, mature, and long-suffering, while Min-u is petulant, unpredictable, and selfish. Yun Kae-hwa's task, then, in her assignment as surrogate mother and domestic worker, is to help Min-u "grow up," which involves learning to responsibly assume the duties of conventional patriarchal masculinity by accepting his role as a father, becoming better at his profession (i.e., becoming a better actor and performer), and acknowledging the separate careers of his public and private personae.

A key scene signaling Min-u's maturation and the turning point in Min-u's attitude toward his daughter literalizes Min-u's exchange of superficial star image for parental responsibility. When his daughter goes missing at a department store, Min-u responds by instinct as a concerned parent, declaring his relationship to the child to the crowds that swarm him when he enters the shopping complex. After a period of fruitless

Fig. 6. *Oh! My Lady*'s literal depiction of the star's superficial image

searching, Min-u finally finds his daughter clutching the hand of a life-sized promotional cutout of his image, next to a display of clothing. Disoriented, the child looks up, expectantly, at the photograph of her father. As he approaches the child, he apologizes to her for his neglect, and substitutes his living body for his image (figures 6 and 7). From that point onward, he assumes responsibility for her care, now that he has effectively sacrificed his public image for his private life. This event changes his relationship to Kae-hwa as well, as he comforts her over her distress at losing Ye-ŭn, the small child, and later protects her from press scrutiny and fan backlash when the scandalous news breaks of Ye-ŭn's existence.

This scenario envisions wish fulfillment for the viewer in its realization of the fantasy conveyed by media convergence and participatory media cultures—that the fan's consumption of the star image is a two-way relay, a mode of caretaking and a form of intimacy with the celebrity. The industry practices of talent management in K-pop, in particular, provide another register of intertextuality, supporting the fantasy of fans as loving caretakers who shape the idols, supporting them from their early days as trainees through their artistic maturation as representatives of a national culture industry with global reach. Since the standard practice of producing idol stars in Korea involves systematic recruitment and training of young talent,[8] the claim that the stars are simply manufactured products of thoroughly commercialized entertainment often arises among the in-

Fig. 7. Min-u's exchange of superficial star image for parental responsibility (*Oh! My Lady*)

dustry's critics.[9] Indeed, as a sector of commodified mass culture, K-pop's relation to Korean TV drama and vice versa helps to normalize the practices and institutions of manufactured celebrity images, domesticating these processes in the association between everyday life and idol stars in the dramas' plot lines and in the quotidian rhythms of broadcast television. *Oh! My Lady*'s gesture of incorporating fan dynamics into the romance plot intensifies the association of public identity and self-commodification.

Theatricality, Performance, and Social Fact in *The Greatest Love*

The most obvious difference between *The Greatest Love* and *Oh! My Lady* is the former's decidedly satirical approach to the industry practices of what Eun-Young Jung in this volume calls "Hallyu K-pop." *The Greatest Love* bases its narrative on the challenges and rewards of an unlikely romance between a washed-up former pop idol star and an A-list film actor at the height of his popularity across Asia and on the verge of crossover success into Hollywood.[10] The drama has been widely praised for its self-reflexive critique of the mechanics of celebrity construction in Korea, especially the conflicts between the stars' interests and the hard-nosed business decisions of the stars' management companies, who are solely interested in preserving the celebrity as a source of profit. A major plot element in *The Greatest Love* is the failure of idol group managers to protect their young employees from the pressures of life in the public eye. Much of the satirical humor also comes from the show's depiction of variety show television programming, another site in which Hallyu idol culture meets domestic broadcast television's intimate public. Since many K-pop idols are featured in Korean variety shows, these shows are privileged texts within Hallyu K-pop fandoms, circulating in many of the same online streaming and video-sharing platforms as Korean TV dramas and K-pop music videos (see Sangjoon Lee's analysis of YouTube, fansubbing sites, and licensed diasporic media channels in this volume).

The show's main target of criticism is a cruel public, protected by the anonymity of the Internet and provoked by sensationalist news media. The heroine, Ku Ae-jŏng, is the former leader of a popular girl group, Kukpo Sonyŏ ("National Treasure Girls"—a humorous reference to the contemporary idol group Girls' Generation [Sonyŏ Sidae] and the 1980s pop duo Kukpo Chamae ["National Treasure Sisters"]), who struggles to draw an income off her waning celebrity status by appearing on variety shows where she often has to endure humiliating gags. The backstory to the breakup of the group explains Ae-jŏng's precipitous fall as the result of her attempts to protect and care for her group-mates. When the drama begins, she has long suffered passionate hatred from former fans because of rumors that her ambitions for a solo career caused the group to disband. As a perpetual target of public criticism, Ae-jŏng is the most sympathetic of drama heroines—plucky, determined, optimistic, and hardworking, in spite of the unfairness of her persecution by antifans.

Tokko Chin, on the other hand, is adored by the public, though his public image contradicts his private actions, which are arrogant, entitled, selfish, and insecure. In a scene that demonstrates the extent of his solipsism, as the entire nation tunes into a sports broadcast to cheer on Korean swimming star Park Tae-hwan in an international meet, Tokko Chin roots for defeat, so that he won't lose a lucrative advertising contract to the athlete. The irony of this gesture emerges in his arrogant self-designation as *kungmin paeu* or "the nation's actor." As one of the most sought-after celebrities in the country, Tokko Chin appears literally everywhere, on a sea of advertisements and product packaging; *The Greatest Love* critiques the value of the star image as a commodity that helps sell other commodities, while simultaneously engaging in the standard practice of product placement for show sponsors. The unavoidability of Tokko Chin's image be-

Fig. 8. The power attributed to public critique via participatory media is so exaggerated in *Greatest Love* that, in a fantasy sequence, Ku Ae-jŏng imagines negative web forum comments as a weapon, shooting her with words.

comes a source of tension in the couple's courtship. In episode 5, after Tokko has confessed his feelings to Ae-jŏng and she replies that she does not have any inclination to become involved with him, his offended response is "I'll make you think of me always." Later, she finds that she cannot escape his image, as it endorses everything from soft drinks to toiletries, both domestic and imported—in particular, his image frequently appears on the packaging of the multinational Glaceau Vitamin Water, one of *The Greatest Love*'s sponsors. Confronted by a smirking image of Tokko that adorns a shampoo bottle in her bathroom, she indignantly turns the image away, finding it impossible to avoid him even in the most private of spaces. The metajoke, of course, is that Ae-jŏng, unlike the beguiled public, feels affronted by the intimacy implied by consumption of the star image.

Both celebrities' public images contrast with their "real" personalities, thus emphasizing the disparity between public presentation and "authentic" selfhood. This is a long-standing opposition that drama scholar Marvin Carlson traces to classical conceptions of theater. However, Carlson notes a shift in the meaning of performance, with the growing imbrication of theories of performance and social phenomena. He writes, "It is hardly an exaggeration to say that in the study of social phenomena today metaphors of theater and performance are so common that they have become almost transparent, while conversely, in the study of theater, a similar critical dominance is currently held by the metaphors and the *topoi* of social analysis" (2002, 238). What Carlson refers to here is the emergence of the interdisciplinary field of performance studies, generated from an overarching reversal in the relation between the terms *performance* and *theatricality*. Whereas performance and theatricality were once considered basically synonymous, with the development of the concept of performativity in language[11] and gender, the terms took on opposed meanings such that theatricality came to signify behavior that seemed "not natural or spontaneous" and performativity became, in contrast, the mechanism by which subjectivity is "'performatively constituted,' precisely by the 'ritualized production' of codified social behavior" (240).[12] Carlson argues that the conceptual developments by which "theatricality and performance have come to be posited as rhetorically oppositional terms" (239) have inadvertently revived the conventional opposition between "'authentic' or 'meaningful expression of the self and the 'empty rituals' of theatricality" (240). This return to convention has had the unfortunate effect of reifying the distinction between "self" and "role," reinforcing theatricality's negative connotations of deception or illusion (240).

Against the conservatism of this opposition, which implies an authentic self that precedes or can be differentiated from the performance of social roles that Judith Butler and others assert actually constitutes the subject, Carlson notes that "theatricality . . . has built into it a doubleness, or a play between two types of reality" (244) rather than presenting a mendacious, second-order representation of reality. These two types of reality are what *The Greatest Love* affords access to, in its dramatization of both performance as theatricality, for instance, in Tokko Chin's public appearances and advertising images, and performance as a structure of subjectivity and the embodied enactment of social reality. *The Greatest Love* shows the interplay of performance-as-theatricality and performance-as-sociality to be the very mechanism of the establishment of social fact—those aspects of social life that are discursively produced yet have material effects.

The Greatest Love presents this imbrication of theatrical and performative realities in its dramatic development. After Ae-jŏng and Tokko have fallen in love, they must keep their relationship a secret, for the sake of maintaining the monetary value of Tokko's public image and also to shield Ae-jŏng from Tokko's fans, who would retaliate against her via online web forums and other social media sites for devaluing Tokko's public persona. The couple's concerns turn out to be well founded; when Tokko's manager learns of their relationship, she doesn't hesitate to admit that she would go to any lengths to protect Tokko's image, including sending him overseas to work on Hallyu publicity projects while she set to work destroying their relationship, to keep him from being tainted by association with a lesser celebrity. It is clear that the reality of the couple's affections cannot offset the no less real ways that they can do harm to each other through the incompatibility of their public images.

When Tokko's heart implant begins to malfunction, necessitating an open-heart surgery with a slim survival rate, the drama establishes an inverse relationship between Tokko's physical life and the vitality of his public image. To solve the problem of the public's hatred of Ae-jŏng, Tokko gambles on the possibility that if he dies, he will be able to transfer the public's goodwill to Ae-jŏng, by arranging for the posthumous release of a public statement of his feelings for her and then betting on her ability to win over his fans through a demonstration of public mourning over his loss. By linking Tokko's physical death to the elevation of his public image via the abstraction of Tokko's identity from his embodiment, *The Greatest Love* expresses the play between performative and theatrical realities. "The two contrasting functions" are "mutually reinforcing to achieve a more powerful total effect" (Carlson 2002, 245), that is, to allow the perception of the constitutive tension between the two registers of public and private realities, both of which are shaped by social forces that precede the individual at the same time that they rely on the variables of the individual's particular experiences and identifications. As expected from *The Greatest Love*'s romantic comedy genre, Tokko survives his surgery, and the couple lives happily ever after. However, they continue to navigate the perils of public existence.

Conclusion: Publicity and Hallyu 2.0

Though *Oh! My Lady* and *The Greatest Love* share a preoccupation with revealing the mechanisms of celebrity and the pressures of publicity, they're quite different in the ways that metatextuality functions ideologically in their narratives. In *Oh! My Lady*, the figure of the public actually reinforces the viewer's attachment to the drama's celebration of patriarchy. The perceived critical distance afforded by the metafictional dimensions of the storyline (the netizenry, paparazzi, and media reports, which play out the fantasy of "stars—they're just like us") reinforces attachment to the drama's fantasy scenario of shaping/parenting the perfect masculine object. Through its intensified attention to the artifice of the celebrity image, the drama displaces the artifice of the shows' manipulation of gender and class identity to the peripheries of the viewer's attention. *The Greatest Love*, on the other hand, reminds the viewer of the ambiguous construction of social fact by practically doing away with the category of "natural" behavior. It does this by foregrounding the theatricality of all forms of public subjectivity, which reminds the viewer of the conventionality of even what appears authentic and spontaneous.

Though the dramas present contrasting illustrations of metatexuality's mystifying and demystifying functions, they nonetheless index an overarching preoccupation with the contemporary subject's need to juggle multiple social roles and identities in the realm of publicity—a facet of technological mediation and the estrangement catalyzed by cultural contact in a period of increased transnational exchange. One grim implication of the crystallization of split identity, in the way it is visualized in Korean television, may be the consolidation of forms of publicity vis-à-vis mass media such that the popular media are *expected* to dictate the terms of social relations and civil society in the service of consumerism as a national and transnational pastime. As *Radio Dayz* suggests, the serial melodrama is mainly a vehicle for advertising commodities and for producing a sentimental public; in this sense, the form and function of Korean TV dramas has changed little, despite the transformation in media ecologies and the development of multiple technologies for content delivery and a participatory Internet culture. Moreover, the rise in metafictional narratives signals the preoccupation with publicity that arises when identifying with a public means relating to oneself as a commodity. In the many dramas that thematize celebrity, including dramas in which political popularity and celebrity converge (for example, *City Hall* [Sit'i Hol, 2009]), criticisms of the public indicate nostalgic attachment to "authenticity" as fixed identity, to resist transformations of the public sphere resulting from, among other factors, Korea's increasing investment in digital communications infrastructure, neoliberal policies in education, labor, and development, and a rapidly receding history of popular mobilization.

On the other hand, however, Korean culture industries' appeal to transnational audiences via social media, as strategies to capture global market share, may unexpectedly counter the forces of media consolidation. If the consumption of these dramas by viewers outside of the boundaries of national-cultural citizenship imaginatively incorporates these viewers into the national public of collective witnessing, this undoubtedly affects the signifying function of such a "public." The dramatic tension between public and private identities unleashed by dramas like *Oh! My Lady* and *The Greatest Love* cannot be as easily resolved as their narratives suggest, despite their attempts to naturalize the split according to conventional social categories. The critical capacity of Korean TV dramas' metatextuality suggests that the Internet's decentralization and diffusion of reception sites create the conditions for unpredictable appropriations and creative resignification of Hallyu commodities. Read in this light, Korean TV drama's current obsession with metatextuality suggests that media consumption remains a dynamic and contested arena for the construction of models of public participation and social relations, rather than a monolithic apparatus for shaping consumer behavior.

NOTES

1. Examples include *Rough Cut* (2008, dir. Jang Hoon), *200 Pounds Beauty* (2006, dir. Kim Yong-hwa), *The Actresses* (2010, dir. E J-yong), *Full House* (KBS, 2004), *Worlds Within* (KBS, 2008), *You Are Beautiful* (SBS, 2009), and *Dream High* (KBS, 2011).

2. In this volume, Youjeong Oh, in her essay on the material conditions of Korean TV drama production, and Seung-Ah Lee, in her analysis of JYJ fan activism and civic consciousness, detail the national constraints of the Korean television landscape, while also highlighting the important role that television plays for promoting Hallyu.

3. See Jenkins's *Textual Poachers* (1992) for an account of fan activity as creative appropriation.

4. For an analysis of celebrity that historicizes precisely this relationship of the celebrity as public sacrifice, see Joseph R. Roach's *It* (2007).

5. Sun Jung contextualizes *Full House*'s appeal to fans in Singapore, extending the reach of both K-pop and Korean TV dramas beyond East Asia into Southeast Asia, in an account of Rain's embodiment of hybrid aesthetics and gender ideals in her *Korean Masculinities and Transcultural Consumption* (2011). See chap. 3 "Rain, Global Masculinity, and Singaporean Fans: Fly Anywhere, Click Anytime."

6. *Oh! My Lady* is somewhat unique in that it pairs a young idol with an older actress who is playing a character seven years older than the male love interest. While the nuna-dongsaeng (older sister–younger brother) romance is becoming more common, reflecting, in my observations, a fantasy of heterosexual women in their thirties who see in a younger generation of men a more desirable view of gender relations, it is still rare to see a pairing like the one presented in this drama. Even more anomalous is the fact that the female lead is a divorced, single mother. Other examples of nuna-dongsaeng dramas include *The Woman Who Still Wants to Marry* (Ajikto kyŏrhon hagosip'ŭn yŏja, 2010), *My Sweet Seoul* (Talk'omhan na ŭi tosi, 2008), and *Fox, What Are You Doing?* (Yŏuya mŏ hani? 2006).

7. S.M. has developed Super Junior subgroups including Super Junior-M (the M stands for Mandarin). Recently, S.M. artist Henry Lau, an Asian-Canadian of Hong Kong and Taiwanese heritage, debuted as S.M.'s first male solo artist in thirteen years. Many S.M. idols also perform in musicals, for example, SHINee's Key and Onew.

8. K-pop is produced by entertainment companies that control the formation, training, image, and music selection of their groups. BoA, an idol singer who's found wide success across Korea and Japan, was a trainee of S.M. from age eleven, and released her first album at thirteen. Members of the YG boy group Big Bang trained for six years (from their early teens), before debuting in 2006. Idol groups are now debuting with members as young as twelve. http://seoulbeats.com/2012/06/the-babies-of-k-pop-how-young-is-too-young/. Accessed June 3, 2012.

9. In the closing chapter of *Korean Masculinities and Transcultural Consumption* (2011) Sun Jung summarizes the arguments of Korean media critics who also cite the deceptiveness of idol appearances in variety shows and reality TV programs, in which they are claimed to reveal their "true" personalities. I would argue that the pop idols' appearances in reality television serve a purpose similar to their crossover appearances as actors in the metatextual television drama: to reinforce a split between their pop performer identity and another identity that seems in comparison to offer for consumption a semblance of intimacy, whether in the form of an image of the star's "real" personality or in the form of a character to whom the viewer can develop a sentimental identification.

10. This character satirizes cases like those of Hallyu stars Rain and Lee Byung-hun, who have appeared in a number of commercial Hollywood films, including *Speed Racer* (dir. the Wachowski Bros., 2008), *Ninja Assassin* (dir. James McTeigue, 2009), *GI Joe: The Rise of Cobra* (dir. Stephen Sommers, 2009), and *GI Joe: Retaliation* (dir. John M. Chu, 2013). Unsurprisingly, the Korean stars have been racially typecast in these productions and relegated to virtually nonspeaking roles that emphasize action and athleticism.

11. J. L. Austin pioneered speech act theory, theorizing the performativity of language.

12. Here, Carlson quotes Judith Butler, whose influential theory of performativity was developed in *Gender Trouble: Feminism and the Subversion of Identity* (1990) and *Bodies That Matter* (1993).

WORKS CITED

Butler, Judith. 1990. *Gender Trouble: Feminism and the Subversion of Identity.* New York: Routledge.

Butler, Judith. 1993. *Bodies That Matter.* New York: Routledge.

Beng Huat, Chua, and Koichi Iwabuchi. 2008. "Introduction: East Asian TV Dramas: Identifications, Sentiments and Effects." in *East Asian Pop Culture: Analysing the Korean Wave,* ed. Chua Beng Huat and Koichi Iwabuchi. 1–6. Hong Kong: Hong Kong University Press.

Carlson, Marvin A. 2002. "The Resistance to Theatricality." *SubStance* 98/99, vol. 31 (2–3): 238–50.

Jenkins, Henry. 1992. *Textual Poachers: Television Fans and Participatory Culture.* New York: Routledge.

Jenkins, Henry. 2006. *Convergence Culture: Where Old and New Media Collide.* New York: New York University Press.

Jung, Sun. 2011. *Korean Masculinities and Transcultural Consumption: Yonsama, Rain, Oldboy, K-Pop Idols.* Hong Kong: Hong Kong University Press.

Keenan, Thomas. 1993. "Windows of Vulnerability." In *The Phantom Public Sphere*, ed. Bruce Robbins, 121–41. Minneapolis: University of Minnesota Press.

Lewis, Lisa A., ed. 1992. *The Adoring Audience: Fan Culture and Popular Media.* New York: Routledge.

Roach, Joseph. 1997. *It.* Ann Arbor: University of Michigan Press.

Warner, Michael. 2002. *Publics and Counterpublics.* New York: Zone Books.

8

From Diaspora TV to Social Media

Korean TV Dramas in America

Sangjoon Lee

Korean TV dramas debuted on the airwaves of the United States in 1975, exclusively for overseas Korean communities in an entry-port city, Los Angeles. They then began circulating through two Korean diasporic media outlets: Korean-language TV stations and video rental stores. The latter were in Koreatowns in major metropolitan cities, such as Los Angeles, New York, Chicago, San Francisco, Washington, DC, and Atlanta. This well-maintained, two-channel system has, however, considerably frayed in the new millennium as U.S. consumption patterns of Korean dramas expeditiously migrate toward video-streaming websites like YouTube, Hulu, and Netflix, and online-based fan communities whose ethnic identity is not necessarily Korean. Since the early 2000s, myriad illegal web services and social media networks have provided, shared, and disseminated Korean TV dramas, along with K-pop, to the mainstream users/viewers in the United States, eventually resulting in the first legitimate video-streaming service DramaFever.com. The aim of this chapter is to historicize and analyze the distribution, circulation, and reception of Korean TV dramas in the United States, from diasporic TV, exclusively for Korean immigrants, to the mainstream media market, in the age of social media.

Korean immigrants in the United States were quintessential post-1965 settlers, along with Vietnamese, Indian, and other Southeast Asian refugees. This was when the Immigration and Nationality Act of 1965 eliminated the nation-origin quota system based on race that had been the basis for American immigration policy since the 1920s. The law, instead, focused on immigrants' skills and family relationships with citizens or permanent residents.[1] These new "post-1965" communities have therefore political and social agendas different from the preceding groups from Asia: the Japanese and Chinese. Korean immigrants also stand apart as they are—markedly, for the first generation—maintaining their "imagined community" within American society. Almost all post-1965 Korean immigrants departed from Korea, a culturally homogeneous society. They speak only one language, and do not have indicative regional characteristics in customs and food habits. This largely monolingual/monocultural background of Korean immigrants gives them an advantage over other multilingual immigrants groups in retaining their ethnic attachment.

As Korean immigrants strive to get settled, however, they find themselves in paradoxical situations. They have voluntarily left their old homeland but remain emotionally attached to it; they aspire to become a part of their new "home," but are blocked by language and cultural barriers like many other immigrants from Asia (Zhou and Cai 2002, 423). In light of this, Korean-language newspapers played a vital role in the immigrants' lives during the 1970s and 1980s. Hurh Won-moo and Kim Kwang-chun studied the adaptation patterns of Korean immigrants in Los Angeles. Throughout their in-person interviews with 622 people, they noted that 78 percent of respondents subscribed to Korean-language newspapers. Nearly half of the respondents did not read American newspapers at all (Hurh and Kim 1984). Therefore, ironically, to acquire the information and assimilate to the host society, Korean immigrants relied on Korean diasporic media outlets. The oldest Korean-language newspaper in the United States is *Hankook Ilbo* (Han'guk Ilbo), established in 1969 in Los Angeles. All other newspapers duplicated stories originating from Seoul, with local news added here in the United States. As Yu Euiyoung argues, "They constantly reinforce traditional values and nationalism. They are either pro- or anti-Korean government and community based autonomous papers are rare." He adds, "Korean television broadcasts in LA similarly reinforce traditional values and Korean nationalism. Broadcasts start with the Korean national anthem and Korean news and their main features are dramas and comedies produced in Seoul" (Yu 1983, 39). Korean-language TV stations in the United States began airing imported "homeland" television dramas, news, and entertainment programs as early as 1975, but it was not until 1983 that the community embraced a full-fledged Korean-language television station in the U.S. cable network system.

The Emergence of Diaspora TV

Hamid Naficy (1993), while examining Iranian exiles and their media in Los Angeles, suggests there are three types of minority TV in the United States: ethnic, transnational, and exile TV. Ethnic TV refers to television programs primarily produced in the host country by long-established indigenous minorities, such as Black Entertainment Television (BET). Exilic TV is produced "by exiles living in the host country as a response to and in parallel with their own transitional and provisional status" (62). Television programs produced by Iranians, Arabs, and Armenians fall within this category. His last category, transnational TV, is operated by products imported from the homeland. Korean, Japanese, Chinese, and Vietnamese programs, and Spanish-language national networks like Univision and Telemundo, fit this category (62–63). A decade after his initial theorization, Naficy (2003) revised and updated this last category by replacing "exilic TV" with "diaspora TV." In his new definition, diaspora TV programs are made "usually by local, independent, minority entrepreneurs for consumption by a small cohesive population that, because of its diaspora status, is cosmopolitan, multicultural, and multilingual" (53). In this context, Naficy is still referring to Iranian-, Arabic-, and Armenian-language TV stations that belong to a "decentralized global narrowcasting" as opposed to multi/transnational media conglomerates-driven "centralized global broadcasting" such as AP (Associated Press) or CNN (Cable News Network).

Naficy's grouping of "transnational TV," however, does not suit all diasporic experiences. For example, Stuart Cunningham and Tina Nguyen (2000 and 2003) show that for most Vietnamese in North America and Australia, the concept of "home" is a denied category while "the regime" continues in power, and that sophisticated video programs produced by the Vietnamese diasporic communities are exported back to Vietnam. Adding to this, Chinese-language TV complicates notions of "home," "exile," and "diaspora," as Chinese diasporas are composed of three significantly different demographics—those originating from the People's Republic of China, Hong Kong, and Taiwan—and their cultural interests and investments reflect this diversity (Sinclair et al. 2000; Zhu 2009). Halleh Ghorashi argues that diasporic understanding of homeland signifies "not a place to return to but rather a domain or an idea that serves as one of the available discourses within the present negotiation of identity" (2003, 133) and, from this point of view, Chinese-language TV stations in the United States have been transforming their cultural, political, and ideological identities since the early 1980s.

The case of Korean-language TV is another conspicuous counterexample of Naficy's model. SRI-Gallup Organization for the International Channel Network reported in the early 1990s, according to Naficy, that the channel's Chinese, Korean, and Japanese viewers "by far prefer programming produced in their native homeland over programming produced in their host country" (2003, 52). His definition of transnational TV is mostly based on this statement but is only appropriate if we consider the early phase of Korean-language TV stations in Los Angeles. Naficy noted that the Korean-language broadcasts in the United States are produced by Korean Broadcasting System (KBS) in Korea, a government-controlled body, and imported and distributed for broadcast in the United States by the Korean government-owned Korean Television Enterprises (KTE). As a result of such outside assistance, Korean producers of both TV and radio enjoyed a degree of stability and security that "producers of diaspora television can only dream about" (52).

By contrast, and countering Naficy's argument, most Korean-language TV stations, other than KTE, were launched by local, independent, minority entrepreneurs,and they have been producing a significant portion of local news, talk shows, documentaries, home-shopping shows, and even comedy programs at their own studios in both English and Korean—although most television content watched by Korean immigrants still remains "transnational." Having started as transnational TV, Korean-language channels have gradually transformed to diaspora TV by increasing the number of locally produced programs. Accordingly, this chapter refers to Korean-language broadcasts in the United States as "diaspora TV," which includes elements of both the "diasporic" and the "transnational," and whose identity has been in constant flux.

The formation of the first Korean diaspora TV station in Los Angeles was, as discussed above, not fostered by the producers in the host country, but by the homeland's KBS. Korean Television Enterprises (KTE), owned by KBS, was inaugurated in Los Angeles on July 1, 1983. Prior to this, two locally financed and initiated broadcasters in Los Angeles, Korean Television Broadcast (KTB) and JoongAng Television Broadcast (JTB), had leased several hours of station time on KSCI (aka LA 18) and aired selective programs shipped directly from Korea. In the early 1980s, there was noticeably negative sentiment toward the Chun Doo-hwan (Chŏn Tu-hwan) regime in Korea among Korean immigrants, conspicuously so after the Gwangju (Kwangju) Democratization Movement in 1980. The Korea Intelligence Agency (KCIA) operated its branch office in Los Angeles, based in the Consulate General of the Republic of Korea in Los Angeles, to make sure the emigrant community was not too critical of the Chun regime. KTB and JTB were both categorized as being liberal and therefore "dangerous" because of their critical opinions toward the home country's totalitarianism.

As a consequence, KTB and JTB were forced to stop operation and KTE was established in 1983 after merging KTB and JTB. KTE became the only Korean diaspora TV in Southern California and was able to block-book many of the prime-time hours of KSCI, pushing out other Asian competitors (Holley 1986). Ray Beindorf, then president of KSCI, pointed out that Koreans are "the ones best equipped to buy time and put on the programming" (Cerone 1989). Other metropolitan cities—Chicago, Washington, DC, and New York, where the majority of Korean immigrants resided—began operating their own Korean diaspora TV stations. Unlike in Los Angeles, KBS did not establish branch offices. Instead, locally owned grassroots independent cable TV stations began airing Korean programs.[2] Korean diaspora TV stations targeted a very specific audience: exclusively Korean immigrants, a marginalized group in the marginalized ethnic "ghettos" of U.S. society. But this narrow-target market had already been dominated by a Korean-language video rental business, and that led to more complicated constraints.

Korean Diaspora TV, Koreatown Video Rental Businesses, and Competition

One of the most salient but rarely scrutinized subjects in the Korean diasporic media is the video rental business in major metropolitan cities, which holds an eminently narrowed, target-based business model. The circulation flows and distribution circuits of non-broadcast media products that connect the countries of origin—film and video—have been explored by many media scholars of diasporic Indian, Chinese, Vietnamese, and Latino audiences' audiovisual media consumption patterns. While examining the mediation of consensus regarding "Indianness" in the diaspora, Aswin Punathambekar observes that, for example, post-1965 migration to the United States was comprised mainly of educated professionals and their families but, in the early 1980s, people from a less-educated, largely merchant-class background began migrating to the United States. The number of grocery stores rapidly increased all over the country during the period and it is these stores that served as "initial points of distribution for the video cassettes" (Punathambekar 2005, 154–55). VHS tapes are widely available to the diasporic audience, often with English subtitles to accommodate younger generations. "In the Indian diaspora," Vijay Mishra notes, "video is one of the key markers of leisure activity. . . . It is also a not uncommon method of transmitting cultural events (weddings, anniversaries, even deaths of significant people such as Raj Kapoor) from the homeland to the diaspora or from diaspora to diaspora" (Hu 2006, 94).

The beginning of the Korean video business and its patterns had shared elements with both Indian- and Chinese-language diasporas, but there was one key distinctive aspect: the Korean diaspora spoke only one language, Korean. Sociologist Kyeyoung Park finds that Korean immigrants began to enter the fruit and vegetable business as greengrocers in New York in 1971. This was pioneered by a group of newcomers who entered the United States via Latin American nations, particularly Argentina. By the early 1980s, Korean-Korean competition in the greengrocery market business grew fierce. Greengrocers began to sell flowers and additional grocery items, establish salad bars, and finally began renting VHS tapes (Park 1997, 51). Subtitles were not provided and, as a consequence, Korean TV dramas were circulated exclusively among Korean immigrants and yuhaksaeng (students studying abroad) who easily accessed homeland popular culture.

The Korean-language video market has long been tightly controlled by two major networks in Korea: KBS and MBC (Munhwa Broadcasting Corporation). To quote one video store manager in Manhattan, interviewed in February 2012, "In the 1980s and 1990s, there were two content distributors in New Jersey. We signed contracts with distributors each year who deal with either KBS or MBC. We gave the distributors their fees each month and they gave us packages. We couldn't choose." Both KBS and MBC established their own distribution branches in Los Angeles, San Francisco, San Diego, Atlanta, and New Jersey. Video store owners couldn't choose from catalogs but had to take what the distributor offered. The trader was always given only one master copy, usually two weeks after the original program aired in Korea, but was authorized by the contract to make as many copies as necessary from his own blank tapes. Each store paid approximately USD 1,200 to each distribution unit. To protect video stores and maximize the profits, KBS and MBC adopted a new strategy in the late 1980s: holdŭbaek (hold back). With this new policy, diaspora TV stations had to wait at least four weeks after the master tape had been delivered to the video stores. This holdŭbaek system helped the video stores mobilize huge profits. During the heyday of video stores, from the late 1980s to the mid-1990s, KBS alone collected roughly USD 7 million each year.

By the late 1990s, the stabilized two-channel system—Korean diaspora TV stations and Koreatown video rental services—had been well maintained in the United States; however, with the new millennium the media ecosystem drastically transformed, thanks to the development of digital technologies and the advent of Hallyu. Korean dramas have gained phenomenal popularity all over Asia since the *Winter Sonata* (Kyŏul yŏn'ga, 2002) syndrome in Japan and *Jewel in the Palace* (Tae Changgŭm, 2003–4), *Full House* (P'ul hausŭ, 2004), and *The 1st Shop of Coffee Prince* (K'ŏp'i P'ŭrinsŭ 1-hojŏm, 2007) in China, Singapore, and Taiwan during the mid-2000s. Korean TV dramas in the United States, in response, have actively been consumed by Asian and non-Asian users via online video-streaming services. The importance of Korean diaspora TV that connects Korean immigrants to their "home" culture, politics, and society has therefore exceedingly diminished since then, as the next-generation audience in the United States began actively embracing Korean TV dramas.

Escape from the "Ghetto": New Systems, New Outlets, and New Audiences

It is difficult to trace exactly when Korean TV dramas finally escaped from the Korean immigrants' "ghetto," and began penetrating the mainstream U.S. media market. The most conspicuous turning point was presumably the founding of the California-based YA Entertainment, the first official importer and distributor of Korean TV dramas outside of Korean diaspora media in America. YA Entertainment embarked on the manufacture and distribution of Korean TV drama DVDs in 2003. Tom Larsen, president of YA Entertainment, stated: "We have conducted multiple surveys over the past five years, surveying thousands of Korean drama 'fans' in the U.S. Interestingly, only 5 percent of respondents described themselves as 'Korean.' Therefore, roughly 95 percent of the people purchasing our Korean drama DVDs are not of Korean descent. The majority are Caucasian, Japanese-American, Chinese-American and Filipino-American. And we are also finding strong growth in the Vietnamese-American and Latino/Hispanic communities" (Larsen 2008, 141).

In the survey, close to 64 percent of Korean drama fans are based on the West Coast and, interestingly enough, Korean TV dramas garner a loyal following among America's baby boomers, as more than 60 percent of respondents are older than 40 (Anon. 2006). In 2004, YA Entertainment provided its DVD box sets to Borders, Best Buy, and Barnes and

Noble as well as major online retailers like Amazon.com and YesAsia.com. Larsen said, "Translating and subtitling are the most important part of the production process. If the package and the drama are great, but the English subtitles are terrible, people will feel likely they have wasted their money. We (YA) focus on producing high-quality subtitles geared for native English speakers" (2008, 142).

While YA Entertainment began distributing Region 1 DVD sets that feature newly translated English subtitles, the youth fans of Korean popular culture, unlike middle-aged consumers for the well-packaged DVD box sets, have increasingly been watching and sharing their favorite Korean TV dramas in cyberspace. If the Internet-based fan communities have shaped new outlets for Korean TV dramas in the United States and elsewhere, then how have YA Entertainment and online fan communities influenced the existing two-channel distributions and consumption of Korean TV dramas among the Korean diaspora?

The most eminent impact is the near-collapse of the Korean video rental business. According to the U.S. Department of State report in 2010, KBS America's annual video sales revenue dropped by over 50 percent since 2006. In 2006, KBS America had grossed USD 7.1 million, but in 2008, revenue declined to 5.8 million. Then, in 2010, KBS only collected USD 3.3 million (Anon. 2011a). I conducted a series of interviews with video store owners in New York and New Jersey between February 26 and March 2, 2012. According to six owners in Manhattan, Elmhurst, Flushing, Fort Lee, and Palisade Park, it was 2003 and 2004 when they felt that something in their business was going wrong. By the early 2000s, although the business was not as prosperous as in the 1990s, most Korean diasporas, Korean Americans, and Korean Students were still renting videotapes at Koreantown video rental stores. However, around 2004, sales began an alarming drop; the pace of decrease was unprecedented.

Korean diaspora TV stations were also severely wounded, not only by the factors above but also by the home country's ambitious venture, KBS World. On June 1, 2001, KBS launched its first satellite broadcasting service, TV Korea. It soon changed its name to KBS World. With selective programs from KBS, this satellite channel aimed at strategic foreign markets, including Japan, China, Latin America, and North America. With this new satellite service, KBS no longer needed to cooperate with the Korean diaspora TV stations, considering that the company could directly distribute television programs to the Korean diasporic and Asian American communities, as well as possible extensions to the mainstream media market in the United States, Europe, and elsewhere.

With the unprecedented success of Korean cultural products all over Asia, Korean TV dramas began circulating in the United States outside of the Korean "ghetto," first among Asian American youths, then mainstream media consumers who finally noticed the wave during the second half of the decade. More importantly, these new fans of Korean dramas do not necessarily participate in the present two-channel system. Alternately, they are consuming, sharing, and participating in cyberspace via fan-based websites such as mysoju.com (now mysoju.tv), Viki.com, DramaCrazy.net, and allkpop.com. At this end, DramaFever.com, the first legitimate online video streaming service, conducted its first beta test in 2009. Its business model was the first attempt to incorporate dispersed online fan communities, Asian American youths, "baby boomer" consumers of YA Entertainment DVDs, yuhaksaeng, and potential users scattered online.

From Diaspora TV to Social Media

Henry Jenkins uses the term "pop cosmopolitanism" to refer to the ways that "the transcultural flows of popular culture inspires [sic] new forms of global consciousness and cultural competency" (Jenkins 2006, 156). He argues that young Americans distinguish themselves from their parents' culture through their consumption of Japanese anime and manga, Bollywood films, and Hong Kong action films. The most intriguing discussion in his essay is the role of "grassroots intermediaries" in shaping the flow of Asian cultural goods into Western markets. Jenkins closely examines two groups: the South Asian diasporic community and Western fans of Japanese anime, known as otaku. From immigrant grocery stores where Indian film VHS tapes were first circulated to the massive distribution campaigns of major Bollywood products to Western markets, the United States and Britain now account for 55 percent of international Bollywood ticket sales. On the other hand, anime entered the U.S. media market through small distributors who initially targeted Asian immigrants, mostly Japanese immigrants. However, anime soon traveled to newly created fans, mostly in the U.S. colleges, with the help of "fansubbing" (Gonzalez 2007; Lee 2011).[3] Disney-Miramax picked up Miyazaki Hayao's *Princess Mononoke* (Mononoke-hime, 1997) in 1999 and Miyazaki's Studio Ghibli subsequently became a household name in U.S. pop culture. David Desser, on the other hand, argues that during the mid-1990s the Hong Kong cinema entered into "its transnational and globalized capacity due in part to the massive Chinese diaspora" (Desser 2005, 219). The role of "the new cinephilia," according to Desser, emerged at this juncture through pirated DVDs and VCDs, as well as through Chinatown video rental stores that helped non-Chinese-speaking Americans access the content. The new cinephilia is hence the "product of global communication formation and film production sites centered in global cities, the cosmopolitan centers of cultural production as well as cultural consumption. And the genres favored by the new cinephiliac are those favored by the young Asian and Asianized Euro-American subjects living in these new global cities" (213).

Korean TV drama is the newest entry in this transnational cultural products flow. At the time they were conducting research, Jenkins and Desser had probably never met any fans of Korean TV dramas in the United States outside of Koreatown. In addition to this, Korean drama does not fit well into their frames. First, the Korean diasporic market is tiny compared to the vast Indian and Chinese diasporas' global networks, and no language/cultural diversity is involved. The Korean diasporic media had never been considered "important" to either the Korean or the U.S. media industries. Second, pirated VCDs or DVDs were not circulated in Koreatown. Korean dramas had exclusively been rented out via VHS tape formats, even up until the mid-2000s. Third, in contrast to American otaku who contributed a major role to the initial introduction of anime in the United States, fans of Korean dramas outside of Korean communities had mostly been young Asian Americans and online fan communities that were scattered in Indonesia, Thailand, Vietnam, Singapore, Australia, and Canada—in other words, the Hallyu phenomenon. This generated immeasurably large online fan communities, and their network reached the United States around the mid-2000s.

It was two young Korean Americans who noticed this new trend before the competition began. Seung Bak and Suk Park were working in the U.S. media industry and instantly embarked on a business: They are the founders of DramaFever.com. "During my business trip to Asia, I noticed the immense popularity of Korean dramas," said Suk Park, who was born in Korea, raised in Spain, and educated in the United States. Park and his friend Seung Bak decided to research the consumption patterns for Korean TV dramas in the United States. "We noticed a business opportunity," Park continued, "when we found over two dozen pirate online sites servicing this content illegally with no real legal alternative for users" (Anon. 2010). Their initial research indicated that almost six million unique users watch Korean dramas on illegal video streaming websites in North America every month, such as bada.us (now bada.tv), jebangsong.com (now jebangsong3.com), and monorich.com (closed) for ethnic Koreans and DramaCrazy.net, Viki.com, mysoju.com (now mysoju.tv), Crunchyroll.com, and the Chinese website tudou.com for non-Korean speakers. Their business idea was simple: turn the existing illegal services into legitimate ones.

However, the biggest challenge was to persuade content owners in Korea. It took over eight months before Park and Bak finally signed their first licensing agreement with MBC in late 2008. KBS and Seoul Broadcasting System (SBS) followed shortly after. DramaFever opened with a beta version in January 2009, and it was August before the website was fully operational. Park and Bak had maintained good relationships with fansubbing communities in Southeast Asia, and immediately after DramaFever was officially launched, these voluntary translators have been helping the company spend less on subtitling. But who are those fansubbers and why they are dedicating themselves to these painstaking labors?

In the past, consumption of certain types of Korean popular culture required a degree of Korean proficiency, which limited the participation of non-Korean speakers, including second-generation Korean American youths whose Korean was not as fluent as their parents'. But since the 2000s, Korean popular culture has become a source of shared reference and connection among some Asian American youths through the spread of Hallyu. Asian American youths' consumption of Korean TV dramas, hence, should be accounted for as "decisive factors" that have transformed the industry completely. In light of this, Jung-sun Park argued, "Transnational (im)migrant youth are key players in the transnational cultural flows, as exemplified by Korean American youths' roles as consumers, disseminators and potential creators of popular culture across the Pacific" (2004, 163). Through the spaces of social network services, fans of Korean TV dramas around the world set up online fan communities and share their knowledge, affections, and translations with other members, no matter what their nationalities are.

Brian Hu, while observing online fan communities such as D-Addicts.com, Soompi.com, and AsianFanatics.net and their forums for the popular Korean drama *Love Story in Harvard* (Lobŭ sŭťori in Habŏdŭ, 2004), calls them "affective translation communities." Regarding linguistic translation, subtitle files are made by fansite members themselves and are timed to play with the pirated video files circulating among members of the communities above. Translation is, according to Hu, "intimately tied to the logic of community." These groups are communities because there is "an understanding that users from around the world contribute their individual linguistic knowledge for the greater good of the collective. The work of translation itself is indicative of the group's collective emotional investment" (Hu 2010, 38).

Seung Bak, cofounder of DramaFever, told the author during an interview at the company's small and cramped Manhattan office: "About 30–40 percent of our subtitles come from the fansubbers." Bak continued, "Two fansub communities, Haru2subS and With S2, have closely been working with us. They are dedicated fans of Korean dramas and they are happy to see their works [subtitles] appear on a legitimate web service like ours." According to Bak, fansubbers of Korean TV dramas are mostly students and middle-aged housewives in Southeast Asia, particularly Indonesia, Singapore, and Philippines. They do not meet in person while actively communicating, sharing, and collaborating through the online communities.

The labor generally operates in four divided stages: uploading, initial translating, typing, and editing/proofreading. For example, Bak explained, "The leader of one of the communities is a high school student living in Dubai, United Arab Emirates, whose ability in Korean is very limited. He instead controls the whole procedure and working with community members whose ethnic, gender, and educational backgrounds are immensely diverse. The last part, proofreading, is largely done by Asian American members who reside in East and West coasts in America." As a compensation for their voluntary labors, DramaFever acknowledges each translator's name or ID at the end of each episode. As the company grew, the more skilled "fansubbers" were willing to work with DramaFever, and therefore the quality of the subtitles was gradually increased.

In February 2009, only one month after its official launch, DramaFever reached 200,000 unique users visiting the website. To everyone's surprise, the number climbed up to four million in April 2013. However, the real surprise was not in the number of unique users. It was the users' demographics that made the company even more promising. Who exactly is watching Korean TV dramas on DramaFever? Bak said, "Surprisingly, non-Asians make up 71 percent of the viewers, led by Caucasians (40 percent), African Americans (18 percent), and Hispanic (13 percent). Asians make up the remainder, which means only 29 percent." Then who are these 40 percent Caucasians? Bak answered, "These are the people who won't get a Korean cable channel or rent or buy DVDs in Koreatown." With these unexpected user demographics, DramaFever was able to negotiate with mainstream media outlets.[4] Hulu approached the founders, and DramaFever set up its own channel on the Hulu platform in June 2010, with YouTube and Netflix following shortly thereafter.

Fig. 9. A screenshot of "best kiss of the year" category of DFA 2013 (DramaFever awards). Used with permission.

By multiplying distribution platforms for its legitimate video contents, DramaFever is now diversifying its user demographics, from existing fans of Korean TV dramas to the mainstream American audiences who have not been exposed to Asian popular cultural products. DramaFever is, nevertheless, not the only video-streaming service of Korean TV dramas, nor is it the exclusive provider. A number of start-up sites such as Viki and Crunchyroll are specifically servicing this growing demand. The competition is therefore getting fiercer.

On March 21, 2013, *USA Today* published a special report entitled "American Audiences: I Want My International TV." The writer discussed DramaFever, Viki, and Crunchyroll as apparent examples of the new trend, and wrote, "TV viewers' appetites are going global as streaming technology broadens their options . . . from India's Bollywood and Korean dramas to Japanese anime and Nigerian movies, more obscure foreign titles are legally accessible—often for free with a few clicks" (Anon. 2013a). Once a vibrant platform of illegally circulated anime fansubbing, Crunchyroll was founded in 2006 by a UC Berkeley graduates Kun Gao and his college friends. Crunchyroll has been strong in introducing new anime titles to U.S. fans. In other words, it was a home of the U.S. otaku. But, as investments from venture capital came in, the company had to transform its identity into a legitimate one. Crunchyroll gradually removed all copyright-infringing materials from the site and made an official deal with TV Tokyo, a major broadcaster of anime in Japan (2013a). The company began servicing Korean dramas by taking over licensed Korean dramas of YA Entertainment after it shut down in November 2011. On the other hand, a Singapore-based Viki has been focused on Korean, Taiwanese, and Japanese TV dramas since its inception. "There's a billion people watching premium content online and 85% of what they're watching is not from Hollywood." Razmig Hovaghimian, founder of Viki, stressed: "We're going after that 85%" (Holmes 2011). The ever-growing market of international TV programs in America led video-streaming platforms to turn their attentions to newer territories—Chinese-language and Spanish-language dramas. DramaFever was not an exception.

In July 2012, DramaFever closed a round of funding amounting to USD 7 million in investments from AMC Networks, German media giant Bertelsmann, and Mexico's NALA Investments (Roxborough 2012). DramaFever is now planning to expand its repertoire, including the addition of Chinese-language and Spanish-language titles. A new site called DramaFever Latino was launched later in 2012 in response to the rapidly growing number of Hispanic users. Isabel, a TV series from Spain, quickly became one of the company's "five most-watched TV series" (Martinez 2013), and DramaFever has acquired new titles from Argentina's Telefe and Artear, Brazil's Bandeirantes, and Chile's TVN. "From day one," Bak stressed, "we never targeted the ethnic communities; this was about tapping into the cross-cultural, multiracial community that was clearly demanding this service."

Given that DramaFever is now targeting more broad ethnic communities in the United States, then in which platforms are Korean immigrants consuming homeland TV dramas? Traditional users of the Korean diaspora media are still watching TV dramas through the Korean diaspora TV, but those indigenous broadcasting companies have been losing most of their loyal consumers and their influence to the communities have been greatly diminished under these rapidly changing media environments. As figures 9 and 10 indicate, by 2005, Korean immigrants were the largest consumers of ethnic TV among all Asian Americans. But soon most Korean diaspora TV stations had to face the unexpected growth of online-based video-streaming services. According to Nielsen, in 2011, Asians/Pacific Islanders consumes more Internet content than any other group, visiting 3,600 web pages in February—about 1,000 more than their counterparts. Although they watch the least amount of TV (3 hours and 14 minutes per day), they stream the most online video, averaging 10 hours and 39 minutes in February—more than double the overall mean of 4 hours and 20 minutes (Pearson-McNeil and Hale 2011).

To survive, Korean diaspora TV increased the number of in-house programs to include local and nationwide news, talk shows, documentaries, and home-shopping shows. But as a strategy it appears this was both too late and ill conceived. MKTV, for example, started a new 24/7 cable TV channel called Korean News Network (KNN) in 2009. It aimed at consolidating a nationwide network with other Korean diaspora TV stations in the United States. However, within only a year, KNN had to reduce the number of its products and also airtime, as almost one-third of its stations went bankrupt in 2010. By September 2011, most Korean diaspora TV stations no longer aired the dramas of KBS, MBC, and SBS, and therefore their futures remain uncertain.

Korean diaspora TV stations had been facilitated by the homeland government as a propaganda apparatus aiming to scrutinize any antiregime activities and generate favorable attitudes toward the totalitarian government during the 1980s. Each president, Chun, Roh Tae-woo, Kim Young-sam, and even Kim Dae-jung, had invited Korean diaspora media executives to meetings with opinion and business leaders among overseas Koreans in the United States. With the Hallyu phenomenon, nevertheless, the old model of broadcasting homeland television programs to overseas Koreans is suddenly considered obsolete and not "innovative" or "creative" enough. And DramaFever had replaced the former sources. Without any support from homeland and local communities, after nearly three decades, the Korean diaspora TV is now preparing to end its history of Korean community service in the United States. In May 2013, Bak and Park were seated at a table with Park Geun-hye, newly elected president of Korea. They were invited as one of the leading entrepreneurial ventures representing innovation and success around the world that the new government, under the catchphrase of a "creative economy," has sought after as the nation's new engines of sustainable growth. Suk Park proclaimed at the meeting, "We've always believed that through the distribution of Korean content we are increasing Korea's country brand and promoting its culture and global initiatives. We are proud to have been part of this event" (Anon. 2013b).

Conclusion

This chapter has traced and historicized Korean TV dramas' consumption in the United States from the 1980s' diasporic TV stations and video rental

Fig. 10. An Internet meme with E.T. and Do Min-jun character from a hugely successful TV drama *My Love from the Star* (Pyŏl esŏ on kŭdae, 2013). Used with permission.

stores to the first legitimate video-streaming website, DramaFever. Before the new millennium, Korean TV dramas had rarely been consumed by the audiences outside of the market of the Korean diaspora. These TV stations in the United States had never imagined viewers other than ethnic Koreans and, consequently, by the late 1990s, the dramas had been distributed, circulated, and consumed exclusively by immigrants (mostly first generation) and Yuhaksaeng via two dominant channels: Korean diaspora TV stations and Koreatown video rental stores. It was not until the early 2000s that programs from Korea, particularly television dramas, began airing with subtitles when the waves of Hallyu lapped at America's two coasts, driven as they were by digital technologies. Just before this, sociologist Karim H. Karim wrote:

> Global migration trends have produced transnational groups re-
> lated by culture, ethnicity, language, and religion. Whereas mem-
> bers of some of these groups had generally operated small media
> (weekly newspapers, magazines, radio and television program-
> ming) to meet the information and entertainment needs of their
> communication activities, the emergence of digital technologies is
> enabling them to expand such communication activities to a global
> scale. (Karim 1998, 1)

Riding these waves of digital technologies, the advent of Hallyu meant
that Korean TV drama began plugging into massive flows in the global
media ecosystem. After three decades, its consumption in the United
States finally and decisively departed from the marginalized "ghetto."

On June 9, 2013, the Abu Dhabi–based daily newspaper *The National*
delivered an article titled "Brace for an Era of Global TV." David Mattin,
staff reporter, proclaimed, "Online content platforms mean the biggest
television events aren't necessarily country-specific; rather they are global
phenomena . . . and that, of course, is because television is no longer delivered via televisions, instead it's delivered via online space." At the end of
the article, Mattin proclaimed: "a new generation of truly global television
stars will soon be with us" (Mattin 2013). We are now witnessing a new
chapter of global TV. When will the next chapter begin? Will U.S. audiences embrace Korean soap opera stars? Only time will tell.

NOTES

1. The first Korean immigrants that came to the United States were generally laborers, exiles, and picture brides, comprising a negligible portion of all Asian immigrants.
By 1965, the total number of legal immigrants from Korea was just 54,852 (Daniels
1976, 3–4). However, this modest number has markedly increased since the mid-1960s.
Between 1965 and 1980, 299,000 Koreans immigrated, trailing only the Filipinos among
Asian groups in the number of new arrivals (Yu 1983, 24). According to the U.S. Census,
as of the year 2000 there were approximately one million ethnic Koreans living in the
United States; about a quarter of them lived in Southern California.

2. As host to the second-largest Korean population in the United States, New York
initiated its Korean diaspora TV, The Korean Channel (TKC), in March 1986. According
to Han Sang-gi, president of TKC, he aired Korean television programs under the company title of Daehan Broadcast, mainly television dramas, variety shows, and news, every Sunday morning from 9:00 to 10:30 through New York's UHF channel 47 beginning
in 1982. TKC was among the first group of minority television stations of New York's
Brooklyn-Queens Cable System, the first major cable TV system in New York's outer
boroughs. TKC aired on the cable channel from noon to midnight Monday through

Saturday, and from 11:00 a.m. to 11:00 p.m. on Sunday (Han 1994, 129–45). It became a twenty-four-hour channel in 1991.

3. According to Wikipedia a fansub is "a copy of a foreign movie or television [commonly anime] show which has been subtitled by fans in their native language ... [and] shared amongst other fans." For more insightful discussion about this cultural phenomenon, see Gonzalez 2007 and Lee 2011.

4. The unprecedented success of DramaFever made KBS reconsider its strategy in the United States. As KBS World was now providing programs—30–40 percent TV dramas, 20 percent variety shows/comedies, 20 percent news, and 20 percent documentaries—to satellite services such as Dish Net and Direct TV, the company, via its U.S. branch KBS America, advanced into the Internet business in the United States by launching MVIBO.com in March 2011. MVIBO.com has, however, failed to gain attention from Korean TV drama fans as the company cannot provide communities for users.

WORKS CITED

Anon. 2006. "Korean TV Dramas Surprisingly Embraced by U.S. Audiences." YA Entertainment Press Release, August 10.

Anon. 2010. "Korean 'Drama Fever' Spreads among US Fans." *Korea Times*, January 27.

Anon. 2011. "Internet Tsunami: Decline of KBS Video Contents Sales in the United States." Unidentified document.

Anon. 2013a. "American Audiences: I Want My International TV." *USA Today*, March 21.

Anon. 2013b. "DramaFever Recognized as Industry Leader by South Korean Government." PRWeb, May 15.

Cerone, Daniel. 1989. "Around the World in a Day at KCSI-TV Channel 18." *Los Angeles Times*, February 5.

Cunningham, Stuart, and Tina Nguyen. 2000. "Popular Media of the Vietnamese Diaspora." In *Floating Lives: The Media and Asian Diasporas*, ed. Stuart Cunningham and John Sinclair, 91–135. St. Lucia: University of Queensland Press.

Cunningham, Stuart, and Tina Nguyen. 2003. "Actually Existing Hybridity: Vietnamese Diasporic Music Video." In *The Media of Diaspora*, ed. Karim H. Karim, 119–31. New York: Routledge.

Daniels, Roger. 1979. "American Historians and East Asian Immigrants." In *The Asian American: The Historical Experience*, ed. Norris Hundley Jr., 1–25. Santa Barbara, CA: Clio Books.

Dator, Jim, and Yongseok Seo. 2004. "Korea as the Wave of a Future: The Emerging Dream Society of Icons and Aesthetic Experience." *Journal of Future Studies* 9 (1): 31–44.

Desser, David. 2005. "Hong Kong Film and the New Cinephilia." In *Hong Kong Connections: Transnational Imaginations in Action Cinema*, ed. Meaghan Morris, Siu Leung Li, and Stephen Chan Ching-kiu, 205–22. Durham: Duke University Press.

Ghorashi, Halleh. 2003. *Ways to Survive, Battles to Win: Iranian Women Exiles in the Netherlands and the United States*. New York: Nova Science Publishers.

Gonzalez, Luis Perez. 2007. "Fansubbing Anime: Insights into the 'Butterfly Effect' of Globalization on Audiovisual Translation." *Perspectives: Studies in Translatology* 14 (1): 260–77.

Han, Sang-ki. 1994. *CATV Unyŏngnon: Shich'ŏngja Hwakpo rŭl Wihan Mak'et'ing Chŏnnyakkwa Kyŏngyŏnggibŏp (How to Operate CATV: Marketing Strategy and Management Know-How for Retaining Customers).* Seoul: NANAM Publishing House.

Holley, David. 1986. "Accused of Political Bias in LA Programs: South Korean Ownership of TV Firm Admitted." *Los Angeles Times,* February 11.

Holmes, Sam. 2011. "Singapore Start-Up Sees Gold Mine in Foreign Language TV." *Wall Street Journal,* June 23.

Hu, Brian. 2006. "Bollywood Dreaming: Kal Ho Naa Ho and the Diasporic Spectator." *Post Script: Essays in Film and the Humanities* 25 (3): 93–104.

Hu, Brian. 2010. "Korean TV Serials in the English-Language Diaspora: Translating Difference Online and Making It Racial." *Velvet Light Trap* 66: 36–49.

Hurh, Won-moo, and Kwang-chun Kim. 1984. *Korean Immigrants in America: A Structural Analysis of Ethnic Confinement and Adhesive Adaptation.* London: Associated University Press.

Jenkins, Henry. 2006. "Pop Cosmopolitanism: Mapping Cultural Flows in an Age of Media Convergence." In *Fans, Bloggers, and Gamers: Exploring Participatory Culture,* 152–72. New York: NYU Press.

Karim, Karim H. 1998. "From Ethnic Media to Global Media: Transnational Communication Networks among Diasporic Communities." Working Paper WPTC 99-02, Transnational Communities Series.

Larsen, Tom. 2008. "Whetting U.S. Appetite for Korean TV Dramas." In *Korean Wave,* ed. The Korea Herald, 141–10. Seoul: Jimoondang.

Lee, Hye-Kyung. 2011. "Participatory Media Fandom: A Case Study of Anime Fansubbing." *Media, Culture and Society* 33 (8): 1131–47.

Martinez, Laura. 2013. "DramaFever Boosts Spanish-Language Content." *Multichannel News,* April 16. http://www.multichannel.com/dramafever-boosts-spanish-language-content/142758.

Mattin, David. 2013. "Brace for an Era of Global TV." *The National,* June 8.

Naficy, Hamid. 1993. *The Making of Exile Cultures: Iranian Television in Los Angeles.* Minneapolis: University of Minnesota Press.

Naficy, Hamid. 2003. "Narrowcasting in Diaspora: Middle Eastern Television in Los Angeles." In *The Media of Diaspora,* ed. Karim H. Karim, 51–62. New York: Routledge.

Park, Jung-sun. 2004. "Korean American Youth and Transnational Flows of Popular Culture across the Pacific." *Amerasia Journal* 30 (1): 147–69.

Park, Jung-sun. 2010. "Korean American Youths' Consumption of Korean and Japanese TV Dramas and Its Implications." In *Feeling Asian Modernities: Transnational Consumption of Japanese TV Dramas,* ed. Koichi Iwabuchi, 275–300. Hong Kong: Hong Kong University Press.

Park, Kyeyoung. 1997. *The Korean American Dream: Immigrants and Small Business in New York City.* Ithaca: Cornell University Press.

Pearson-McNeil, Cheryl, and Todd Hale. 2011. "Dissecting Diversity: Understanding the Ethnic Consumer." Nielsen Consumer Report, May 19. http://www.nielsen.com/us/en/newswire/2011/dissecting-diversity-understanding-the-ethnic-consumer.html.

Punathambekar, Aswin. 2005. "Bollywood in the Indian-American Diaspora: Mediating a Transitive Logic of Cultural Citizenship." *International Journal of Cultural Studies* 8 (2): 151–73.

Roxborough, Scott. 2012. "AMC Networks, Bertelsmann, NALA Invest in Online Video Site DramaFever." *Hollywood Reporter*, June 12. http://www.hollywoodreporter.com/news/amc-bertelsmann-nala-invest-dramafever-336156.

Sinclair, John. 2006. "From Latin American to Latinos: Spanish-Language Television and Its Audience in the United States." In *Global Traffic and Local Cultures in Film and Television*, ed. Sylvia Harvey, 119–31. Eastleigh, UK: John Libbey.

Sinclair, John, and Stuart Cunningham. 2000. "Go with the Flow: Diasporas and the Media." *Television and New Media* 1 (1): 11–31.

Sinclair, John, Audrey Yue, Gay Hawkins, Kee Pookong, and Josephine Fox. 2000. "Chinese Cosmopolitanism and Media Use." In *Floating Lives: The Media and Asian Diasporas*, ed. Stuart Cunningham and John Sinclair, 35–90. St. Lucia: University of Queensland Press.

Yu, Eui-young. 1983. "Korean Communities in America: Past, Present, and Future." *Amerasia* 10 (2): 23–52.

Zhou, Min, and Guoxuan Cai. 2002. "Chinese Language Media in the United States: Immigration and Assimilation in American Life." *Qualitative Sociology* 25 (3): 419–41.

Zhu, Ying. 2009. "Transnational Circulation of Chinese-Language Television Dramas." In *TV China: A Reader on New Media*, ed. Chris Berry and Ying Zhu, 221–42. Bloomington: Indiana University Press.

PART 4.

Global Receptions of Hallyu 2.0

9

Hating the Korean Wave in Japan

The Exclusivist Inclusion of Zainichi Koreans in *Nerima Daikon Brothers*

Hye Seung Chung

In the past few years, much of the scholarly discourse on Hallyu has high-lighted the transnational fandom for one particular star, Bae Yong-joon (Pae, Yong-jun; known affectionately as Yon-sama in Japan). His whole-some persona and matinée-idol looks in KBS (Korean Broadcasting System)'s twenty-episode serialized TV drama *Winter Sonata* (Kyŏul yŏn'ga, 2002) unexpectedly sparked a social phenomenon in Japan, be-coming a cult hit among middle-aged and older female viewers. Upon his first visit to Japan in November 2004, reports of an unprecedented 5,000 Japanese female fans—many of whom waited overnight in hopes of catch-ing a glimpse of their idol—swarming Yon-sama at Narita Airport were sensationalized by both Japanese and South Korean sports newspapers and entertainment magazines (Jung 2011, 34). Approximately one thou-sand eager fans reportedly continued to stalk the actor to his hotel, jos-tling one another for a fleeting look at their star. Some even threw them-selves in front of his car. At the end of the day, ten women received treatment for fractures, bruises, and sprains (Onishi 2004). In September 2009, when Bae visited Japan to promote his book on Korean culture and tourism, his unabated popularity was evidenced by the presence of 45,000 fans, including Hatoyama Miyuki, wife of the then-Japanese prime minis-ter, who attended a promotional event at Tokyo Dome (Cho 2009).

Many newspaper reports and scholarly essays have accounted for the economic and cultural impact of the Yon-sama craze, which generated an estimated USD 3 billion in profits (Cho 2005, 167–68), inclusive of revenues deriving from tourism and the sales of ancillary merchandise such as DVDs, postcards, photo books, calendars, lunch boxes, and fashion accessories (Miller 2008, 18–19). Less attention, however, has been paid to the patriarchal, xenophobic backlash against the Korean Wave in Japan.[1] Perhaps the best-known example of the anti-Hallyu movement in Japan is Yamano Sharin's comic book entitled *Hating the Korean Wave* (Manga Kenkanryu), which became a bestseller in 2005 and generated three sequels (published in 2006, 2007, and 2009).

A lesser-known case study can be found in "Sarang Heyo with My Balls" ("Ore no Otama de Sarangheyo"), an episode of TV Tokyo's *Nerima Daikon Brothers* (Oroshitate Myujikaru Nerima Daikon Brazazu), which originally aired on January 15, 2006. This adult-themed musical anime series showcases the adventures of two brothers, Hideki and Ichiro. These daikon farmers-by-day and band singers-by-night live with their cousin Mako. In the aforementioned episode, Mako falls victim to the lure of Hallyu Pachinko,[2] a nearby gambling establishment, where Korean Wave star lookalikes—physically unattractive Korean men who changed their appearance through plastic surgery—seduce and swindle middle-aged Japanese women with gigolo-like swagger. Enraged, Hideki and Ichiro intervene and attack the Korean pachinko parlor, only to be captured by its Yon-sama-esque owner. After being tied up, the brothers are pickled alive inside a giant kimchi pot, where they hang upside down. Meanwhile, Mako is nearly raped by the lewd Korean pachinko owner. Boosted by "kimchi power" (in much the same way that another cartoon character, Popeye, might be with spinach), the Japanese brothers break the pot, save the pink-haired "damsel in distress" in the nick of time, and punish the Korean aggressor by robbing him.

This episode's colliding discourses of nationalism, patriarchy, xenophobia, and (post)colonialism can be teased apart by examining contemporary Japanese anime culture, as well as the Yon-sama phenomenon, which otherwise generated positive images of Korea and Zainichi Koreans (Korean residents in Japan) among the Japanese populace. After surveying the Yon-sama craze and its impact on Zainichi Koreans, this essay will problematize what I call the "exclusivist inclusion" of Zainichi characters in the anime program, a disarming cultural production that pokes fun at excessive Hallyu fandom. Under the pretext of a zany, satiric comedy, the aforementioned *Nerima Daikon Brothers* episode reinforces socially constructed differences between Japanese and Koreans. In this age of social media and the DIY digital revolution, such images can easily go viral and be uncritically consumed by anime otaku (fans) with little foreknowledge of Korean-Japanese relations. Available stateside and internationally (via Amazon, Netflix, Hulu, and YouTube) with English subtitles, *Nerima Daikon Brothers* is not simply an obscure, late-night television program that a smattering of local audiences might have stumbled upon, but rather a widely consumed part of global Japanese popular culture that captures the hearts and minds of otaku around the world. Indeed, the show's extended postbroadcast life on the Internet compels us to carefully examine its politics of race, ethnicity, nationality, and gender through the lens of global multiculturalism—beyond the scope of the Yon-sama phenomenon in Japan.

Japanese Women's Love of Yon-sama and Its Impact on Zainichi Koreans

In his study of Japanese middle-aged women's fandom of *Winter Sonata*, Mori Yoshitaka argues that the popular Hallyu TV drama is an unprecedented intervention in the history of Japanese culture's relationship with Korea for three reasons: (1) It changed negative stereotypes of Korean people and culture in Japan; (2) it rendered visible what formerly had been a marginalized fan demographic (middle-aged and geriatric women, between the ages of thirty and seventy); (3) it affected the social and cultural lives of fans whose interest in Korean culture increased significantly after their exposure to the drama (Mori 2008, 130–31). As one of Mori's interviewees put it, after watching *Winter Sonata* many Japanese women felt that "Korea got closer. . . . [W]e love Korea" (139).

Some of the younger fans took love for a fictional character perhaps too seriously and embarked on a quest to find their dream Korean man in real life. For example, Yoshimura Kazuma, a telephone operator in Hiroshima, became one of the 6,400 young Japanese women who signed up with Rakuen Korea, a Japanese-Korean matchmaking service whose popularity soared after NHK's successful broadcasting of *Winter Sonata* (which aired four times between 2003 and 2005). According to a 2006 *Washington Post* report, the twenty-six-year-old telephone operator squandered thousands of dollars in her search for a perfect Korean husband, flying to Seoul ten times and taking the bullet train to Tokyo for seven blind dates (Faiola 2006, A01). The Hallyu-affected bachelorette offered a rationale, stating, "South Koreans are so sweet and romantic—not at all like Japanese guys, who never say 'I love you.'" However, she also admitted, "Maybe I'm living in a fantasy world. Maybe I'm looking for the TV stars I can't really have. But we are all allowed a dream, aren't we?" (A01).

Perhaps one of the most significant effects of the influx of the Korean Wave in Japan is that which is experienced by Zainichi Koreans. In her 2005 interview with *Chosun Daily* (Chosŏn Ilbo), Wang Su-yeong, a Korean poet living in Japan for over thirty years, confides, "They used to blame me if there happened to be discarded garbage in the neighborhood. After the Yon-sama boom, the same people now boast that they have a Korean neighbor. . . . Bae Yong-joon restored our self-confidence" (Kim 2005, A23). A Zainichi interviewee cited in Sun Jung's book *Korean Masculinities and Transcultural Consumption* confesses, "Japanese people used to treat us as if we were not human beings, but after Yon-sama, their attitudes have been changed completely" (2010, 37). Such uplifting testimonials may tempt the reader to jump to the premature conclusion that the Yon-sama phenomenon is a postcolonial panacea to current problems underlying Korean-Japanese affairs, from the lingering pain of the colonial past to the discrimination and predicament of Zainichi Koreans in Japan. However, a more probing investigation of the Zainichi reception of *Winter Sonata* and the Hallyu phenomenon reveals the contradictions and complications associated with co-opting Zainichi Koreans' bodies as "'tokens' to represent the [Hallyu] culture" (Han et al. 2007, 166–67).

In their focus-group study of forty Zainichi Korean viewers of *Winter Sonata* in 2005, Min Wha Han and his co-researchers discovered ambivalent reactions among Korean residents of Japan about the Japanese celebration of Hallyu, despite the fact that such recognition improved their own status in Japanese society. One respondent indicated that the Japanese public's interest lies only in "Korean celebrity culture," but many of them still don't know why "Zainichi Koreans are in Japan" (167). Another Zainichi viewer is equally skeptical, and deems the whole phenomenon "funny":

> Well, I will admit [Hallyu] made our life here easier, because basically you can't imagine what kind of discrimination we had to face in our daily lives. . . . But the flip side of it is that this [Hallyu] is the only thing the Japanese know about Koreans. . . . And politicians are using [Hallyu]. (168)

Yet another respondent is more explicitly negative about Hallyu, suggesting that the Japanese can use the phenomenon as an excuse to "cover up the history," and absolve their collective responsibility to address the oppression of Korean people and Zainichi Koreans (168).

Indeed, as eloquently pointed out by these Zainichi viewers, popular culture and its associated fan cultures cannot provide solutions to deep-rooted historical and political problems. The conflation of contemporary Korean popular culture and a historically oppressed minority group in Japan proves to be problematic despite the immediate benefits that the latter group has received in the process. Zainichi Koreans are a distinct diasporic identity, one that resulted from Japanese colonialism. During the colonial period (1910–45), two million Koreans were relocated to Japan. Many of those individuals were forcibly mobilized as wartime laborers. After Korea's liberation in 1945, an estimated 1.3 million returned to the homeland and the remaining 700,000 Koreans decided to stay in Japan (Han et al. 2007, 160). Although most of this sizable diasporic population firmly established their livelihoods and families in Japan, the Japanese government stripped them of Japanese nationality in the wake of Korean independence. No longer colonial citizens, Zainichi Koreans were subject to Japan's Alien Registration Law, and had to carry a registration card with fingerprints until 1991, when they were granted the status of "special permanent residents" (Iwabuchi 2008, 253). Many Zainichi Koreans chose *not* to naturalize into Japanese citizenship because of the Japanese government's strict assimilation policy, which required them to forsake their ethnic and cultural identity, including Korean names, in exchange for citizenship. Because Zainichi Koreans were excluded from the traditional job market—all public-sector jobs were officially open to Japanese nationals only until 1972—they came to seek opportunities in the service and entertainment sectors: in particular, yakiniku (Korean barbeque) restaurants and pachinko parlors (Lie 2008, 73). According to statistics provided in John Lie's *Zainichi (Koreans in Japan): Diasporic Nationalism and Postcolonial Identity*, "Zainichi owned 90 percent of the roughly 20,000 yakiniku restaurants in Japan in the 1990s . . . [and] an estimated 70 to 80 percent of the 18,000 pachinko parlors, which generated turnover twice that of the Japanese automobile industry and even exceeded the South Korean GNP in 1994" (73). Predominantly Korean ownership of Japanese pachinko parlors attracted the attention of Western news agencies for its impact on the North Korean economy, since a significant portion of pachinko cash has been reportedly channeled into Pyongyang through Zainichi Koreans sympathetic to North Korea. Although no concrete data are available, some economists believe it to be "the single biggest source of revenue for North Korea" (Seidman 2012).

Gambling is prohibited by the Japanese Penal Code (Articles 185, 186), which states that "a person who gambles shall be punished by a fine of not more than 500,000 yen," and "a person who gambles habitually shall be punished by imprisonment with labour for not more than three years." In spite of this, the pachinko industry raked in a revenue of USD 230 billion in 2007 (Takiguchi and Rosenthal 2011).[3] Although pachinko is a popular leisure activity enjoyed by millions of men and women from various age groups (from 18 to 80), according to recent local reports the once male-dominated culture is becoming "increasingly female-friendly," with clean, modern facilities attracting young and old alike (Nakagawa 2011). Indeed, pachinko addiction is considered a growing social problem for Japanese women. According to Japan's Health Ministry statistics in 2009, 750,000 women are compulsive gamblers (Anon. 2012). Health experts comment that women are particularly vulnerable to pachinko addiction "due to the pressures they disproportionately face—child-rearing, caring for elderly relatives, abusive or inattentive husbands, inadequate income" (Anon. 2012).

Noteworthy here is the fact that both Hallyu and pachinko are addictively consumed by the same demographic of Japanese women—middle-aged housewives with disposable income and leisure time, and with emotional longing to escape from their domestic routines. Moreover, precisely because pachinko is the only industry in Japan (other than yakiniku restaurants) dominated by Zainichi Koreans, one can make superficial ethnic connections between these two completely different types of entertainment for women. What is particularly noteworthy is that when anti-Hallyu sentiments began to percolate through Japanese popular culture, synchronized attacks were made on Korean popular culture (the competitor), Japanese women (the consumers), and Zainichi Koreans (symbols of Korea within Japan). As mentioned earlier, the progenitor of the anti-Hallyu movement in Japan is Yamano Sharin's manga *Hating the Korean Wave*, which became an instant hit, selling 360,000 copies during its first six months of publication.[4] Tange Akihide and Yamanaka Susumu, editors at Shinyusha (the publisher of Yamano's comic book), collectively offer a rationale for this unexpected success: "The 'Hate Korea' feelings have spread explosively since the World Cup. . . . We weren't expecting there'd be so many [anti-Korean readers]. But when the lid was actually taken off, we found a tremendous number of people feeling this way" (Onishi 2005).

Centering on a university history circle that sets out to investigate the history of Japanese-Korean relations, *Hating the Korean Wave* is the apotheosis of a more general anti-Korean movement that began in 2002, when South Korea and Koreans were accused of cheating to advance in that year's FIFA World Cup finals and for taking advantage of Japan and the Japanese for their own economic and political agendas. Furthermore, the manga makes racialized distinctions between handsome, Caucasian-looking Japanese characters and unattractive, slant-eyed Zainichi Koreans who are grossly caricatured as duplicitous foreign agents bent on subverting Japanese national interests. This representational strategy ironically evokes U.S. anti-Japanese propaganda during World War II, which tried to justify the wartime internment of American citizens of Japanese descent. In a special section devoted to *Winter Sonata* at the end of his book, Yamano Sharin summarily dismisses middle-aged or elderly female fans as mindless, gullible dupes being manipulated by media practitioners and promoters to advance Korea's economic interests. Along with the first sequel to *Hating the Korean Wave*, Yamano Sharin published another Korea-themed manga, *Zainichi Map: Seeking out Korea Towns* (Zainichi no Chizu: Koria Taun Tambo) in 2006. In this latter book, the author focuses exclusively on anti-Zainichi themes, and sends warnings to younger Japanese women who might be interested in dating ethnic Korean men by portraying them as monstrous, deviant, and opportunistic foreigners. The female protagonist Mizuho fails one relationship after another with Zainichi dates, who turned out to be obsessive stalkers, anti-Japanese radicals, or "genetically defective" men who die mysteriously at a young age.[5] In a heavy-handed attempt to undo the Hallyu effects on the Japanese populace in general and women in particular, Yamano's comic books strategically include Zainichi Koreans in the narrative only to advocate their further exclusion and segregation in Japanese society. Such a paradoxically exclusivist inclusion of Zainichi Koreans in the anti-Hallyu movement is a telling indicator that the Korean Wave is a mixed blessing for ethnic Koreans living in Japan without benefits of citizenship and equal protection.

Daikon-Legged Women and Gigolo Zainichi Men: The Inverse Rape Metaphor and Historical Revisionism in *Nerima Daikon Brothers*

In *Anime: From Akira to Howl's Moving Castle*, Susan J. Napier admonishes the "ignorance" betrayed by Disney-friendly American viewers who habitually ask the culturally naive question, "Why is anime so full of sex and violence?" (2005, 9). For her, this is the wrong question to ask, since anime is not simply a Japanese equivalent to American cartoons primarily, if not entirely, catering to child and young adolescent audiences. Napier elaborates:

> Essentially, anime works include everything Western audiences are accustomed to seeing in live-action films. . . . Japanese television studios produce around 50 animated series a year. . . . Animated films are also far more important in Japan than in the West, amounting to "about half the tickets sold for movies." (6–7)

For the author, anime is a cultural phenomenon that deserves serious critical inquiry not only because it reaches broader demographics in Japan but also because it provokes viewers to "work through certain contemporary issues in ways that older art forms cannot" (4).

Although Napier constructs a simplistic binary between American cartoons of the Disney tradition and multi-genre, adult-oriented Japanese anime, without taking into account such edgy, mature stateside programs as Comedy Central's *South Park* (1997-) and Cartoon Network's Adult Swim shows, the primary role of anime as a contested terrain of hegemonic national ideals of class, gender, race, and ethnicity should be taken more seriously in a "pictocentric" Japanese cultural context (7). For this reason, a relatively obscure, minor production such as Watanabe Shinichi's zany twelve-episode musical anime series *Nerima Daikon Brothers* can and should be recuperated as a significant cultural barometer of the anti-Hallyu, anti-Korean movements gaining traction in Japan. The series was programmed after midnight in its original run on TV Tokyo in 2006 due to its risqué subject matter: sexual violence, nudity, masturbation, incestuous desire, and homosexuality.[6] In his analysis of the Cold War–era, American B-movie *Invasion of the Body Snatchers* (1956), Stuart Samuels states, "All films are . . . ideological and political . . . [and] contain the values, fears, myths, assumptions, point of view of the culture in which they are produced" (1998, 204). He goes on to argue that not only do films "*reflect*, embody, reveal, mirror, symbolize existing ideologies," but also they "*produce* their own ideology, their own unique expression of reality . . . by reinforcing a specific ideology or undercutting it" (204). Like its print predecessor (Yamano Sharin's aforementioned manga), the "Sarang Heyo with My Balls" episode of *Nerima Daikon Brothers* reinforces dehumanizing stereotypes of Zainichi Koreans and endorses dominant social values in the process of producing its own (counter)ideology of the anti-Hallyu. In other words, as a popular text, *Nerima Daikon Brothers* can be construed as an "arena of consent and resistance," to borrow the words of media theorist Stuart Hall, "where hegemony arises, and where it is secured" (Hall 2006, 453).

Set in the Nerima Ward, an area on the outskirts of Tokyo that is famous for daikon (radish) production, the anime series follows the exploits of Hideki, a twenty-five-year-old daikon farmer who dreams of building a concert dome and becoming a pop star, and his gang: his effeminate brother Ichiro (who works as a paid companion for women or gay men at a host club), his pink-haired cousin Mako from Okayama (the object of Hideki's incestuous affection), and a pet panda. Toward the beginning of the episode, Hideki's farm is invaded by a group of middle-aged women who steal radishes from his patches to pay their gambling debts to the neighboring Hallyu Pachinko. From the onset, Hallyu is stereotypically associated with the Zainichi pachinko business and kimchi, a staple of Korean cuisine. In this unlikely scenario, gigolo-like Zainichi companions tell broke women that they will accept a variety of kimchi ingredients—cabbages and radishes—in lieu of cash. Jumping on the pachinko bandwagon is Mako, who extorts gambling money from Hideko through blackmail (threatening to inform on his incestuous desire to her parents/Hideko's aunt and uncle).

To his bewildered brother, Ichiro explains that Hallyu Pachinko has recently lured female patrons away from his host club. The shady business practice of Hallyu Pachinko is revealed in an expository musical sequence unfolding from the perspective of the owner, who takes center stage in his establishment and is dressed like Yon-sama, wearing the star's signature horn-rimmed glasses and muffler. The Korean man croons:

> We put sweet love into our pachinko balls.
> Your companions have the faces of Korean Wave stars you love so
>   much.
> They're actually all fake, plastic-surgery faces, though.
> Squeeze [it] out of them, bleed those hags dry of all their money.

During this musical sequence, we learn that Zainichi hosts in the pachinko parlor are in fact buck-toothed, ugly con artists who are turned into handsome Hallyu star lookalikes via a conveyor belt plastic surgery line. The exposition scene shows how these deceitful gigolos "bleed" money out of unsuspecting older patrons who, charmed by their companions' handsome looks and sweet nothings (the repeated phrase "Sarang heyo" or "I love you"), mindlessly order a large amount of pachinko balls and expensive alcohol to please their servers.

After learning the "truth" of Hallyu Pachinko, Hideki is enraged that his incestuous love interest Mako has been lured into the web of Zainichi seduction and swindling. He intervenes and catches his cousin in the midst of being pampered by yakiniku-serving hosts in the pachinko par-lor. Exerting his authority as a male relative (and, by implication, a guard-ian of her chastity), Hideki admonishes Mako, telling her, "You're clean and adorable and sweet, and your body mustn't be in places like this." This line is tellingly spoken in front of a series of identical pachinko slot ma-chines covered with pictures of Yon-sama and Korean letters phonetically inscribing "Pachinko." In other words, a Zainichi pachinko is inappropri-ate for Mako, a nineteen-year-old Japanese girl (who is presumed to be a virgin despite her girly flirtations), not only because it is a gambling estab-lishment but also because it is a potential site for sexual contact between Japanese female patrons and their seductive Korean hosts posing as Hal-lyu stars. Contrary to Hideki's blind belief in her innocence, Mako is ap-parently prone to the temptation of debauchery and thus becomes an easy target for Zainichi swindlers. Her weakness for both gambling and foreign men is subsequently expressed in her solo musical sequence (entitled the "Pachinko Requiem") where she confesses to have been "cleaned out" by a number of ethnic pachinko parlors: Korean, Russian, Indian, Chinese, and Mexican.

Hideki's antagonism to Hallyu Pachinko reaches its peak when a pla-toon of Korean Wave pachinko tour buses storms into his farm and ruins his radish field on the pretext that the route is a shortcut to their destina-tion. Inexplicably, Mako comes to embody anti-Korean feelings after wit-nessing this scene and fires up against what she calls "an international crime." In a low-angle shot (framing her heroically from below), the fe-male crusader yells, "Those evildoers who disturb the peace of Nerima, no, of Japan—we'll take back their ill-gotten money!" Prompted by Mako, Hideki and Ichiro concoct a scheme to rob Hallyu Pachinko—or rather, retrieve what the pachinko has disingenuously taken from Japanese women—and teach duplicitous Zainichis "a lesson." Their ill-fated mis-sion backfires when the Yon-sama-posing owner incarcerates Hideko and Ichiro in a giant kimchi pot while attempting to rape Mako on his desk (with a traditional Korean painting in the background serving as a re-minder of the perpetrator's identity). Reminiscent of the notorious "Gus Chase" sequence in D. W. Griffith's *The Birth of a Nation* (1915), in which a lecherous black renegade captain stalks an innocent young Southern belle in the woods, the (attempted) rape scene in *Nerima Daikon Brothers* is particularly disturbing because of its foregrounding of the attacker's eth-nicity through constant references to yakiniku, kimchi, and gochujang (red pepper paste).

To seduce the Japanese virgin, the ethnic Korean man proposes, "Want to come with me to Seoul and eat yakiniku?" In a fantasy scene, the inter-ethnic couple is shown dining in an authentic Korean restaurant in Seoul, where Mako enjoys barbeque and asks her companion, "Aren't you going to eat? Why not?" A shock cut takes us back to the owner's room in the pachinko parlor, where the lustful Zainichi man in his underwear springs up like a frog, shouting, "Because I'm going to eat you." Both scenes turn out to be fantasies of Mako, who wonders if yakiniku is what he really wants with her (unbeknownst to her, a sinister-looking Zainichi propri-etor is gazing her with a lustful look behind her back). When Mako turns around and faces the Korean man, he is seen drooling like an animal in anticipation of a wild feast. In an extreme close-up, the overexcited man confesses, "I just start drooling when I picture spicy things." A threatened Mako falls to the ground and asks her would-be-rapist, "What spicy things?" The Zainichi man bursts into a song:

I like kimchi.
I love kimchi.
I have an irresistible passion for kimchi, you see.
You're my kimchi.

While the kimchi-crazed man uses scissors to cut away the cabbage costume being worn by Mako (her camouflage gear), Hideki and Ichiro, bound and hanging upside down, are seen in the process of being fer-mented in an oversized kimchi jar in a storage room.[7] Unfortunately for their captor, "kimchi power" transforms the Nerima brothers into Hulk-like muscular monsters whose oversized bodies break the pot prison.[8] Back in the office, the aroused Zainichi chases after Mako in slapstick fashion, calling her "my little kimchi" and himself "a Korean Wave man . . . a man who loves kimchi." Tasting a jar of Korean red-pepper paste with his finger, the rapist looms over a terrified Mako and declares, "It's time to start the adult-man-and-woman, hot-and-spicy love showtime." His re-pulsed victim yells, "I don't want to do it with this kimchi geezer." As if responding to her desperate cry, Hideki and Ichiro break the wall with their kimchi-boosted biceps. Confident and self-righteous, the trio turns Hallyu Pachinko upside down, exposes the grotesque faces of Zainichi men (whose plastic surgery is mysteriously undone during the crack-down), and leaves the establishment with bags of kimchi-stained pachinko cash (which had been stored in a kimchi jar). The Nerima brothers do not take advantage of the stolen cash, as an army of Hallyu-crazed women return to claim their money, more desirable to them for its kimchi smell, and turn the brothers' radish farm into a war zone when the Self-Defense Forces mobilize to quell the commotion.

The episode exceeds what is generally permissible in U.S. animated parodies and satires, such as *South Park* and *Family Guy* (1999–2002, 2005–), by explicitly depicting Zainichi Koreans as literally ugly con artists whose criminal behavior, foreign lifestyles, and deviant sexuality threaten both the racial homogeneity of the Japanese nation and the chastity of Japanese women.[9] Despite the presumably parodic and satiric intent of the animators, it is hard to imagine a similar scenario of sexual violence involving an African American perpetrator, a Caucasian American victim, and constant references to spicy, ethnic food. To apply Hall's theory of popular culture, the aforementioned episode simultaneously engages the dialectic of "consent and resistance." It exposes the social problems of pachinko addiction and excessive media fandom (which can jeopardize personal well-being and public safety if pushed too far). In resisting the effects of the Korean Wave and critiquing gambling addiction among women, however, the episode reinforces xenophobic stereotypes of Zainichi Koreans as criminals, sexual deviants, and two-faced opportunists. The middle-aged women who fall for the Korean Wave and gigolo-like servers are habitually called "hags," and their legs are pejoratively compared to daikons (stressing their lack of physical beauty). Conflating a cultural counternarrative (anti-Hallyu) with a masculinist, nationalist, and neocolonialist narrative of vigilantism and exclusion (anti-Zainichi), *Nerima Daikon Brothers* offers an unsettling yet familiar historical revisionism wherein victims morph into perpetrators. The inverse rape metaphor—where Korean men pose a sexual threat to Japanese women—explicitly challenges one of the most notorious colonial atrocities, one that still angers many Koreans: the Japanese Imperial Army's sexual slavery of tens of thousands of Korean women as "Comfort Women" during the 1930s and 1940s.

As Koichi Iwabuchi puts it, "What is most imperative is for the Japanese to relieve resident Koreans of the burden of postcolonial engagement by considering what they can do, together with resident Koreans, to deconstruct an exclusive notion of 'the Japanese' and 'the Koreans'" (2000, 73). The "Sarang Heyo with My Balls" episode of *Nerima Daikon Brothers* does the opposite. In its gross amplification of cultural and ethnic differences between Japanese and (Zainichi) Koreans, the anime series ceases to operate as a lighthearted, satiric jab at foreign popular culture (Hallyu), and implicates itself within an oppressive ideological system of segregation, exclusion, and discrimination.

At Your Fingertips: Watching *Nerima Daikon Brothers* in the United States

Contributors of this volume (Sangjoon Lee and Dal Yong Jin, in particular) observe the crucial role that social media and digital technologies have played in disseminating Hallyu 2.0 products, including Psy's "Gangnam Style," the most watched YouTube video of all time (with more than 2 billion views as of June 2014). Despite the potential for user empowerment provided by social networking and video-sharing sites, scholars of new media collectively acknowledge the limitations of such Web 2.0 sites, propelled by user-generated content, as facilitators of the public sphere. For example, Alla Zollers asserts that "although [social networking sites] can encourage participatory democracy, they can also extend the structures of capitalism and further hegemonic ideals" (2009, 611). Similarly, Douglas Kellner and Gooyong Kim caution against the deficiency "in rationality . . . silliness, narcissism, or worse" exhibited in many YouTube products (2009, 632). For this study, what is particularly noteworthy is the role of the Internet and social media as public platforms conducive to the replaying, remixing, and refashioning of politically incorrect humor being fetishized by today's teenagers and twentysomethings (be they "frat boys" or "hipsters") in the industrialized West.

As mentioned earlier, *Nerima Daikon Brothers* is widely available with English subtitles at Amazon, Netflix, Hulu, YouTube, WatchCartoonOnline.com, and other websites, and has left an indelible virtual footprint in the shifting sands of Internet-based media distribution. Unlike its American counterparts such as *South Park* or *The Simpsons* (1989–), whose online circulation is restricted because of their parent companies' copyright protection policy, every episode of *Nerima Daikon Brothers* can be streamed instantly anywhere and anytime. More importantly, the latter program is not subject to the regulatory protocols of U.S. network or cable shows, the racial and ethnic representations of which are monitored by cultural watchdogs and prone to postbroadcast modifications based on external pressures (as exemplified by the controversial Muhammad episodes of *South Park* season 14 [2010]).[10] Given the unregulated open access to *Nerima Daikon Brothers* on the Internet, the anime series warrants critical scrutiny.

For cultural outsiders who might stumble upon and consume the "Sarang Heyo with My Balls" episode online, it would be optimistic to believe that a "negotiated" or "oppositional" decoding practice might be employed for the sake of "seeing through" or simply acknowledging its problematic ethnic representations (Hall 1980).[11] During an in-class screening of the episode at a prestigious East Coast liberal arts college a few years ago, I had to stop the video in the midst of its aforementioned depiction of the attempted rape scene, owing to the fact that the offensive images had become unbearable, difficult to swallow. One student, a die-hard aficionado of Japanese anime, spoke up and defended the episode on the basis that it is a satire, and thus should be elevated above any criticisms that might deflate a fan's enthusiasm. He conjectured that Japanese audiences might have a different sense of humor and even called for "cultural tolerance" for the series' overt political incorrectness. It was apparent to me that, for all the student's good intentions (in terms of generating dialogue and proffering a counterbalancing argument), he had little foreknowledge of Korean-Japanese relations, and had not been sufficiently sensitized to the history of discrimination faced by Zainichi Koreans. What struck me most deeply was his unwillingness to acknowledge that the episode's humor relies upon a racist conception of ethnic alterity and intraregional difference, something that he would likely have recognized in a U.S. program. This classroom-based incident furthered my conviction that the "Sarang Heyo with My Balls" episode *matters* in the U.S. context and should not to be dismissed as a minor footnote to the Yon-sama (anti)fandom in Japan, a phenomenon that remains virtually unknown stateside. A minor text it might be, but its potential to disseminate distorted images of monstrous Koreans to a new generation of YouTube users worldwide suggests that a major critical intervention is needed to guide informed consumption of this and other cyber popular culture texts suffused with regressive racial content.

NOTES

1. Much English-language scholarship on Hallyu in Japan focuses on Japanese audiences' fandom of *Winter Sonata* and its lead actor, Bae Yong-joon. Notable works on this topic include Hirata 2008; Lee 2010; Miller 2008; Mori 2008; and Jung 2010. While there have been several essays published on the subject of anti-Korean discourses in Japanese popular culture (Sakamoto and Allen 2007; Yamanaka 2010), their focus is almost exclusively on Yamano Sharin's controversial comic book *Hating the Korean Wave* (Manga Kenkanryu), rather than antifandom of the Korean Wave. Hallyu antifandom in Korea's Asian neighbors remains an understudied subject that deserves wider academic attention.

2. Pachinko is a combination of arcade games and pinball/slot machines.

3. Pachinko players win balls that are exchanged for tokens or prizes—instead of cash—in the parlor, thus bypassing antigambling statutes. Players eventually cash in their wins at a designated exchange post outside the establishment.

4. By October 2007, 780,000 copies of the *Hating the Korean Wave* manga series (the original and its first sequel) had been sold in Japan (Yamanaka 2010).

5. Mizuho's first boyfriend, a recent Korean immigrant, forces her to date him with a "Korean style" harassment-and-intimidation technique. The Japanese woman ultimately changes her telephone number and moves to different places twice to escape from the Korean man's obsessive pursuit. Her second boyfriend, a closeted Zainichi whose ancestors migrated to Japan during the colonial period, hides his identity for a long period of time and, once outed, tries to convince his Japanese girlfriend to accept his radical anti-Japanese ideology. The third boyfriend, a naturalized Japanese citizen, appears to be a perfect match for her but dies unexpectedly of a genetic disorder. Ostensibly serving as a "tour guide" to Japan's Korea towns (where Mizuho, along with her coworker Sana, roams in search of a new Korean boyfriend), the manga *Zainichi Map* reinforces Japanese social prejudices that Zainichi are not suitable dates or marriage prospects for Japanese women because of their destructive behavior and unassimilable foreign traits.

6. In its original run, TV Tokyo scheduled the series in the 1:30–2:00 a.m. slot on Sundays from January to March 2006. It was rerun on AT-X, the anime television network, in the 10:30–11:00 p.m. slot on Wednesdays from February to April 2006.

7. Prior to their raid on Hallyu Pachinko, Hideki, Ichiro, and Mako make a nocturnal visit to Nine Dragon Pawn Shop, where the proprietor (whose voice was provided by the series' director, Watanabe Shinichi) loans them vegetable-shaped garments for their covert operation, in exchange of song-and-dance entertainment. Initially, the Nerima brothers and their cousin mistake the costumes as magic suits invisible to Koreans and their customers in the pachinko parlor. Much to their disappointment, the loaned items possess no such power and the trio is captured by the Zainichi owner and his henchmen.

8. It is worth noting that the episode seems to acknowledge and privilege some "good Korean things" (kimchi/food/ethnicity) while rejecting "bad Korean things" (Zainichi men/racialized masculinity).

9. Similar to *South Park*, *Nerima Daikon Brothers* wages war on political correctness and commits "equal-opportunity" offense against different marginal groups, including middle-aged women, ethnic Koreans, and homosexuals. In the first episode (entitled "Please Touch My Nerima Daikon"), for example, a gay casting director of a talent agency is depicted as a sinister sexual predator who takes advantage of young boy musicians.

10. After the April 14, 2010, airing of *South Park*'s two hundredth episode (entitled "200"), in which the prophet Muhammad is shown disguised in a bear suit, the show's creators, Matt Stone and Trey Parker, received a warning from Revolution Muslim, a radical Muslim group based in New York City. The second half of the two-part episode (entitled "201") aired the following week with additional audio bleeps and image blocks marked "Censored." *South Park*'s Facebook discussion boards were bombarded with negative posts by Muslims expressing their frustration over offensive depictions of the Prophet. The two controversial episodes were permanently removed from digital distribution on the Internet (South Park Studios, Netflix, iTunes, Hulu, and Amazon on Demand) and never reaired on Comedy Central. Also, both episodes were omitted from the Region 2 DVD release intended for European and Middle Eastern markets.

11. Included in the Region 1 DVD release of *Nerima Daikon Brothers*, vol. 1, distributed by ADV Films (now Funimation Entertainment), are liner notes with a glossary of

a few keywords and character names related to the series. For her entry on Korean Wave Pachinko, Sarah Alys Lindolm, the translator of the animation and author of the liner notes, emphasizes the sinister connection of Zainichi-owned pachinkos (yakuza backing and pachinko cash flow to North Korea). Seemingly endorsing the director's decision to couple "the yakuza/Korea connection [of] pachinko money" with "the extreme influence of the 'Korean Wave' on Japanese pop culture," the American cultural gatekeeper provides no background information about the history of Japanese colonialism in Korea and controversies surrounding the treatment and status of Zainichi Koreans.

WORKS CITED

Anon. 2012. "Pachinko Addiction a Growing Problem for Japanese Women." *JapanToday*, February 8. http://www.japantoday.com/category/kuchikomi/view/pachinko-addiction-a-growing-problem-for-japanese-women. Accessed October 21, 2012.

Cho, Jae-hyon. 2009. "Undying Popularity for Yonsama." *Korean Times*, October 1. http://www.koreatimes.co.kr/www/news/special/2009/10/178_52849.html.   Accessed October 21, 2012.

Faiola, Anthony. 2006. "Japanese Women Catch the 'Korean Wave.'" *Washington Post*, August 31.

Hall, Stuart. 1980. "Encoding/Decoding." In *Culture, Media, Language*, ed. Stuart Hall, Dorothy Hobson, Andy Lowe, and Paul Wills, 128–38. London: Hutchinson.

Hall, Stuart. 2006. "Notes on Deconstructing the Popular." In *Cultural Theory and Popular Culture: A Reader* ed. John Storey, 442–53. Athens: University of Georgia Press.

Han, Min Wha, Arvind Singhal, Toru Hanaki, Do Kyun Kim, and Ketan Chitnis. 2007. "Forced Invisibility to Negotiating Visibility: *Winter Sonata*, the *Hanryu* Phenomenon and *Zainichi* Koreans in Japan." *Keio Communication Review* 29: 25–36.

Hirata, Yukie. 2008. "Touring 'Dramatic Korea': Japanese Women as Viewers of *Hanryu* Dramas and Tourists on *Hanryu* Tours." In *East Asian Pop Culture: Analyzing the Korean Wave*, ed. Chua Beng Huat and Koichi Iwabuchi, 143–55. Hong Kong: Hong Kong University Press.

Iwabuchi, Koichi. 2000. "Political Correctness, Postcoloniality and the Self-Presentation of 'Koreanness' in Japan." In *Koreans in Japan: Critical Voices from the Margin*, ed. Sonia Ryang, 55–73. London: Routledge.

Iwabuchi, Koichi. 2002. *Recentering Globalization: Popular Cultural and Japanese Transnationalism*. Durham: Duke University Press.

Iwabuchi, Koichi. 2008. "When the Korean Wave Meets Resident Koreans in Japan: Intersections of the Transnational, the Postcolonial and the Multicultural." In *East Asian Pop Culture: Analyzing the Korean Wave*, ed. Chua Beng Huat and Koichi Iwabuchi, 243–78. Hong Kong: Hong Kong University Press.

Jung, Sun. 2010. *Korean Masculinities and Transcultural Consumption*. Hong Kong: Hong Kong University Press.

Kellner, Douglas, and Gooyong Kim. 2009. "YouTube, Politics, and Pedagogy: Some Critical Reflections." In *Media/Cultural Studies: Critical Approaches*, ed. Rhonda Hammer and Douglas Kellner, 615–35. New York: Peter Lang.

Kim, Kwang-il. 2005. "Ilbon iut kwa insa hagŏra" (Greet Your Japanese Neighbors). Chosŏn Ilbo (*Chosun Daily*), January 10: A23.

Lee, Hyangjin. 2010. "Buying Youth: Japanese Fandom of the Korean Wave." In *Complicated Currents: Media Flows, Soft Power and East Asia,* ed. Daniel Black, Stephen Epstein, and Alison Tokita. Victoria, Australia: Monash University Publishing. http://books.publishing.monash.edu/apps/bookworm/view/Compli cated+Currents/122/xhtml/chapter7.html. Accessed June 11, 2013.

Lie, John. 2008. *Zainichi (Koreans in Japan): Diasporic Nationalism and Postcolonial Identity.* Berkeley: University of California Press.

Miller, Laura. 2008. "Korean TV Dramas and the Japan-Style Korean Wave." *Post Script* 27 (3): 17–24.

Mori, Yoshitaka. 2008. "*Winter Sonata* and Cultural Practices of Active Fans in Japan: Considering Middle-Aged Women as Cultural Agents." In *East Asian Pop Culture: Analyzing the Korean Wave,* ed. Chua Beng Huat and Koichi Iwabuchi, 127–41. Hong Kong: Hong Kong University Press.

Nagakawa, Ulara. 2011. "Pachinko: Japan's Lifesaver or Time Waster?" CNNGo, September 16. http://www.cnngo.com/tokyo/play/pachinko-japan%E2%80%99s-lifesaver-or-time-waster-061302?page=0,1. Accessed October 21, 2012.

Napier, Susan J. 2005. *Anime: From "Akira" to "Howl's Moving Castle."* New York: Palgrave Macmillan, 2005.

Onishi, Norimitsu. 2004. "What's Korean for 'Real Man'? Ask a Japanese Woman." *New York Times,* December 23. http://www.nytimes.com/2004/12/23/international/asia/23JAPAN.html. Accessed October 21, 2012.

Onishi, Norimitsu. 2005. "Ugly Images of Asian Rivals Become Best Sellers in Japan." *New York Times,* November 19. http://www.nytimes.com/2005/11/19/international/asia/19comics.html. Accessed October 21, 2012.

Sakamoto, Rumi, and Matthew Allen. 2007. "'Hating the Korean Wave' Comic Books: A Sign of New Nationalism in Japan?" *Asia-Pacific Journal: Japan Focus,* October. http://www.japanfocus.org/-Rumi-SAKAMOTO/2535. Accessed June 11, 2013.

Samuels, Stuart. 1988. "The Age of Conspiracy and Conformity: *Invasion of the Body Snatchers* (1956)." In *American History/American Film: Interpreting the Hollywood Image,* ed. John E. O'Connor and Martin A. Jackson, 203–17. New York: Ungar.

Seidman, Gary A. 2012. "Pachinko Politics, Korean Missiles: Can Japan's Money Deter North Korea's Missiles?" MSNBC.com, August 15. http://www.msnbc.msn.com/id/3073092/t/pachinko-politics-korean-missiles/. Accessed October 21, 2012.

Takiguchi, Naoko, and Richard J. Rosenthal. 2011. "Problem Gambling in Japan: A Social Perspective." *Electronic Journal of Contemporary Japanese Studies,* Article 1. http://www.japanesestudies.org.uk/articles/2011/Takiguchi.html. Accessed October 21, 2012.

Yamanaka, Chie. 2010. "The Korean Wave and Anti-Korean Discourse in Japan: A Genealogy of Popular Representations of Korea 1984–2005." In *Complicated Currents: Media Flows, Soft Power and East Asia,* ed. Daniel Black, Stephen Epstein, and Alison Tokita, Victoria, Australia: Monash University Publishing. http://books.publishing.monash.edu/apps/bookworm/view/Complicated+Currents/122/xhtml/chapter2.html. Accessed June 11, 2013.

Zollers, Alla. 2009. "Critical Perspectives on Social Networking Sites." In *Media/Cultural Studies: Critical Approaches,* ed. Rhonda Hammer and Douglas Kellner, 602–14. New York: Peter Lang.

10

Consuming the Other

Israeli Hallyu Case Study

Irina Lyan and Alon Levkowitz

While Korea and Israel have been enjoying the prosperity of political and economic relationships since the 1990s, Korean popular culture has gained popularity in Israel only since the late 2000s with the advent of Hallyu 2.0. According to Dal Yong Jin (see his chapter in this volume), the shift toward Hallyu 2.0 has occurred as a result of technological development and fans' involvement with social media. Unlike government and industry-driven Hallyu 1.0, the fan-driven Hallyu 2.0 has gone beyond Asia. The Israeli case study of a non-Asian and non-Western setting can demonstrate the power of technology and social media to create new maps of Hallyu distribution. The phenomenon of Korean popular culture spreading around the world has aroused great interest in academic circles, although it still concentrates mostly on East and Southeast Asian regions (Chua and Iwabuchi 2008; Shim 2006; Chua 2008). Considering this gap, it is important to address the question of how Israeli Hallyu fans negotiate their identity in the process of cultural consumption through their active involvement with online communities of Korean popular culture. Ethnographic discourse and survey analysis show that Korean culture audiences in Israel, like in other places of Hallyu fandom,[1] are not passive recipients in a unidirectional process, but rather cultural agents that construct "Koreanness" adapted to the local environment. This hybrid process is mediated by virtual communities that generate feelings of being the "Other," belonging to a community of fans, and even a sense of mission in disseminating Korean culture in Israel.

Korea in Israel

Until the 1988 Seoul Olympics, Korea was an "obscure nation" not only in Israel but also around the world (Kim 2007; Chung 2011; Keane 2006). The lack of knowledge about Korea stems from the limited trade and the lack of cultural exchange between the two countries. The beginning of the peace process in the Middle East in the 1990s and the decreased fear of Korean companies from the Arab boycott of any company that trades with Israel led to the growth of political and economic relations between Korea and Israel (Levkowitz 2012). This disparity was gradually dissolving, but Korea's cultural influence in Israel was still imperceptible.

The shift toward cultural acknowledgment of Korea came in the late 2000s with the introduction of Hallyu in Israel. In 2006, the first Korean TV drama, *My Lovely Sam-Soon* (Nae irŭm ŭn Kim Sam-sun, 2005), was aired on the Israeli cable soap opera channel Viva. It gained such popularity that it paved the way for the next thirty Korean TV dramas broadcast on the same channel. In 2008, the Israeli national newspaper described the popularity of Korean TV dramas in Israel as a "revolution" of cultural taste (*Ynet* 2008). This revolution, initiated by the Viva channel, boosted the creation of dozens of online Korean culture fan communities that initiated the subsequent Hallyu 2.0 era.

An example of this change toward recognition of Korean culture can be seen in the Korean government's attitude toward Israeli Hallyu. In 2011, the (then) Korean ambassador to Israel, H. E. Ma Young-sam, joined a meeting of members of the Israeli Hallyu fan club (figure 11). After greeting the audience, the ambassador asked if they knew who Bae Yong-joon (Pae, Yong-jun) was. The audience shouted "Yes!" He stated that that evening he felt like the star of *Winter Sonata* (Kyŏul yŏn'ga, 2002), which evoked a highly emotional response. In the eyes of the Israeli fans, this meeting symbolized the success of Hallyu in Israel (*Korea JoongAng Daily* 2011).

The phenomenon of Israeli Hallyu can be approached by examining the role of online fan communities and striving to understand how the local environment is unique or similar to other locales. Contrary to the simplistic view of the unidirectional cultural flow from center to periphery—or from America to the rest of the world—current research brings an example of a bidirectional cultural flow between Korea and Israel. Cultural engagement with more peripheral and foreign cultures to compare to the American and European "center" in the so-called process of "recentering globalization" (Iwabuchi 2002) has only recently become evident.

Fig. 11. Ambassador Ma Young-sam meets members of the Israeli Hallyu fan club. Photo by Limor Lechniak. Used with permission.

Hallyu Is Going Global

The globalized nature of Korean popular culture consumption should be understood within cultural globalization theories. Featherstone (1990) defines globalization as "trans-societal cultural processes which take a variety of forms, some of which have preceded the inter-state relations into which nation-states can be regarded as being embedded, and processes which sustain the exchange and flow of goods, people, information, knowledge and images which give rise to communication processes which gain some autonomy on a global level" (1). This global age is characterized by endless cultural opportunities, as if the world has become a "global supermarket" of cross-cultural consumption. Within this metaphor, although individuals perceive themselves as possessing a specific cultural identity, they can also acquire additional ones in a cultural supermarket. Therefore, individuals negotiate their cultural identities through consumption by seeking a home in this global marketplace (Mathews 2000).

The most salient characteristic of Hallyu is that, as a global wave, it is generated outside Korea,[2] and is usually foreign to its fans (Chua 2008). What is of particular interest in a phenomenon such as Hallyu is the way in which agents confer local meaning upon foreign content. This process of negotiation between global and local, so-called glocalization, assumes that global products are consumed by locally contextualized audiences who create their own meanings and subsequently process them to serve their own social and cultural needs (Robertson 1994). Most global products that are designed for the international market are specifically and intentionally produced to be as universal and "culturally odorless" (Iwabuchi 2002) as possible and cater to the needs, abilities, and interests of audiences worldwide. However, even products that aim to be culturally neutral need to be further localized by local audiences (Lemish and Bloch 2004).The Korean origin of Hallyu, therefore, poses a challenge to its localization in Israel.

Hallyu as the Other

Academic studies have attempted to explain the major success of Hallyu by proximity, close cultural and historical affinity with Asian sentiments (Chua and Iwabuchi 2008). However, these explanations cannot elucidate the Israeli case, where Korean culture is perceived as exotic, distant, and different. Thus, if the consumption of Hallyu in East Asian countries is the consumption of similar and familiar products,[3] in the Israeli case it is the consumption of the unfamiliar Other. Concurrently, as Edward Said (1979) points out, the Other is always a reflection and a projection of ourselves. Thus, fans' consumption of Hallyu is based on their hybrid reading of different and similar, known and unknown, familiar and exotic media contents. Moreover, most of the research on Hallyu neglects not only the non-Asian countries, but also the impact of local microinteractions and social online networks of fans (Noh 2010; Schulze 2013; Otmazgin and Lyan 2013), which have become the driving force of Hallyu 2.0. The purpose of our study is to investigate how the Korean TV drama phenomenon is received within the Israeli context and to examine the transnational transfer of meanings and values by fan communities.

Method: Qualitative Internet Research

This study used qualitative Internet research that includes an analysis of both online and offline data in order to explore the significance of "the multiple meanings and experiences that emerge around the Internet in a particular context" (Orgad 2009, 34). It combines various methods in an attempt to triangulate different sources of information such as community ethnography, media text analysis, and electronic survey descriptive statistics. First, we visited different Internet-based social networks of Korean drama fans, and conducted close textual analysis of two major fan communities, ASIA4HB.com and South Korea Lovers, to typify main themes. ASIA4HB.com (abbreviation for "Asia for Hebrew") is a volunteer organization that has been operating since 2010. The site contains K-pop, Korean films, and Korean TV dramas translated by volunteers into Hebrew. It is the largest Korean TV drama fan club, with more than five thousand members. There are dozens of additional smaller Israeli fan clubs excluded from this research, with the exception of one fan club called South Korea Lovers. This Facebook-based fan club is open to group members only. An Israeli woman founded the website in 2011; since then, the fan club has grown to almost two thousand members (as of February 2014). It is esteemed by fans as one of the most active fan clubs of Korean pop culture with 24/7 postings and commenting. In contrast to ASIA4HB's translation project, South Korea Lovers places an emphasis on communal sharing of K-pop and pictures of Korean actors and singers. In addition to these two communities, one of the authors (I.L.) has managed a Facebook page called "Korea: Culture and Language" since 2011 with more than two thousand members (as of February 2014); its main purpose is to promote Korean culture in Israel beyond its popular culture. This forum created an opportunity for online participant observation and familiarization with the research subject.

In addition to virtual participation, we participated in actual meetings, held informal discussions with members, and attended Korean cultural events organized by the members themselves or by the Korean Embassy and the Korean community in Israel, such as Korea Day (since the early 2000s), Quiz on Korea (since 2010) and K-pop Festival (since 2013). We also tracked local media coverage of the phenomenon, and followed up with a close textual analysis of ten Israeli newspaper articles and two TV programs on the theme of Israeli Hallyu. Based on a discourse analysis of communities' entries, informal discussions with fans, and media texts, the electronic survey's questions mainly pertained to issues of recognition and exposure to Korean TV dramas as well as an awareness of the country of origin. Even though Hallyu includes different types of texts, this analysis concentrates on Korean drama for two reasons: First, it seems to be the most popular genre to capture the interest of Israeli audiences, to date.

Second, Israeli Hallyu originated from Korean TV drama, and this study attempts to trace this localized phenomenon from its beginnings. The Israeli interest in K-pop that characterizes Hallyu 2.0 usually stems from Korean TV drama, or is accompanied by it.

The survey contained several background questions, nine questions pertaining to Korean TV dramas with several options, forty-seven questions pertaining to the dramas with numeral options from 1 ("definitely no") to 7 ("definitely yes"), and finally four open-ended questions on what viewers (dis)like about Korean TV dramas and what makes it so special in general and for the female audience in particular. The survey was conducted among Korean TV drama fans in Israel and was disseminated via fan forums in different social networks, such as Facebook, Tapuz, Viva, Agenda, and others. A total of 395 completed questionnaires were collected from 390 females and only five males. To identify active drama viewers who qualified for the survey, participants had to have seen at least three dramas in the past. With an estimated more than five thousand Korean drama fans in Israel, this questionnaire sample represents almost 10 percent of the research population, a relatively high percentage. Survey results identified the main characteristics of the research population and major themes of Israeli Hallyu fandom. Subsequent readings classified the accounts in each of these themes and selected groups of specific examples.

Research Population

One of the most prominent characteristics of Hallyu fans both worldwide (Chua and Iwabuchi 2008; Kim et al. 2007; Schulze 2013; Noh 2010) and in Israel is that the majority of fans are females. Still, the gendered nature of Hallyu fandom in Israel is striking and we are going to provide a possible explanation later in this chapter (according to the survey, only 1 percent of respondents are males). Regarding age, almost one-third of survey participants were between the ages of eighteen and twenty (mean = 28.71, median = 24, SD = 12.95). As a part of Hallyu 2.0 influences, this age group's better mastery of technological devices could explain its more active participation in virtual communities as well. Another indicator of the rather young age of Israeli fans is that 46 percent of the survey participants are high school or university students and 67 percent are single. The survey also included the religion variable of Judaism and three levels of religiosity, traditional (31 percent), religious (13.1 percent), and orthodox (1.8 percent), to determine the relationship between the level of religiosity[4] and viewing Korean TV drama.[5] A high percentage (46 percent) of participants indicates a strong relationship between TV dramas and its popularity within the religious sector.

An additional characteristic is that every virtual community is usually led and facilitated by moderators and a small number of active members. Passive members support community life by their silent and anonymous presence on a somewhat regular basis. Thus, active members are more visible and relevant for the purpose of this research. To draw a line between a consumer and a fan, the survey asked respondents to rate their levels of addiction to Korean TV dramas on a 1-to-7 scale. Sixty percent responded with 7, "definitely yes," whereas 28 percent answered with a less definite 4–6 score (mean = 6.22, SD = 1.31). The most important characteristic of the research population is that 95 percent of fans had never been to Korea, and began to experience Korean culture mostly through Korean TV dramas (see table 5); therefore, Korean culture in Israel is mediated by the

TABLE 5. Activism of Israeli Hallyu Fans

Survey question	Percentage of answers "definitely yes" on 1 to 7 scale	Mean	Standard Deviation
"I feel a part of the Korean drama lovers' community"	41%	5.26	2.026
"I regularly enter forums and share with other fans my experiences from Korean television dramas"	15%	3.32	2.247
"Because of Korean television dramas I tasted Korean food"	25%	3.62	2.595
"Because of Korean television dramas I became interested in Korean music"	53%	5.46	2.118
"I am trying to participate in Korean cultural events organized in Israel"	8%	2.18	1.905
"I learned some Korean by watching Korean television dramas"	67%	6.20	1.364
"I would like to visit places related to Korean television dramas"	67%	6.19	1.482
"I am 'addicted' to Korean television dramas"	60%	6.22	1.310
"I knew very little about Korean culture and Korean people before I started watching Korean television" dramas"	38%	3.72	2.583
"I personally know Korean people who live in Israel"	3%	1.63	1.402

consumption of popular culture as an unknown and distant Other—at least, that is how it begins.

Findings: Consuming the Other

> [What is special about Korean TV drama?] Unknown and
> unfamiliar, the difference between advanced West and old-fashioned
> Asia, deviation that causes curiosity. It's almost like seeing a
> discovered African tribe (from the survey).

Similar to other consumers of popular culture around the world, Israeli viewers of Korean TV dramas are active interpreters of the text. They negotiate their viewing experience by their own knowledge, cultural context, and gendered identity and preferences. In the Israeli Hallyu case, Korean popular culture is consumed as a whole construct—Korean TV drama becomes a gateway to a broader interest in Korean culture. As can be seen from above citation, the Otherness or "foreignness" (Chua 2008) became the source of attraction to Korean popular culture. The exposure to a different culture requires self-identification as well. Fans construct their own cultural identity by holding up the Other as a mirror (Goldshtein-Gideoni 2003). As the findings section will detail, this mirror both fills the gap of something lacking in the host culture and is reminiscent of one's own culture. The research findings were divided into three major themes: Fan as the other, the Other as a mirror, and the Other as a mission. All of these themes move from the micro level of self to the macro level of community—from fan as a stereotyped individual to the sense of a welcoming community, and from (female) idealization of Korean culture to the communal effort to promote it in Israel. These themes also track the process of domestication of the Other, from being "they" to becoming "us," and vice versa.

Fan as the Other

> [Journalist:] How does your environment react [to your addiction to
> Korean TV dramas]? [Ora, the interviewee:] Everybody says I'm
> tralala ["crazy"]. They don't understand how it happened. [They ask
> me,] "What is it with you and the Koreans?" (From the Channel 10
> TV program Viva Korea, 2011).

In their book *Fandom: Identities and Communities in a Mediated World*, Gray, Sandvoss, and Harrington (2007) argue that fans are the subject of ridicule in mainstream society. To challenge "the firm desire to understand fandom solely as other" (2), they procure recent fandom studies on power relations, identity construction, and creative consumption to demonstrate the complex nature of fans and their fandom. By liking the Other, one becomes the Other him-/herself. This ability of fans to (re)interpret and manipulate popular cultural texts indicates that one's own identity has both positive and negative aspects (Baym 2000; Darling-Wolf 2004).

One of the positive effects is the empowerment of cultural identity. For example, 39 percent in our survey reported that they felt special and unique by watching Korean TV dramas (mean = 5.04, SD = 2.199). On a visual level, Facebook users creatively adopted a Korean identity by using profile pictures of Korean actors and singers, translating and creating names in a Korean style and language. However, some fans concurrently feel that they are becoming outsiders in their own family and circle of friends. The negative stereotype is composed of three different constructs: exotic Korean culture, the low status of the TV drama genre, and its being stereotyped as a female leisure activity. One of the members of the Facebook group South Korea Lovers, for instance, complained about her friends: "It's so annoying. I write something on my [Facebook] wall about Koreans and all my friends think somebody has hacked my account. 'I can't believe that you really like these Chinese!!' Come on, what's the problem? Is it forbidden to like something different? If I wrote something about Americans, does that mean that nobody hacked my account?" It is evident that Korea is not yet the "accepted" Other, even though Israel is a culturally heterogeneous (Ram 1999), and there is a demand for exotic cultures and a fascination with Otherness (Hall 1992). Korean products are more salient and even exotic in Israel than those from other places such as the United States and Europe. Among East Asian countries, Korea is more remote from China and especially Japan, whose dominant presence is felt in Israeli daily life (Goldshtein-Gideoni 2003; Daliot-Bul 2007; Lemish and Bloch 2004).

The second reason for the poor acceptance of Korean popular culture in Israel is its union with the TV drama genre. As one survey respondent complained, she is "a teacher with a master's degree and despite that everybody mocks [her] because of this addiction [to Korean TV dramas]." Similar to professional and educational hierarchies, this leisure activity, together with soap operas, has low status in the hierarchy of fandom (Gray, Sandvoss, and Harrington 2007; Baym 2000). Moreover, it is strongly connected with a female audience, which further lowers the fans' status. Sport fandom, for example, is rarely mocked because it is high in the hierarchy and occupied predominantly by males (Gosling 2007). According to both survey results and larger observations, female gender emerged as a central variable influencing the construction of meaning in Hallyu consumption. For example, in January 2013 the moderator of South Korea Lovers asked for introductions—of the one hundred respondents, only seven were males.

To better understand the feminized nature of the audience for Korean drama, we asked survey participants to explain why women, more frequently than men, like Korean dramas. The most common answer was connected to females' natural attraction to romantic and emotional dramas. Social norms of masculinity in Israel also define consumption of TV drama as a solely female leisure activity. In addition, women presented themselves as more open to being exposed to different cultures and experiences than are men. Moreover, both Korean dramas and Viva—the TV soap opera channel that broadcasts them—target mostly female audiences. Despite this fact, most respondents believed that men would enjoy Korean drama. Consequently, Korean-culture communities are also dominated by female audiences, which prevents men from joining for fear of being stereotyped as feminine.

The Israeli media also added to the exotic image of both Korean TV dramas and the fans of those dramas by dismissing them as Others. In 2011, Israeli Channel 10 broadcast a TV program called *Viva Korea* on Israeli Hallyu that enraged the fan community. The male journalist who investigates Hallyu in Israel, Yinon Mills, does not hide his incredulity regarding the phenomenon, asking how "it's possible to become addicted to ridiculous love stories from Asia." He meets several active female members from the fan community, and mocks them, wondering how they fell into Korean TV dramas. The program ends with the journalist joking that he became addicted himself, watching dramas and repetitively saying, "What trash!" The program's participants, who were initially glad for the opportunity to share their fandom on a somewhat popular TV show, were horrified by the final result. In keeping the entertaining tone the program aimed for, fans were depicted in a humiliating way by mainstream media. The program was also criticized for its choice of a male journalist to cover (female) dramas, a journalist whose attitude demonstrates the gendered spaces of the public sphere. This space leaves women no room to represent themselves in an equal or superior way.

As an alternative, Hallyu fans create and join female spaces of fan communities. This belonging draws borders between "us" and the rest of Israeli society,[6] which can be mocking and impatient toward the Other, and even hostile toward its followers. The community can give them confidence and a strong sense of identity, sometimes for the first time. Therefore, such communities serve needs beyond the goal of sharing information (Noh 2010; Otmazgin and Lyan 2013). Based on their love of Korean culture, some members become virtual friends, and some become friends beyond virtural reality, organizing face-to-face meetings or going to cultural events together. The encounters can be very personal and unconnected to Korean content that occasioned them: personal remarks sharing depression, happiness, or fatigue, taking an exam, liking another person, and so on. The space itself is welcoming, and there are frequent remarks on belonging to an online community, as if to a physical space. The sense of belonging and togetherness is one of the fundamentals of such communities, beyond the fandom. These virtual communities become a shelter for sharing fandom without fear of being mocked or misunderstood while idealizing and longing for the Other.

The Other as a Mirror

> [What is special about Korean TV drama?] Modesty and Korean
> cultural values make watching dramas enjoyable, without any
> concern/fear of "wrong" content. In general, it's a fact that we are
> influenced by what we watch. If we don't watch only regular dramas
> [American and South American], I think the generation's behavior
> would be better and calmer. (From the survey)

One of the recurring themes that explain Israeli audiences' admiration for Korea is respect for Asian values. In this sense, by looking at the Other, one is longing for something that is lacking in one's own culture. The Other as a mirror fills the void as a person adopts the alien culture (Goldshtein-Gideoni 2003) and is also a reminder of something lost and forgotten. For example, according to an article in *Korea JoongAng Daily* about an interview with three Israeli fans of Korean drama, "[They] seemed especially impressed that Koreans in the dramas still maintain a respect for the elderly, a value they said they thought Israelis are losing. 'When I was young, we behaved like that with our grandfathers and grandmothers, but today, it's not the same,' Nomi Poraty said. 'Respect is nice. We shouldn't be too strict about it, but we should keep it'" (*Korea JoongAng Daily* 2011). As another Korean drama fan emphasizes, "The special thing about Korean dramas is their culture and different attitude from Israel toward various topics such as love, family honor, and values. These topics are forgotten and have lost their value here in Israel, and that's why it's so fun and exciting to see that it still exists in other places" (from the survey). Survey results also showed that 67 percent agree that they appreciate the family values of honor that are expressed in Korean drama (mean = 6.30, SD = 1.383), and 61 percent even think that Israelis should learn from Koreans (mean = 6.27, SD = 1.259).

As a part of idealizing the Other, participants admire the beauty of Korean actors, singers, and landscapes. The "exotic" perspective of Korean TV drama is reminiscent of a tourist consuming foreign landscapes (Chua 2008). This consumer response varies, from posting Korean stars' photos, to expressing admiration for their looks and abilities or dreams and for Koreans and Korea. The attraction to the visual aspects of Hallyu has a strong impact. Moreover, respondents frequently cited the beauty of Korean men, as well as the actors' performance and talent, as reasons why especially women like Korean TV dramas. But the enchantment with Korean TV dramas goes far beyond physical appearance or talents, to longing for the Other as an escape from reality. In Korean TV dramas, the Israeli woman finds an image of ideal men and distant love that she cannot find in real life:

(Why do women in particular watch Korean TV dramas?) I think that women like me have found a connection (to Korean TV dramas) because they struggle to find true love. . . . I personally found myself withdrawing further and further away from Israeli men. . . . Korea gave me a hope of (finding) a different type of man. Women are more sensitive to small differences that are the most important in cultures. Korean culture, which is all about manners, tenderness, honor, and care at all costs for the family and spouse certainly enchants women that suffer from cynicism, rudeness and almost complete ignorance of beauty, [and] pure and real feelings in our culture. (From the survey)[7]

This polarized view of the two cultures has therapeutic effects. Fandom here is a tool of female empowerment rather than solely an aesthetic experience. It also shows how women consume differently than men because of a difference in socialization. In their feelings of idealization, survey respondents clearly preferred Korean dramas to other Asian TV dramas and Latin American melodramas. They explained their preference by the naïveté, purity, and simplicity of feelings expressed in Korean drama, especially in contrast to Western-style TV dramas. As a result of these qualities, Korean TV drama was said to be appropriate for every age, for family viewing, and for religious audiences as well (46 percent of survey respondents identified themselves with some level of religiosity) (see table 6).

While most fans admire this ideal of simple purity, a certain group of activists set a goal of promoting Korea in Israel, with different levels of involvement. The findings show that the sense of mission comprises one of the main characteristics of Korean drama fans in Israel.

The Other as a Mission

Please pass a message to all Koreans in South Korea how many people love them and their culture here in Israel; let them know how much love we have for them. And let Israelis know that there are Koreans and they are amazing. (From the survey)

TABLE 6. Idealization of Korea and Koreans through Hallyu Consumption

Survey question	Percentage of answers "definitely yes" on 1 to 7 scale	Mean	Standard Deviation
"I appreciate Korean family values of honor that are expressed in Korean television dramas"	67%	6.30	1.383
"I think that Israelis should learn a lot from Koreans"	61%	6.27	1.259
"I'm attracted to the beauty of Korean actors"	71%	6.42	1.159
"It tend to fall in love with Korean actors"	47%	5.43	1.937
"I would like to marry a Korean person"	27%	3.87	2.476
"I would like to stay in Korea for a period of time"	52%	5.27	2.281
"I would like to move to Korea"	25%	3.65	2.394
"I prefer Korean television dramas to other Asian television dramas"	61%	6.06	1.644
"I prefer Korean television dramas to Latin-American television series"	74%	6.55	1.098
"Korean television drama is appropriate for every age"	64%	6.22	1.410
"Watching Korean television dramas was a life-changing experience"	32%	4.95	1.883

Together with a sense of exclusiveness and uniqueness shared by the community of Israeli fans, they share the mission of spreading Korean culture in Israel. On a macro level, the Korean government recognizes the potential of Hallyu, and has become an active agent in promoting and exporting it overseas. Korean pop culture is used as a "soft power" to establish a presence outside Korea (Shim 2006; Chua 2012; Otmazgin 2011). But with the introduction of Hallyu to Israel on the micro level of consumption alone, the number of Israelis interested in Korean culture has grown from tens to thousands. For example, 38 percent of respondents claimed in the survey that they knew about Korean culture before their exposure to Hallyu (mean = 3.72, SD = 2.583), but 73 percent fell in love with it after their exposure (mean = 6.53, SD = 0.996). Although direct experience with Korea and Koreans is limited by physical distance, fans (re)create "Koreanness" solely on the basis of cultural products. Israeli entrepreneurs of Korean culture re-create it in the global context inside local communities. As part of this process, Korea has become more accessible in the local language, Hebrew, particularly as a result of ASIA4HB's voluntary translations.

There are similar fansub (fan-subtitled) communities around the world that translate Korean TV dramas into different languages and upload subtitles online. As a result, the Internet has become the ultimate source of information on Korea and its popular culture, and the tool for global fan activity that transcends time and space, allowing fans to negotiate their fandom as a group. Hallyu 2.0 relies on fans and their freedom to illegally download and watch dramas on the Internet (in contrast to broadcast television), which enables the dramatic spread of TV drama in the local language. It is evident that the sense of mission is an important part of fan identity in any effort to connect the two cultures. A somewhat high percentage of 35 percent of respondents feels that they are spreading Korean culture in Israel (mean = 4.87, SD = 2.151). Besides translation, the activities vary from feeling proud of the Israeli media attention given to Korean drama fans to causing friends to fall in love with the drams. Some fans also create communities and petitions to bring Korean stars to Israel or to place pressure on the Viva TV channel to import more dramas. In their attempt to promote fandom, fans seek to legitimize their own identity through the social environment. The goal here in some way is to cease being the Other and liking the Other, and finally find a home and recognition of their fandom and themselves.

Conclusion: Is Korea Here?

> I can't explain my personal connection to these dramas, I feel at
> home. . . . I'm dying to go [to Korea] and I have a feeling that when I
> arrive, I'll feel like I came home. (From the survey)

In contrast to the field of Korean studies, Israeli media and academic studies have already announced, "Japan is here." Indeed, Japanese culture has been very popular in daily Israeli life since the 1980s (Goldshtein-Gideoni 2003; Daliot-Bul 2007; Lemish and Bloch 2004). However, the Hallyu of the late 2000s reached Israel and has the full potential of finding a home there as well. Once regarded as marginal, Korean culture has currently reterritorialized in Israel, mostly in online fan communities. Because of the cultural and geographical isolation between the two countries, the Israeli community brings Korea to Israel. It is still too early to discuss Korea in terms of "here," but it is definitely in the process of "in between."

Chua (2008; 2012) refers to Hallyu fandom in East Asian regions as the simultaneous process of distancing and identification. We would like to make the general point that every fan vacillates through this process. In the case of Israeli fans, the process begins with an attraction to foreignness, but after familiarizing themselves with it, they feel as if "at home." The metaphor of "symbolic pilgrimage" fits to this process of homecoming—"a sense of rejoining a community" without leaving the chair (Brooker 2007, 162). In this way, Hallyu's media-consumption process is the metaphorical journey that transforms the cultural identity of the fan (Mathews 2000). The fan making this journey goes back and forth in the liminal space between, perceived as both home and "promised land," known and unknown, and familiar and ideal.

NOTES

1. See, for example, Seung-Ah Lee's chapter on JYJ fandom and Youjeong Oh's chapter on active viewers that engage in TV drama production, both in this volume.

2. See JungBong Choi's chapter in this volume on the definition of Hallyu.

3. But see Beng Huat Chua's (2008) paper that questions the proximity and similarity of "Asia" as a homogeneous construct.

4. This is an accepted measurement of religiosity in Israeli studies that varies from the traditional stream, which observes some of the Jewish religious traditions and whose followers perceive themselves as neither religious nor secular; to the religious mainstream; and to the ultraorthodox.

5. Since the survey was conducted in Hebrew, the language limited this study to Jew-

ish Israelis. Palestinian fans, for example, consume and participate in communities in Arabic and/or English (Otmazgin and Lyan 2013).

6. The JYJ Republic metaphor in Seung-Ah Lee's chapter in this volume is another good example of fandom community.

7. See, for example, Kim et al. 2007 for a very similar representation of ideal love in the "Yon-sama syndrome."

WORKS CITED

Baym, Nancy K. 2000. *Tune In, Log On: Soaps, Fandom, and Online Community*. Thousand Oaks, CA: Sage.

Brooker, Will. 2007. "A Sort of Homecoming: Fan Viewing and Symbolic Pilgrimage." In *Fandom: Identities and Communities in a Mediated World*, ed. Jonathan Gray, Cornell Sandvoss, and C. Lee Harrington, 149–64. New York: New York University Press.

Chua, Beng Huat. 2008. "Structure of Identification and Distancing in Watching East Asian Television Drama." In *East Asian Pop Culture: Analysing the Korean Wave*, ed. Beng Huat Chua and Koichi Iwabuchi, 73–89. Hong Kong: Hong Kong University Press.

Chua, Beng Huat. 2012. "Delusional Desire: Soft Power and Television Drama." In *Popular Culture and the State in East and Southeast Asia*, ed. Nissim Otmazgin and Eyal Ben-Ari, 35–81. New York: Routledge Taylor & Francis Group.

Chua, Beng Huat, and Koichi Iwabuchi. 2008 "Introduction: East Asian TV Dramas: Identifications, Sentiments and Effects." In *East Asian Pop Culture: Analysing the Korean Wave*, ed. Beng Huat Chua and Koichi Iwabuchi, 1–12. Hong Kong: Hong Kong University Press.

Chung, Hye Seung. 2011. "Medium Hot, Korean Cool: Hallyu Envy and Reverse Mimicry in Contemporary U.S. Pop Culture." In *Hallyu: Influence of Korean Popular Culture in Asian and Beyond*, ed. Do-Kyun Kim and Min-sun Kim, 63–90. Seoul: Seoul National University Press.

Daliot-Bul, Michal. 2007. "Eroticism, Grotesqueness and Non-sense: Twenty-First-Century Cultural Imagery of Japan in the Israeli Media and Popular Culture." *Journal of Intercultural Studies* 28 (2): 173–91.

Darling-Wolf, Fabienne. 2004. "Virtually Multicultural: Trans-Asian Identity and Gender in an International Fan Community of a Japanese Star." *New Media and Society* 6 (4): 507–28.

Featherstone, Mike. 1990. "Global Culture: An Introduction." In *Global Culture: Nationalism, Globalization and Modernity*, ed. Mike Featherstone, 1–14. London: Sage.

Goldshtein-Gideoni, Ofra. 2003. "'Japan Is Here?'—Japan as Cultural Alternative in Israel of 2000s." *Israeli Sociology* 1: 193–218 (in Hebrew).

Gosling, Victoria K. 2007. "Girls Allowed? The Marginalization of Female Sport Fans." In *Fandom: Identities and Communities in a Mediated World*, ed. Jonathan Gray, Cornell Sandvoss, and C. Lee Harrington, 250–60. New York: New York University Press.

Gray, Jonathan, Cornell Sandvoss, and C. Lee Harrington. 2007. "Introduction: Why Study Fans?" In *Fandom: Identities and Communities in a Mediated World*, ed. Jonathan Gray, Cornell Sandvoss, and C. Lee Harrington, 1–16. New York: New York University Press.

Hall, Stuart. 1992. "The Question of Cultural Identity." In *Modernity and Its Futures*, ed. Stuart Hall, David Held, and Tony McGrew, 273–325. Cambridge: Polity Press.

Iwabuchi, Koichi. 2002. *Recentering Globalization: Popular Culture and Japanese Transnationalism*. Durham: Duke University Press.

Keane, Michael. 2006. "Once Were Peripheral: Creating Media Capacity in East Asia." *Media, Culture and Society* 28 (6): 835–55.

Kim, Choong-soon. 2007. *Kimchi and Information Technology: Tradition and Transformation in Korea*. Seoul: Ilchokak.

Kim, Samuel Seongseop, Jerome Agrusa, Heesung Lee, and Kaye Chon. 2007. "Effects of Korean Television Dramas on the Flow of Japanese Tourists." *Tourism Management* 28 (5): 1340–53.

Lemish, Dafna, and Linda-Renee Bloch. 2004. "Pokémon in Israel." In *Pikachu's Global Adventure: The Rise and Fall of Pokémon*, ed. Joseph Tobin, 165–86. Durham: Duke University Press.

Levkowitz, Alon. 2012. "Korea and the Middle East Turmoil: A Reassessment of South Korea–Middle East Relations." *Korean Journal of Defense Analysis* 24 (2): 225–38.

Mathews, Gordon. 2000. *Global Culture/Individual Identity: Searching for Home in the Cultural Supermarket*. London: Routledge.

Moon, Gwang-lip. 2011. "Israeli Fans Latch On to Ever-Mobile K-Pop Wave." *Korea JoongAng Daily*, July 11. Accessed January 26, 2014. http://koreajoongangdaily.joinsmsn.com/news/article/article.aspx?aid=2938596.

Noh, Sueen. 2010. "Unveiling the Korean Wave in the Middle East." In *Hallyu: Influence of Korean Culture in Asia and Beyond*, ed. Do-kyun Kim and Min-Sun Kim, 331–67. Seoul: Seoul National University Press.

Orgad, Shani. 2009. "Question Two: How Can Researchers Make Sense of the Issues Involved in Collecting and Interpreting Online and Offline Data?" In *Internet Inquiry: Conversations about Method*, ed. Annette N. Markham and Nancy K. Baym, 33–60. Thousand Oaks, CA: Sage.

Otmazgin, Nissim. 2011. "A Tail That Wags a Dog? Cultural Industry and Cultural Policy in Japan and South Korea." *Journal of Comparative Policy Analysis: Research and Practice* 13 (3): 307–25.

Otmazgin, Nissim, and Irina Lyan. 2013. "Hallyu across the Desert: K-Pop Fandom in Israel and Palestine." *Cross-Currents: East Asian History and Culture Review* 9: 68–89. Accessed January 26, 2014. https://cross-currents.berkeley.edu/e-journal/issue-9.

Ram, Uri. 1999. "Between Weapons and the Market: Israel in an Age of Glocality." *Israeli Sociology* 2 (1): 99–145 (in Hebrew).

Robertson, Roland. 1994. "Globalisation or Glocalisation?" *Journal of International Communication* 1 (1): 33–52.

Said, Edward. 1979. *Orientalism*. London: Viking.

Schulze, Marion. 2013. "Korea vs. K-Dramaland: The Culturalization of K-Dramas." *Acta Koreana* 16 (2): 367–97.

Shim, Doobo. 2006. "Hybridity and the Rise of Korean Popular Culture in Asia." *Media, Culture and Society* 28 (1): 25–44.

Spector, Danny. 2008. "Viva la Rebolusion." *Ynet*, April 1, 2008 (in Hebrew).

11

RIP Gangnam Style[1]

Brian Hu

"Gangnam Style" happened. Past tense. Just months after the video featuring Korean rapper Psy broke out internationally in late summer 2012, American commentators were calling it done. On September 21, E! Online dubbed it "officially over" (Boone 2012). On October 1, *Time* said the "meme" was "killed" (Carbone 2012). CNN Tech proclaimed October 12 "the day 'Gangnam Style' died" (Bellini 2012). Even Psy himself said that his New Year's Eve performance on the popular *Dick Clark's Rockin' Eve* program was "the ending of 'Gangnam Style'" (Wood 2012). In every instance, the cause of death was overexposure. And in every instance, the track, the video, and the dance lived on.

The desire to see "Gangnam Style" dead, to call it the best/worst song of 2012 in order to taper off an end date, even to associate the song with the Mayan apocalypse (Shepherd 2012) and the actual death of forty-six-year-old Eamonn Kilbride, who allegedly died doing the "Gangnam" dance at an office party (Hall 2012), stands in stark contrast to a Korean entertainment industry and Korean government doing everything it could to keep "Gangnam Style" alive, all while shrugging their shoulders over how it was born to begin with. "Gangnam Style" as a national-institutional campaign, to use JungBong Choi's distinction earlier in this volume, caught on quickly, from state-sponsored international megaevents like the Gangnam-styled Busan International Film Festival in October, to world-stage photo ops like Psy's meeting and dance with United Nations secretary general and fellow South Korean Ban Ki-moon. The questions of why Psy blew up, what in him appealed to the rest of the world, and how to keep him—and indeed all of K-pop—from being an international one-hit wonder, began to vex the Korean entertainment industry. Did this seemingly uncalculated pop cultural phenomenon, in overexposing itself to the world, essentially kill Hallyu's dreams of mainstream success in the West? How would the traditional recipes for success, like those observed by Roald Maliangkay in an earlier chapter in this volume, have to be rewritten, or was Psy simply the gargantuan exception that proved that there were no rules?

The nervous ways in which these questions have been lodged and debated in the wake of Psy's unprecedented international popularity, as well as the time-sensitive need to ride his coattails via viral video parodies or special guest appearances, speak to everyone's knowledge that fads have expiration dates, that pop cultural explosions leave nothing but dust. Perhaps because of the foreignness of "Gangnam Style" itself, or perhaps because the public was weary of what happens to Macarenas, Running Mans, and Dougies when they've overstayed their welcome, Psy and his success were never taken as anything but a trend in the United States, even as they time and again defied death. As a Korean-born entertainer who wore his otherworldliness on his sleeve, Psy is in many ways an extreme example of what Sue Collins (2008, 89) has called the "dispensable celebrity" of contemporary reality-TV culture in the United States, whereby outsiders are cast into the mainstream, only to be discarded with a "temporal flexibility" that audiences fully anticipate. It's precisely that imminent expiry, accentuated by the perceived alienness of Psy and the "Gangnam Style" video itself, that accelerated so much creativity, debate, explanation, grievance, suspicion, anxiety, and celebration in late 2012. Before it inevitably vanishes, exploit it, mimic it, dissect it as an allegory for our troubles. Caught in the middle of it all were Asian Americans, a group already marginalized and made invisible in the American mainstream, suddenly lumped together with the ubiquitous Psy and his looming disappearance.

In hindsight, it's easy to pinpoint the qualities that made "Gangnam Style" such an object of fascination and idolatry. Blogs, newspaper articles, even other YouTube videos have all offered their explanations. However, given the notoriously formula-driven mind-set of the Korean pop industry and its calculated strategy for breaking out onto American televisions and concert venues, it would have been nearly impossible to predict that Psy, a portly thirty-four-year-old rapper riding on seemingly excessively local references to Korean leisure culture would have been the one to do it when the sculpted Rain and the choreographed Wonder Girls couldn't. In fact, Psy's presence in the Korean entertainment industry has from the beginning run against the traditional stakeholders of Hallyu and K-pop, incensing governmental bodies, record labels, and independent watchdog groups for obscene lyrics and the promotion of lifestyles deemed inappropriate for youth. He was known as a double dropout from American universities (Boston University, Berklee College of Music), a pot-smoker, and a military conscription-dodger. Like many acts in Korean pop, Psy was famous for distinctive, expressive dancing, but with a dose of mockery: an excess of energy, a swagger to the point of exhaustion, and as flaunted in his "Right Now" (2010) video, a chubby man in a muscle suit looking deeply into the camera daring us to look away. If traditional pop massproduces desires, Psy has us desire his mass. But the joke's neither on him nor the viewer, as it is in a parody like Weird Al's "Fat" (1988). In Psy's videos, the singer's agile, throbbing round body is always juxtaposed with the carbon-copied ones: the lean b-boys and the supermodel-shaped vixens. And it's Psy who's the leader of the pack, the spark for celebration or dancing in the streets, the pied piper of the pop wannabes. The joke's on the K-pop formula itself: behind every beautiful girl or boy group is a decked-out chubby thirtysomething with the fastest, freshest, and most fabulous moves of all.

With 2012's "Gangnam Style," Psy's leadoff single to his sixth album, the joke is extended to Seoul's glitzy Gangnam District, its horse-owners, Benz-drivers, and yoga-practitioners—and the sexy ladies who love them. It's the perfect target for the image-driven Psy. The song's video begins with a shot of a plane and a fawning woman reflected on Psy's sunglasses; luxury surrounds but doesn't faze him, for he's sipping drinks under an umbrella on the beach, as revealed to us by the camera that suddenly zooms to a wider view of his surroundings, a comedic trope repeated four more times later in the video to juxtapose the portly Psy with what culture tells us should be "luxury living." Prancing Psy + Seoul World Trade Center. Creepy Psy + man relaxing in spa. Throughout, Psy struts with an uncommon force, arms flailing and feet bouncing just a bit harder than any other dancer in the shot; he's both the embodiment of everything over the top about the Gangnam lifestyle, as well as the only character in the video who seems to self-consciously appreciate that it's all a performance. These moments are punctuated by moments of environmental excess—a wind machine blowing sticky white material, a spontaneous combustion, slow-motion seduction—that seem the culmination of Psy's exploding energy. The pulsating images of what cultural critic Hua Hsu (2012) calls the video's "vigorous euphoria" are matched by a song whose structure seems designed to thrust the listener from toe-tapping joy to arm-waving bliss to body-shaking delirium and finally to chant-along numbness. The song has an elaborate density ("wall-of-buzzsaw," according to Hsu) that ignites and cools with robotic precision, and is textured by Psy's buzz-phrases ("oppan Gangnam style," "hey, sexy lady!") and comically assured rap-boasting.

For the non-Korean-comprehending audience, Psy's lyrics of upscale romancing are indecipherable, but his cocksure verbal declamation manages to communicate enough for most international listeners. But nothing seemed to better express everything/nothing, while also catapulting "Gangnam Style" into the stratosphere, than the video's signature dance move. Early in the video, Psy is seen marching down a stable, surrounded by horses. He then breaks into a gallop, legs arched open and wrists overlapping and bobbing as if controlling the reins of a horse. In a later variation of the gallop in the video, one arm is extended upward moving in a lasso motion, while the other is horizontal and held toward the chest. The "horse dance," as Psy calls the move in an address at Oxford University (Oxford Union 2012), is performed with a determined seriousness (aided by Psy's ever-present sunglasses), if not a manic seriousness, again juxtaposing the ludicrous with the self-important luxury symbolized by the Gangnam District. Beyond mere mockery though, the horse dance is captivating as a sort of glorious mindless movement. Formally, the move has a simplicity and novelty that invites imitation, which is punctuated by the video's ending in which two lines of ordinary people (a chef, boxer, college graduate, cosplayer, among many others) join Psy in the dance. And yet its awkwardness and unusualness make the dance difficult to perfect, let alone to perform with Psy's swagger, as the video's ending group dance also reveals.

On July 15, 2012, the "Gangnam Style" video was released on the "officialpsy" YouTube channel. The video helped make the song a sensation in Korea, where it peaked on the Mnet and Gaon charts by the end of July for record label YG Entertainment. After gaining traction among K-pop fans around the world, the video was shared on several notable American websites between July 28 and August 3: Reddit, Gawker, Daily Beast, and finally, the sites for CNN and the *Wall Street Journal*. Fueling the excitement during those days were notable blog and Twitter endorsements from music celebrities as diverse as former British pop-idol Robbie Williams ("TRY WATCHING THIS AND NOT SMILING I DARE YOU"), American opera-pop star Josh Groban ("It's a Gangnam Style world, we're just living in it. Amazing video"), and American hip-hop mainstay T-Pain ("Words cannot even describe how amazing this video is"). These early notices, essentially social media "shares" on a mainstream platform, expressed mostly the kind

Fig. 12. Psy introducing the horse dance. (From https://www.youtube.com/watch?v=9bZkp7q19f0.)

of hyperbolic statements that get other shares moving: "Best music video of the year?" asked Gawker (Zimmerman 2012); "Quite possibly the most incredible music video ever made," joked The High Definite (Endswell 2012). Enabled by Facebook shares and Twitter retweets, the "Gangnam Style" video hit 10 million views by the end of this original blast of international notice.

In August and September, the video entered full acceleration mode. Early August saw the video receive a remarkable million views per day. By the end of September, it was receiving over 10 million daily views. Psy made his first U.S. appearance at a Los Angeles Dodgers baseball game on August 20. On August 22, Psy appeared on VH1's *Big Morning Buzz Live* and more significantly, on September 10, he appeared on the high-profile *Ellen DeGeneres Show* alongside Britney Spears. In both television appearances, Psy's on-screen role was to provide simple instructions about how to perform the horse dance, turning fascination with the dance into an incitement to mimicry. Not that the move needed the help, but Psy turned the attention to the viewer, literally asking Ellen DeGeneres' audience to stand up and try out the gallop.

Meanwhile, YouTube users were doing exactly that, posting videos of themselves doing the dance. Possibly the first to do so were Canadian expats in Korea Simon and Martina Stawski, who run the English-language

Korean culture site EatYourKimchi (2012), and who posted a parody video on July 23. Soon, parodies were shared as vivaciously as Psy's original video and became phenomena in themselves, from a lo-fi August 26 video of lifeguards dancing in and around a suburban swimming pool (Roaboat 2012),[2] to a perky August 30 reenactment featuring the duck mascot of the University of Oregon (Goducksdotcom 2012), to a September 1 video featuring babies (including one in Psy's signature blue tuxedo jacket) and their dancing, diaper-disposing, carriage-pushing mothers (Whatsupelle 2012). Many of these early parodies took advantage of the "style" of Psy's video, adapting the juxtaposition comedy format to satirize seemingly any lifestyle possible, in these cases suburban swimming, college mascoting, and yuppie parenting. "Gangnam Style" provided professions, localities, and other identity groups a formula for self-deprecation and self-affirmation before a hungry, international online viewership. In the early months, it seemed that every day saw yet another viral parody, which then did its part to turn those not yet aware back to Psy's original video, adding to its skyrocketing pageviews. Also doing its part was Psy's own mid-September U.S. media tour, which kicked off with the *Ellen* appearance, followed by spots on *TMZ*, NBC's *Today* show, *Saturday Night Live*, and *Chelsea Lately*. On September 20, Guinness World Records crowned "Gangnam Style" the "most liked" video in YouTube history (Barrett 2012). The next day, entertainment site *E!* called "Gangnam Style" "officially over" (Boone 2012).

October to December 2012 could be called the phenomenon's "officially over" months, by which one could mean the months in which timing, momentum, and the sense of the inevitable fall were essential to keeping "Gangnam Style" relevant on the air and online. TV parodies and appearances had to be prime time (*Glee*, *Dancing with the Stars*, *South Park*, Country Music Association Awards), and not just daytime and late night. Celebrity mentions had to be of the highest order—Justin Bieber, Shah Rukh Khan, Cristiano Ronaldo, Ai Weiwei, Ban Ki-moon—to warrant a retweet. With multiple parodies appearing online daily, they were the ones by celebrity reenactment artists (like the Cebu Dancing Inmates from the Philippines) that rose to the surface. Suddenly, creativity and cute parodies of other life "styles" were not enough; there needed to be timeliness and a sense of urgency. The November U.S. election, for instance, provided fodder for parody and Internet buzz. Late-night host Jay Leno used the video to mock Mitt Romney's difficulty appealing to young voters at the Republic National Convention (Tonightshownbc Aug. 2012). The comedy site College Humor released a video entitled "Mitt Romney

Style," which lampoons the candidate by comparing his elite background (and his wife's penchant for equestrian sports) to Psy's Gangnam (Collegehumor 2012). On the day of the final debate between the candidates, animated Obama and Romney engaged in a virtual "dance-off" in another video (ItsOnBTV 2012). Finally, in the most urgent of references, on Election Day President Obama told a New Hampshire radio DJ that he'd seen the video and "can do that move" (Fendrich 2012).

That Obama's public statement was national news was not just a testament to the video's popularity at the highest levels of society. Rather, it was a symbol of the video's utility and short-term exploitability, which had already permeated the market in the form of digital downloads, video games, and Halloween costumes. References to the video in shares and tweets were no longer of the "greatest video ever" variety. The video that was once introduced in news articles and blog entries with the enthusiasm of "In case you missed it . . ." (Thunderstix 2012) was now introduced with the knowing sarcasm of "Unless you've been living under a rock . . ." (*New York Post* 2012). Not only was the Internet teeming with "Gangnam," users were self-conscious that the saturation point was near. Nobody's under the rock. It's over. Past tense. And of course these proclamations of the video's death took on a momentum of their own. If the early references to the video were a race to see who could mention the video first, the later ones were a race to see who could first declare its time of death or scapegoat the celebrity performance or amateur video that killed off the last modicum of cool the video still seemed to possess. There was communal pleasure to be had in bemoaning the video's omnipresence, especially against the looming deadline after which even bemoaning would be considered old news. The video rode this postmortem pleasure all the way to one billion views by December 21, well ahead of its nearest competition, making it the most-viewed video in the history of YouTube.

What has gone relatively unremarked is the extent to which Gangnam stopped being just a social media phenomenon, and even not just a traditional media phenomenon, but a real-life one. In these later months, the impetus to hop online and search "Gangnam Style" on YouTube was often in response to a real-world incident. Grandchildren would show their bemused (and non YouTubing) grandparents the video that inspired the dance they were doing during Thanksgiving dinner, for instance. Partiers would have to show the video to rabbis and priests to explain what they were going to do during bar mitzvahs and weddings. Tens of thousands of sports fans were introduced, however unwittingly, to football players' horse-riding touchdown celebrations or to the "Gangnam Cam" at Philadelphia 76ers home games. Suddenly, the crowning moment of Hallyu 2.0 became a bizarre, nontechnological, and to some extent de-ethnicized, spectacle. The funny-sexy horse-riding was performed as a ritualistic collective dance in moments of religious celebration and at all-American sporting rituals. Offline, it gave families something to talk/dance about across generations. Flash mobs wove the dance and song into the fabric of daily life; just beneath the surface of shopping, strolling, and going to school was the possibility of a "Gangnam Style" breakout. Corporations, nonprofits, and business associations would recruit horse dancers for their events to seem "with it" (and not under a rock) or just to get employees, clients, and supporters "going" to Psy's catchy beats. In this environment of being "caught up" to what the kids were doing, going online to see the video was a means of being coeval with the offline world.

There's more to coevality, though, than just keeping up with the latest fads. The online and offline mimicry (or "reverse mimicry" if we heed Homi Bhabha's colonial interpretation of the concept) of the horse dance reveals discrepancies of power that go beyond cool kids versus square adults. "Gangnam Style" is a perceptively Korean production, Gangnam is a district in Seoul, and Psy was born Park Jae-sang in Korea. While Korean pop culture has grown in popularity among diasporic, niche, and cult audiences in places like the United States, it is far from accepted in the mainstream, just as most of contemporary Asian culture more broadly has not found favor in mainstream American television, film, and music. Is the appetite for "Gangnam Style" then a realization that America has to "catch up" to Korea in the realm of music video amazingness? Are the American parodies and reenactments a way of mimicking the new cultural torchbearer?

These suggestions, while exciting for K-pop fans and stakeholders in the Korean national-institutional campaign to promote Korean culture internationally, don't adequately account for the ways in which the idea of "catching up" in a twenty-four-hour newsfeed culture is precisely the game itself, and that musical novelties and viral stars are only valuable insomuch as their expiration—the proverbial fifteen minutes of fame—is anticipated by all so we can make room for the next act. Sue Collins (2008, 95) writes of the "temporal flexibility" of the dispensable celebrity, and the way in which the industry itself has structured the new second-tier star's rise and fall into a larger system of celebrity scarcity. Collins describes the new star system's stratification between A-list celebrities and lesser ones that come from the pool of amateurs, reality show participants, and outsiders. The system thrives on the sense of "anyone-can-make-it" democracy (which includes racial/ethnic diversity) embodied by the lesser celebrities, but by constructing them as inherently inferior to the A-listers, is able to maintain the scarcity of "true" celebrities and thus keep their values high. The quick-paced revolving door of the dispensable celebrity keeps the star system intact while producing the illusion of access and diversity.

In the case of Psy, mimicry was one of the mainstream's strategies for accentuating his novelty and, consciously or not, keeping him at the lower strata of celebrity, alongside other amateurs and song-and-dance oddballs. In so many of Psy's early American TV appearances, he is brought onstage to teach the celebrity host how to do the horse dance and thus take entertainment value away from himself. As he teaches Britney Spears and Ellen DeGeneres the steps on TV, it's clear who the "real" celebrities are, because they're the ones who get applause for effort, whereas Psy is the one to bring external interest to familiar, preexisting celebrity. The true purpose of Psy's appearance became apparent in an unanticipated on-air aside. Before Psy enters the scene, DeGeneres reminds the audience that Britney Spears had tweeted that she wanted to learn the dance. The host then surprises Spears by bringing Psy out from behind the curtain for the purpose of fulfilling Spears's wishes. The three of them line up and Ellen is giddy for the instruction to begin. Unexpectedly, Psy interjects and says, "By the way, can I introduce myself? Not just dancing." DeGeneres agrees, at which point Psy looks to the audience and says, "I'm Psy from Korea, how are you?" (TheEllenShow 2012). By speaking, in confident English, when he was expected merely to work, Psy exposed the existing celebrity stratification, and perhaps even threatened it. And yet, through the show's mimicry games that followed, Psy was immediately reduced to mere trainer to the stars.

At other times, the mainstream did not even need Psy's physical presence to bolster the "real" A-list through "Gangnam Style." During an appearance on Jay Leno's *Tonight Show*, Hugh Jackman, in town to promote the musical *Les Miserables*, boasted to Leno that Psy had taught him how to do the dance, and he proceeds to demonstrate it for the host and for the audience (TonightshowNBC Dec. 2012). Though they joke that Jackman does the dance incorrectly, Jackman gets the applause—for effort or for demonstrating that he's "with it," however awkwardly and even self-deprecatingly. Jackman's performance of "catching up" to "Gangnam Style" was thus another high-profile reminder that Psy was a novelty to be subsumed and discarded so that the real celebrities could go on doing what they do best.

It's tempting to make the analogy that, as the "real celebrity" is revealed to be in the position of power, so is the "real race" of American celebrity revealed. Psy's Koreanness and Asianness is discarded, as is his budding celebrity, when the dance is subsumed by established white (and sometimes black) celebrities and Psy is marginalized from the stage altogether. As "Gangnam Style" is mimicked throughout the United States, it becomes increasingly perceived online, on TV, and in real life as "transcending race"—that is, turning white. The lyrics may be predominantly Korean, but most fans have no problem with *oppan Gangnam style* or "hey, sexy lady!" while they do a "universal" dance that even the president of the United States claims he can do. Most revealing of the shifting national/racial identity of the phenomenon is the aftermath of Psy's past "anti-American" comments, discovered in an early December by the media. As those reports detail, in 2004, Psy told a Korean audience, in Korean, "Kill those fucking Yankees who have been torturing Iraqi captives," among other incendiary comments. Surprisingly, after a quick apology, Psy escaped further scrutiny by the American media and public. But it could be that, by December, the United States had already annexed "Gangnam Style" and in Americans' minds Psy was already discarded or at least on his way out as a one-hit wonder.

But in fact, the Internet was ready to racialize "Gangnam Style" when tempted. Most notoriously, following Psy's live performance of the song with MC Hammer (a brilliant pairing in celebration of celebrity dispensability) at the American Music Awards on November 18, the twitter-verse erupted with tweets like "I'm pretty sure this is called the American Music Awards #gobacktoasia" and "this is an AMERICAN MUSIC AWARD show not fucking chink music awards" (Public Shaming 2012). Comments like these, as well as their less overtly offensive variations, have triggered defensive positions from critics, especially Asian American ones, who suspect that Psy's mainstream popularity stems from a desire to see Asian masculinity as uncool, clownish, and nonthreatening.[3] In these critiques, Psy is compared to caricatures ranging from Mickey Rooney in *Breakfast at Tiffany's* to William Hung on *American Idol* to Ken Jeong in *The Hangover*. For these critics, many of whom actually admit to enjoying the song, Psy is not just one in a revolving door of dispensable celebrities, but also the latest in the revolving door of stereotypical Asians. In these analyses, the death of "Gangnam Style" only means another one is just around the corner. Other Asian American critics, who have chosen not to enter the chorus against what some see as racism, have responded instead by ignoring the phenomenon for as long as they could get away with it. The anonymous blogger at Ask a Korean! (2012) wrote about his attempt to wait out the storm: "The Korean tried. He really tried to avoid the fad. He thought this was going to blow over in a few days, and everyone will feel a bit silly afterward. But no." Phil Yu from the ever-popular site Angry Asian Man also quipped, "I've been trying to avoid all things 'Gangnam Style'" (Sept. 2012) and forced himself to do the "obligatory 'Gangnam Style' post" a whole month after the video was first posted (Aug. 2012). These critics mistimed the end of "Gangnam Style." As is the case with so much pesky "Asian" culture that calls on Asian American commentators as "ethnic informants," it's sometimes impossible to wait it out given the aggressive incitement to discourse that is race and meme culture in the United States. For those Americans who have relatives that look like rotund Korean troublemakers, or who might be called "Psy" in the schoolyard just as they've been called "Long Duk Dong," "Daniel-San," "Jackie Chan," and "Yao Ming" in the past, this spectacular, hilarious, heart-pumping, and thoroughly amazing track couldn't die sooner.

And yet there was a steady legion of Asian Americans who boldly took to the Internet to embrace "Gangnam Style"—albeit on their own terms. Their medium was not the blog, but video. They didn't try to "beat" the temporality of viral videos the way commentators like Phil Yu tried to do. Instead, they saw in the video's goofy song-of-the-hour charm an opportunity to capture a quirky view of life in all of its ephemerality. If more jaded bloggers chose to wait out the storm of viral-ness's short-term fever, these Asian Americans jumped on the bandwagon, steered it, and indulged in the speed of it all. Ironically, one of the first "Gangnam Style" parody videos produced primarily by Asian Americans was made on the occasion of an event that traditionally symbolizes the opposite of temporary and dispensable frivolity: a marriage.

In late August 2012, as "Gangnam Style" was gaining traction but before Psy's *Ellen* appearance, San Francisco Bay Area couple Stephani Nguyen and Jeremy Ueno were in search of a song that could be the basis of a video celebrating their marriage and their wedding party. A mere week before their September 2 wedding, they stumbled upon Psy's "Gangnam Style," which they noticed had over 15 million views on YouTube.[4] Though neither of them were K-pop fans, they immediately picked "Gangnam Style." In collaboration with Asian American Bay Area production company Lightbulb Videography, the couple concocted a plan to parody Psy's video in various locations throughout San Francisco. As seen in their final video, the locations are casually ordinary: a kid's park, a trolley, a parking lot (LightbulbEnt Sept. 10, 2012). Meanwhile, the settings are populated by the effortless multiculturalism of the wedding party and the random bystanders drawn by and into the horse dancing. In short, this is a self-conscious take on "San Francisco Style," celebrated with vivacity and a taste for mischief. The video incorporates a "flash mob" mentality, embracing an aesthetic of stolen locations, rubbernecking passersby, and a mundaneness shattered by music and dance. In the context of Asian American representation, Stephani, Jeremy, and their friends are no stereotypes. They are simultaneously ordinary and spectacular. In their struts, gestures, and stolen Psy-isms, they seize the opportunity to play the role of a star—even a fifteen-minute one from a production culture of "temporal flexibility." The video seems to acknowledge that a wedding is none other than the one day in an average person's life to be a superstar; referencing a fleeting sensation like Psy doesn't undermine the convincingness of their real-life stardom, but rather propels it to furious heights in a flash of jubilation that everyone can immediately feel and identify thanks to Psy's popularity.

For the group of friends that made up the wedding party, the production of the "Gangnam Style" parody video was also a celebration of friendship in an era of time-space compression. Only five of the ten members of the wedding party were based in the San Francisco area, so the viralness and shareability of the YouTube video gave it legs in the week the team had to prepare remotely. The video was shot on two days: four hours on the Thursday before the Sunday wedding, and just before the wedding itself. Wardrobe was bring-your-own-ridiculousness and the actions were largely improvised on the spot. The video's acceleration as an Internet phenomenon in many ways was mirrored in the speed and giddiness of the shoot. Beyond just borrowing the original video's high-speed antics, the wedding video also borrowed its exploding momentum as a beacon of collective ecstasy. It's an elation that apparently quickly brought the entire wedding party together in the spirit of collaboration. As groom Jeremy Ueno puts it, "If anything, [the video] symbolizes that my wife and friends are a lot of fun and we are lucky to have these great people in our lives that would travel across the country to be with us on this special day and dress up and act stupid in front of the camera." The corollary to Ueno's statement is that not only is the wedding a special occasion for friends to all be together, but that they will all soon be separate again too. For these friends, the wedding is a temporary state of bliss that the videographers strove to capture in all of its energy, and Psy's "Gangnam Style" was the perfect crystallization of that momentary excitement. As evidenced by the wedding video and the circumstances of its production, the fleetingness of "Gangnam Style" gave many of those who mimicked Psy's original video a ver-

Fig. 13. Stephani, Jeremy, and friends doing the horse dance in San Francisco. (From https://www.youtube.com/watch?v=0yr7FW1S5e0.)

nacular with which to memorialize the present—to celebrate it, laugh at it, and then let it go so as to clear the way for the future. The birth of Stephani+Jeremy must be at the cost of the inevitable but glorious death of "Gangnam Style." R.I.P. "Gangnam Style."

NOTES

1. In February 2013, "R.I.P. Gangnam Style" was the "Top Comment" on several extremely popular "Harlem Shake" YouTube videos.

2. The posting of the video led to the termination of the lifeguards. After the media reported their firing, the lifeguards were reinstated.

3. For instance, see Anderson 2012; refresh_daemon 2012; Shigematsu 2012; Lu 2012; and Liu 2012.

4. Details about the background of the production come from Jeremy Ueno, email message to author, June 25, 2013. See also LightbulbEnt (September 14, 2012).

WORKS CITED

Anderson, Crystal "CeeFu." August 27, 2012. "What Does Gangnam Style Mean for (the) US." High Yellow. http://highyellow.me/2012/08/27/what-does-gangnam-style-mean-for-the-us/.

Ask a Korean! September 25, 2012. "The Obligatory Gangnam Style Post." http://aska-korean.blogspot.com/2012/09/the-obligatory-gangnam-style-post.html.

Barrett, Dan. September 20, 2012. "'Gangnam Style' Holds Guinness World Record for Most 'Liked' Video in YouTube History." Guinness World Records. http://www.guinnessworldrecords.com/news/2012/9/gangnam-style-now-most-liked-video-in-youtube-history-44977/.

Bellini, Jarett. October 15, 2012. "Apparently This Matters: R.I.P. 'Gangnam Style.'" CNN Tech. http://www.cnn.com/2012/10/12/tech/web/apparently-this-matters-gangnam-style/index.html.

Boone, John. September 21, 2012. "Why Gangnam Style Is Officially Over (Already)!" E! http://www.eonline.com/news/347518/why-gangnam-style-is-officially-over-already.

Carbone, Nick. October 1, 2012. "Google's Eric Schmidt Dances 'Gangnam Style,' Killing the Meme for the Rest of Us." Time. http://newsfeed.time.com/2012/10/01/googles-eric-schmidt-dances-gangnam-style-killing-the-meme-for-the-rest-of-us/.

Collegehumor. October 8, 2012. "Mitt Romney Style (Gangnam Style Parody)." YouTube. http://www.youtube.com/watch?feature=player_embedded&v=yTCRwi71_ns.

Collins, Sue. 2008. "Making the Most of 15 Minutes: Reality TV's Dispensable Celebrity." *Television and New Media* 9 (2): 87–110.

Eat Your Kimchi. 2012. "Psy—Gangnam Style: Kpop Music Monday." http://www.eatyourkimchi.com/kpop-psy-gangnamstyle/.

Endswell. July 29, 2012. "Psy—Gangnam Style (video)." The High Definite. http://www.thehighdefinite.com/2012/07/psy-gangnam-style-video/.

Fendrich, Howard. November 6, 2012. "'Gangnam Style,' Obama Style?" Associated Press—The Big Story. http://bigstory.ap.org/article/gangnam-style-obama-style.

Goducksdotcom. August 30, 2012. "Gangnam Style Parody—the Oregon Duck." YouTube. http://www.youtube.com/watch?v=mDpgzn7KuzE.

Hall, Richard. December 12, 2012. "'Gangnam Style' death prompts warning to middle-aged men not to attempt the vigorous dance." *The Independent.* http://www.independent.co.uk/news/uk/home-news/gangnam-style-death-prompts-warning-to-middleaged-men-not-to-attempt-the-vigorous-dance-8411905.html.

Hsu, Hua. September 24, 2012. "Why Psy's 'Gangnam Style' Is a Hit With Listeners Who've Never Heard of K-pop." Vulture. http://www.vulture.com/2012/09/psys-k-pop-crossover.html.

ItsOnBTV. October 22, 2012. "OBAMA ROMNEY—GANGNAM STYLE." YouTube. http://www.youtube.com/watch?v=WdFn6xzdZCU.

LightbulbEnt. September 10, 2012. "PSY—Gangnam Style Parody—Bay Area Wedding Music Video." YouTube. http://www.youtube.com/watch?v=0yr7FW1S5e0.

LightbulbEnt. September 14, 2012. "PSY—Gangnam Style Parody Lightbulb Videography Interview with Moving99.7 NOW." YouTube. http://www.youtube.com/watch?v=-8C5q1-q3D0.

Liu, Patricia. December 13, 2012. "Gangnam Style, Racism, and the Evolving Asian Stereotype." Call Me Patricia. http://www.callmepatricia.com/2012/12/13/gangnam-style-racism-and-the-evolving-asian-stereotype/.

Lu, Jenny. October 2012. "Gangnam Style: Analysis of a Sudden Pop Culture Sensation." Hardboiled 16.1. http://hardboiled.berkeley.edu/archived-issues/issue-16–1/gangnam-style-analysis-of-a-sudden-pop-culture-sensation/.

New York Post. December 7, 2012. "WATCH: Best of 'Gangnam Style' 2012." http://www.

nypost.com/p/entertainment/music/watch_best_of_gangnam_style_KlOI-YXzSmHS1HzUpOQchNO.

officialpsy. July 15, 2012. "PSY—GANGNAM STYLE M/V." YouTube. http://www.youtube.com/watch?v=9bZkp7q19f0.

OxfordUnion. November 9, 2012. "PSY | Address Highlights | Oxford Union." YouTube. http://www.youtube.com/watch?v=Nsh1Ej2ADA4.

Public Shaming. November 19, 2012. "Oppa ~~Gangnam~~ Racist Style." Public Shaming. http://publicshaming.tumblr.com/post/36049416072/oppa-gangnam-racist-style-south-korean-pop-star.

refresh_daemon. September 20, 2012. "PSY and the Acceptable Asian Man." Racialicious. http://www.racialicious.com/2012/09/20/psy-and-the-acceptable-asian-man/.

Roaboat. August 26, 2012. "Lifeguard Style (Gangnam Style Remake)." YouTube. http://www.youtube.com/watch?v=fpVmMtUlKQ.

Shepherd, Tory. December 13, 2012. "How Gangnam Style Is Linked to the End of Times." News.com.au. http://www.news.com.au/features/mayan-apocalypse-2012/how-gangnam-style-is-linked-to-the-end-of-times/story-fngjq0bi-1226535943653.

Shigematsu, Tetsuro. October 7, 2012. "Why Asians Aren't Dancing in the Streets Gangnam Style." Huffington Post. http://www.huffingtonpost.ca/tetsuro-shigematsu/gangnam-style-psy-asians-stereotypes-ken-jeong_b_1944294.html.

TheEllenShow. September 10, 2012. "Surprise! Britney Learns 'Gangnam Style' from Psy." YouTube. http://www.youtube.com/watch?v=QZmkU5Pg1sw.

Thunderstix. August 1, 2012. "T-Pain, Robbie Williams, Josh Groban, and Gawker Show Love for Psy's 'Gangnam Style.'" Soompi. http://www.soompi.com/2012/08/01/t-pain-robbie-williams-josh-groban-and-gawker-show-love-for-psys-gangnam-style/.

Tonightshownbc. August 31, 2012. "Romney RNC Entrance—The Tonight Show with Jay Leno." YouTube. http://www.youtube.com/watch?v=LUUGa0vBdTg.

Tonightshownbc. December 13, 2012. "Hugh Jackman Teaches Jay Gangnam Style—The Tonight Show with Jay Leno." YouTube. http://www.youtube.com/watch?v= 7Mxx-B3uVe8Y.

Whatsupelle. September 1, 2012. "Baby Gangnam Style Parody feats. Baby Psy & LA Moms." YouTube. http://www.youtube.com/watch?v=7iheCrwQQlI.

Wood, Mikael. December 31, 2012. "Psy Threatens to Retire 'Gangnam Style' on New Year's Eve." *Los Angeles Times*. http://www.latimes.com/entertainment/music/posts/la-et-ms-psy-gangnam-style-new-years-eve-20121231,0,2662299.story.

Yu, Phil. August 22, 2012. "Obligatory 'Gangnam Style' Post." Angry Asian Man. http://blog.angryasianman.com/2012/08/so-theres-this-thing-called-gangnam.html.

Yu, Phil. September 5, 2012. "Umma Gangnam Style: Mike Song's Mom's Got the Moves." Angry Asian Man. http://blog.angryasianman.com/2012/09/umma-gangnam-style-mike-songs-moms-got.html.

Zimmerman, Neetzan. July 30, 2012. "Did This Underground Hip Hop Artist from South Korea Just Release the Best Music Video of the Year?" Gawker. http://gawker.com/5930283/did-this-underground-hip-hop-artist-from-south-korea-just-release-the-best-music-video-of-the-year.

Afterword

Before the Wave: The Difference and Indifference of Hallyu Beta through 2.0

Abé Mark Nornes

Hallyu Beta

Coediting this volume has been an interesting experience, because it inspired me to think back and through my own relationship to Korean media. I became interested in Asian media—cinema, to be specific—in the early 1980s when I happened to stay in Taiwan for a month at the height of the Taiwan New Cinema. By that point, I had already seen some of the high points of 1950s Japanese cinema, but this was the first time that Asian film had any kind of simultaneity with my own world. I was moved by the films of Hou Hsiao-hsien, Edward Yang, and others, and watching them in theaters with their home audiences was absolutely exhilarating. Up to that point, the only Asian films that reached me in the northern Colorado cow town of Fort Collins were Japanese and Indian art films. These works were invariably vetted by a long process of festival runs and then art film distribution deals, so my experience of them was marked by a significant and palpable *lag*. Few films were less than four or five years old before I had a chance to see them; most came out a decade or two earlier. As a matter of course, none of them were Korean.

Not long after my sojourn to Taiwan I found myself in graduate school at the University of Southern California. I had decided to specialize in Japanese cinema, but was also determined to learn what I could about the other film cultures of Asia. So little was written about cinemas other than Japan that mastering the English-language literature on Asian cinema was a matter of a semester's worth of reading. The only book on Korean cinema was Lee Young-il and Choe Young-chol's overtly nationalist *The History of Korean Cinema* (1988). It left me thinking Korean cinema must be far more interesting than their book suggests.

The only way to test this suspicion was to watch films, but this was not a straightforward matter. This was the tail end of the era when 35mm movie theaters in Little Tokyo and Chinatown catered to their respective ethnic communities. I haunted those theaters weekly. However, Korean films posed a special challenge. Thankfully, USC bordered Koreatown, and I borrowed snowy VHS dubs from nearby grocery stores. However, I then learned that the Korean consulate had a nice collection of subtitled 16mm prints, and they were happy to lend them out at a simple request. It felt like hitting pay dirt.

Looking back, it seems rather extraordinary. Here was a foreign consulate sending film prints to a lowly graduate student, just because he expressed interest. It is a long way from the government support JungBong Choi describes in his essay or, for that matter, the contemporary soul-searching Dal Yong Jin describes around the vexing issue of copyright. Back then the consulate's collection was under the radar, while the dominant ethos of the industry itself was about circling the proverbial wagons. Back in Korea the government was on a decidedly defensive footing. The stories about South Korea in *Variety* and *Hollywood Reporter* were either about the latest government quota for Hollywood product, or about unions releasing snakes into theaters showing American films. Before the wave, it made more sense to protect oneself from the incursion of American popular culture (not to mention Japanese products), rather than make any serious attempt to crack the European and American markets.

Looking back at this early moment in the 1980s and 1990s—before the sea change that spawned the wave—we see that one of the key differences between then and now is the collapse of the temporal lag between media events over there and over here. Los Angeles was certainly better than Colorado, but it most definitely took years for films to make their way to the Korean grocery stores or consulates. One was grateful for any kind of access. How different from today's instant bitstreaming piracy and encyclopedic fansites, not to mention having every film festival catalog on the planet a click away.

Hallyu 1.0

At the turn of the century, the growing popularity of Korean music across the Asian region took a year or two to hit my consciousness. I happened to be living in Tokyo in 2002 and 2003, when BoA released her first Japanese studio album, *Listen to My Heart*, and NHK broadcasted *Winter Sonata* (Kyŏul yŏn'ga, 2002). Both were wildly popular. Hallyu had most definitely arrived on the shores of Japan. It was extraordinary to watch. Suddenly Korea was everywhere, as the PR machines backing the music and television industries were in high gear. I watched *Winter Sonata*, all twenty hours of it, dreaming of drinking games built on Choi Ji-woo's crying scenes—unable to enjoy said games because I couldn't find a single person to watch with me. I understood. This was a far cry from the artful sobriety of Im Kwon-taek or the political fervor of Kim Dong-won, the favorites of my crowd in Tokyo. It is also a far cry from the situation described in our essays by Youjeong Oh, Michelle Cho, Irina Lyan and Alon Levkowitz, and others. Not only have the audiences for Korean television proliferated around the globe, but the producers self-consciously construct both their industry and their programs with this global circulation in mind. Hallyu beta looks quite "provincial" in comparison.

Another striking thing about Hallyu 1.0 was a new vibe humming below the surface—a rhetoric of pride connected to South Korean pop culture's regional popularity. This has only amplified in the subsequent decade thanks to Hallyu's global spread. Indeed, I believe it quietly informs many of the essays in this book, and in ways far more subtle than all the examples of South Korean nationalism that the authors write about. It is actually a familiar dynamic to anyone who has studied film history.

We see this dynamic take root in most of the world beginning in the silent era, when Hollywood took a position of global dominance after World War I. Consider Japan, my own area of expertise. Being an imperial power sporting a highly capitalized economy, Japan swiftly developed one of the most vigorous film industries in the world within decades of cinema's invention. Before the late 1910s, the films were marked by local theatrical conventions and a more formalist logic of construction. This perturbed elite critics, who agitated for change in what came to be called the Pure Film Movement. They called for all sorts of changes, but at a fundamental level it all came down to a push to emulate Hollywood conventions. They called for a break with local conventions, such as those derived from kabuki, and wanted to purge the *onnagata* female impersonator and screen-side narrator called the *benshi* (*pyŏnsa* in Korean). When their narrative film took the shape of the Hollywood films they so loved, Japanese cinema would be shown in America and points beyond. And only then, they argued, would Japanese cinema be cinematic. What they desired, clearly, was a recognition by the other.[1] Value was indelibly linked to the foreign, and especially to Hollywood.

Fig. 14. "The Antichrist Numerology in Gangnam Style." (From http://www.
youtube.com/watch?v=oUbE34XjOgw.)

I sense a similar vibe in the discourses of Hallyu. It is certainly built deeply into government policies and proclamations, as well as in the PR of the entertainment industries. It is evidenced in entertainers' appearances on American television, or any number of Korean directors moving to Los Angeles. Naturally, at this level the nationalism connected to Hallyu is an overt and rather crude version found in the Pure Film dynamic and its global counterparts. But I also find it running softly through much of the academic discourse around the Hallyu phenomenon. Many writers, in this volume and elsewhere, regularly point to a given text's international popularity—albums sold, YouTube clicks—as evidence of the importance of their objects of study. One wonders how well this will age, once the wave breaks.

Hallyu 2.0

Social media supercharges Hallyu, sending it global . . . at least for the time being. Thinking back at the lag between the Korean premiere of a film by

Im Kwon-taek and my viewing of a 16mm dupe from the consulate, the most striking thing about Hallyu 2.0 is the virtual simultaneity of textual circulation. Everything is so immediate. Of course, at one level, this is due to the one-to-many- and many-to-many-points mode of distribution made possible by the proliferation of media platforms. However, the supercharging comes from other features, two of which seem particularly emphatic at this moment in Hallyu 2.0 and which can be powerfully illustrated by Psy's "Gangnam Style."

The first is "sharing," the ability for a consumer to become a distributor, (re) producer, or both at the click of the mouse. This has its roots in the VHS tape, when it became possible for people to dub films that caught their fancy and it became possible to possess moving image texts. When this technology first appeared, this early form of piracy was a powerful experience; one could line one's bookshelves with movies, when before this kind of collection was mainly the surreptitious domain of archivists who enjoyed access to film prints and optical printers.

This all feels rather quaint in the age of Hallyu 2.0. Today, after a text leaves its source—usually through a wide variety of routes—it gets *shared*, not simply *possessed*. Consumers create a digital copy. Some platforms allow them to bounce the text with the click of a button. Many actually "rip" it from the foundation of its maker and turn it into yet another source-point—a process that can proliferate swiftly and globally. Other consumers become producers themselves, taking the ripped digits and playing with them, revising, parodying, critiquing, riffing—transforming the original into something novel and infinitely prolific, sometimes wonderfully profligate.

"Gangnam Style" is surely the ur-text here. This was powerfully demonstrated during the creation of this book. The video was uploaded on YouTube's officialpsy channel on July 15, 2012, three months after the University of Michigan conference that kicked off this project. By the time essay manuscripts were due, many authors had written about the music video. Its popularity was too phenomenal to ignore. Its explosiveness was palpable to Sangjoon Lee and me, as every time we returned to a given manuscript we had to return to YouTube to adjust the latest view count. We finally had to give up—as of the writing of this sentence the figure stands at 1,978,344,771. That is over 300,000,000 more than when I began this section of the essay, and well on its way to 2 billion views. That a fundamentally novel mode of consumption was taking place was brought (literally) home to me on the eve of Psy's passing the billion views mark. My twelve-year-old son sat at his computer watching the video over and over

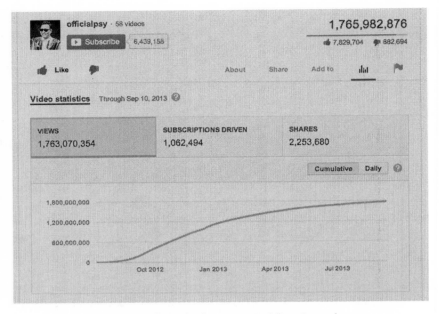

Fig. 15. YouTube's analytics for "Gangnam Style" on September 12, 2013

again, intent on playing his part, on participating in an immediate global event. (He was devastated when he had to go to bed before the counter turned 1 billion.)

The other striking thing about the supercharging of Hallyu 2.0 is the new twist it gives to "word of mouth." In the age of Hallyu beta and 1.0 this was a lucky by-product of the buzz created by marketing campaigns. Now it is the very point of marketing, and it rubs both ways for the producers of media. It is through the sharing-driven word-of-mouth made possible by social media that "Gangnam Style" circulated so intensely, so widely, and for so long. There was probably some kind of advertising campaign for "Gangnam Style"—after all, the music video form is nothing other than an advertising mechanism for audio recordings. However, the video slowly and progressively peeled away from that campaign and took a life of its own, occasionally given renewed vigor by the market engineering of concerts, television appearances, and print interviews. At the same time, word-of-mouth 2.0 can be as destructive as well. The YouTube analytics for Psy's follow-up "Gentleman" show a spike of curiosity after the video's release before falling flat on the floor of the graph.

Unlike the word-of-mouth of Hallyu 1.0, social media often leave a record of the chatter propelling texts around the world. For example, at the height of "Gangnam Style" popularity, the comments box on YouTube was an animated scroll. People around the world were registering their thoughts by the second. Even today the flow is impressive. YouTube puts the total count at 6,318,080.

One thematic thread stands out among all the others in these comments: race. The running conversation is punctuated by a staccato beat of (English-language) racist ranting. YouTube response videos weren't much better. One even performs a nutty numerological analysis of the video, arguing that God was warning us of the end times with Psy representing the anti-Christ (Fig. 14).[2] However, this being social media, every racist comment about "chinks" or "commies" was met with pushback from colorblind fans.[3] This dynamic itself could become the cultural by-product of Hallyu 2.0. For example, here is one YouTube comment by a user named Emily Lewis that spawned tens of thousands of comments, even today:

Reasons why Justin Bieber is better than this. 1. JB can at least speak english unlike_this Barbaric mongol 2. Never disrespect music by singing in an uncultured weird language 3 JB is actually cute and doesn't look like Kim Jongil. 4 JB can actually dance unlike the air humping in this video—5. JB is american so that means he's civilized.—6. JB is not communist like this guy.—7. JB's song's are actually good.—8. JB videos are 1# on all of YT!

Clearly meant to be provocative, these comments prompted a visit to the author's channel page, which revealed that "Emily Lewis" was a troll. That is to say, whoever posted the comments assumed a fake identity to write a fake post that was sure to throw the comments section into turmoil. One can attribute the ploy's success to the substantiveness of its underhanded critique. "Lewis" essentially summarized all the racist gibberish circulating around "Gangnam Style." It inspired tens of thousands of rebukes precisely because it was so "real."

Race is the part of this story—the story of Hallyu beta through 2.0—that seems missing from much of the scholarship of Korean popular culture heretofore. For example, in Kyung Hyun Kim's excellent *Virtual Hallyu: Korean Cinema of the Global Era*, race is a highlighted topic; however, Kim's discussion is primarily regional, not global, and is restricted to representations and not reception. A reconsideration of Hallyu in its 2.0 iteration inevitably orients us toward users and user-producers. This is ex-

Fig. 16. A Twitter exchange reacting to Psy's appearance on the American Music Awards

emplified by Hye Seung Chung's essay on a complex example from Japanese television and Brian Hu's essay on Psy in America.

What interests me, what seems quite fundamental to the entire history of Hallyu, is the pushback by fans—not brutish teenage tweeters or crazy Christians or the 882,594 people that gave "Gangnam Style" a thumbs down. And above and beyond the defensive and passionate fans, I am also fascinated by the indifference of the vast number of consumers who simply don't buy in.

When one looks at the fans of Hallyu, from American college students to middle-aged Japanese housewives, it is this racial and national difference that is part and parcel of the attraction. Hallyu presents an exceedingly complex dynamic between sameness and difference. In the Asian region, sameness sells; turn on a television for its parade of melodrama, sit-com, and variety shows and the similarity from Taipei to Tokyo to Seoul to Beijing is patently striking. At one level, this is surely a matter of producers mimicking what sells. As Roald Maliangkay's essay painstakingly demonstrates, the Korean industry constructed a talent factory floor that spit out version after version of the boy and girl band brand. Yet, despite these textual and industrial similarities, difference is a key ingredient for success. The platoons of gyrating girls may look strikingly similar in Taipei and Seoul, but the expertise of the fans allows them to pick out a subtle panoply of difference involving dress, gesture, language, hairstyle, musical idiom, and much, much more. For all its sameness, it is crucial that it is K-pop and not X-pop.

It seems to me the situation outside of the East Asian region is quite different, and here race is a crucial factor in the Hallyu difference. For fans out and about the globe—a clear and vast minority among all the consumers (or nonconsumers) of Hallyu—race can be a hook for identification among Asian Americans or a vague wellspring of fascination for others. There is also another group, and it is probably far larger than the fan base. Looking at the "Gangnam Style" reception in the English-speaking world, it is clear that much of the pleasure is driven by a camp sensibility: the enjoyment of watching a chubby Asian man with amazing moves, playing to his own failed seriousness at that. By way of comparison, it is likely that American audiences couldn't find the camp value in Girls' Generation when they famously bombed on *The Late Show with David Letterman*, thus bringing a potential crack at the U.S. market to thudding stumble.

Clearly, the vast audience watching Letterman's show that night had the reaction of the other guest, Bill Murray, who sauntered over to the group of girls looking utterly bored. So what of the people who meet Hallyu in its various iterations with a collective shrug? The essays in this collection repeatedly describe forays by Korean artists into Euro-American venues and sputtering, especially when it comes to the North American media environment. Why would this be, considering the fact that few American or British girl and boy groups are any more impressive than their Korean counterparts? Yet, each has met with different success. Actually, *indifference* is the constant here from Hallyu beta to 2.0; this has nothing at all to do with value and everything to do with race, geopolitics, and the unequal terms of modernity.

To invoke an earlier point, Hallyu producers, their fans—and, yes,

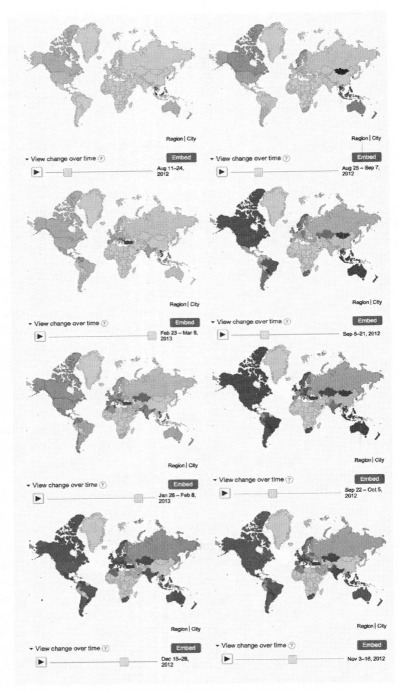

Fig. 17. Google's analytics graphically reveal the Psy tsunami.

their scholars—desire international success and the recognition by the other this implies. At the same time, this is a situation quite unlike that of nearly a century of world filmmakers aspiring to acknowledgment by Hollywood. Despite similar desires, Hallyu artists and producers do not necessarily assume that emulation of Euro-American styles—of dress, sound, or structure—is the first step toward recognition. On the contrary, what is quite striking about Hallyu is the circulation of a regional idiom in music, dance, television, movies, gesture, and genre. The products of Hallyu strikingly resemble what one finds in other parts of East Asia.

This is to say that Hallyu 2.0 is, ultimately, a regional phenomenon at heart. Despite the enthusiasm of a truly global assortment of fans—from Latin America to Israel—this globalized community clearly inhabits a limited, if lively, niche. For most of the world, Hallyu is but a series of gentle lapping waves on far-flung shores. However, the rhetoric Hallyu 1.0 and especially 2.0 presents the phenomenon as nothing less than a global tsunami. Arguably, "Gangnam Style" truly achieved a wave of that scale. Google's graphic analytics (fig. 15, starting from the upper left and moving clockwise) show the music video's tsunami starting in Korea and Southeast Asia, then jumping to Mongolia before slamming into North and South America; by the end of 2012 the search engine was lighting up globally before retreating to Southeast Asia.

If one looks at Psy and acknowledges the way his wave hit and then receded, leaving mud and emptiness, yes this image works quite nicely. However, in East Asia the metaphor actually works quite differently: that is because the waves of Hallyu emanate from the Korean peninsula, only to hit a complex continental shoreline and countless chains of islands. Each sends waves back and forth and in every which direction. This is the true dynamism of Hallyu, one that works quite differently at national, regional, and global levels.

It is this intricate vitality that the authors of this volume grapple with, eschewing a simple textual analysis of the films, TV shows, and music. The media ecology of the digital era has immeasurably enriched Korea's music, television, comics, and cinema, while radically diversifying its reception. This book is testament to that shift. Indeed, this is the Hallyu 2.0 difference, which naturally points us toward the reception context. It is the challenge these authors present to their readers; it was also the contest faced by the contributors themselves. The mindboggling complexity of Hallyu's reception—its global sweep, its multiplicity of (interconnected) media and distribution technologies, its seemingly innate ability to cut across gender, racial, linguistic, and generational boundaries—means any book that attempts to tackle the subject will be pulled in every which direction.

An edited volume like this lends itself to this centripetal energy. Without the charter of an obligatory, overarching argument, authors are relatively free to explore this wide-ranging territory from the worldview of their own particular discipline, generation, personal background, and whatever factors go into the choices scholars make when deciding on where to turn their intellectual investments. This mix was a conceptual conceit of this book (and a diversity of method I have exploited to issue this thoroughly subjective take on Hallyu beta through 2.0). The authors come to this topic from a wide variety of disciplinary and theoretical stances, ranging from the poststructural to the social scientific. For this reason, this afterword refuses to collate and summarize this heterogeneity, but rather trace its history from a particular point of view while celebrating the proliferation of approaches these scholars take to the same phenomenon. For it is simply fascinating to see a field of study transform before one's eyes, within one's life.

NOTES

1. This is the argument of Aaron Gerow's impressive *Visions of Modernity* (2010).
2. third eagle books, "Antichrist Numberology Gangnam Style," Youtube http://www.youtube.com/watch?v=oUbE34XjOgw, accessed September 12, 2013.
3. Although the pushback is heartening, much of it is marred by a misogyny as virulent as the racism it critiques.

WORKS CITED

Gerow, Aaron. 2010. *Visions of Modernity*. Berkeley: University of California Press.
Lee, Young-il, and Young-chol Choe. 1998. *The History of Korean Cinema*. Seoul: Ji-moondang.

Contributors

Michelle Cho (McGill University) is an Assistant Professor of East Asian Studies. Her work on genre translation, celebrity culture, and self-reflexive media appears in journals and edited volumes including *Cinema Journal* and *The Korean Popular Culture Reader* (Duke University Press, 2014). She is completing a book that analyzes the form and function of South Korean genre cinemas in the "Sunshine Policy" decade. Her second project examines the relationship between popular culture, populism, and the postpolitical in South Korea, with a focus on celebrity labor and media convergence.

JungBong Choi (New York University) is Assistant Professor in the Department of Cinema Studies, where he teaches theories of cultural globalization, transnational media/cinema/popular cultures, and the political economy of digital technologies. He authored *Digitalization of Television in Japan: State, Economy, and Discourse* (2008) and edited *Globalization, Television and Japan* (2010), *Unsettling the National in Korean Cinema* (2011), and *Of Transnational-Korean Cinematrix* (2012). His new book, *Global K-pop Fanthropology* (in Korean), and a coedited volume, *K-pop: the International Rise of the Korean Pop Music Industry*, will be published in 2014.

Hye Seung Chung is Assistant Professor of Film and Media Studies at Colorado State University. She is the coauthor of *Movie Migrations: Transnational Genre Flows and South Korean Cinema* (Rutgers University Press, 2015) and the author of *Kim Ki-duk* (University of Illinois Press, 2012) and *Hollywood Asian: Philip Ahn and the Politics of Cross-Ethnic Performance* (Temple University Press, 2006). Her writing has appeared in such journals as *Asian Cinema, Cinema Journal, Historical Journal of Film, Radio, and Television, Journal of Film and Video, Journal of Popular Film and Tele-*

vision, and *Post Script*. She is the coeditor of the *Journal of Japanese and Korean Cinema*.

Brian Hu is the Artistic Director of the Pacific Arts Movement and the San Diego Asian Film Festival. His writings have appeared in scholarly collections and journals such as *Screen*, *Velvet Light Trap*, and the *Journal of Chinese Cinemas*. He received his Ph.D. in Cinema and Media Studies at UCLA and has taught at the University of California San Diego, California State University Fullerton, and the University of San Diego.

Dal Yong Jin (Simon Fraser University) earned his Ph.D. from the Institute of Communications Research at the University of Illinois, Urbana Champaign. He is an Associate Professor at Simon Fraser University, and his major research and teaching interests are on new media and convergence, globalization and media, transnational cultural studies, new media and online gaming studies, and the political economy of media and culture. He is the author of several books, including *De-convergence of Global Media Industries* (2013, Routledge), *Korea's Online Gaming Empire* (2010, MIT Press) and *Hands On/Hands Off: The Korean State and the Market Liberalization of the Communication Industry* (2011, Hampton Press). Professor Jin's recent work has appeared in several scholarly journals, including *Media, Culture and Society*, *Games and Culture*, *Telecommunications Policy*, *Television and New Media*, *Information Communication and Society*, and *Javnost–the Public*.

Eun-Young Jung (University of California, San Diego) is an Assistant Professor of Integrative Studies. She received her Ph.D. in Ethnomusicology along with an Advanced Certificate in Asian Studies, followed by a postdoctoral fellowship in Japanese-Korean Studies, all at the University of Pittsburgh. Prior to her appointment at UCSD, Dr. Jung served as the Assistant Director at the Center for East Asian Studies, University of Wisconsin–Madison. Her research largely focuses on popular music and transnational dynamics in and from East Asia and music, media, race, and ethnicity in Asian American communities in the United States.

Sangjoon Lee (University of Michigan) is Assistant Professor in the Division of Broadcast and Cinema at the Wee Kim Wee School of Communication and Information, Nanyang Technological University in Singapore. Previously, he taught at the University of Michigan, Ann Arbor, where he was also the Curator of Korean Cinema NOW contemporary Korean film series and A2KIFF (Ann Arbor Korean Independent Film Festival) at the Nam Center for Korean Studies. He is currently working on a monograph, entitled *The Asian Film Festival and the Emergence of Transnational Cinema Network in Cold War Asia.*

Seung-Ah Lee (University of California, Los Angeles) is a Lecturer at UCLA and USC (University of Southern California) teaching Korean Studies. She earned her Ph.D. in the department of Asian Languages and Cultures at UCLA. Her scholarly interests include pre-modern popular culture and the most cutting-edge and border-crossing aspects of contemporary popular culture in Asia as well. The recent studies are devoted to resurrections, reinventions, and reinterpretations of several historical heroes in popular cultural products and adaptation practices in Asia. She also has developed recognized expertise on these topics in both public and academic contexts, with multiple media interviews, a book published in Korea titled *JYJ Republic* (2013), and a published article in Korean.

Alon Levkowitz is the coordinator of the Asia Program at Bar-Ilan University in Israel. His research interests include Korean society, culture, history and politics; Asian civil society; Asian regional international organizations; and Asian foreign and security policies. His finished his Ph.D. dissertation in 2004 at the Hebrew University of Jerusalem with the subject "The Defense Policies of Allies: The U.S. versus South Korea, Japan and the Philippines." He teaches Korean politics and history, foreign and security polices in Asia at Bar Ilan University and Hebrew University of Jerusalem. He published articles on Korean security and Korea's relations with the Middle East.

Irina Lyan (Hebrew University of Jerusalem) is a doctoral candidate in the Department of Sociology and Anthropology. Her research interests include Korean business culture and Hallyu fandom. Irina is the co-organizer of the conferences on Korean cultural industries in the Middle East (2013) and "Cultural Geography of the Hallyu" (2014). Her paper on Israeli Hallyu fandom won third prize at the article competition of World Association of Hallyu Studies (WAHS) in October 2013. Irina is a recipient of the Hebrew University Presidential Scholarship (2013–17) and is a Doctoral Fellow at the Truman Research Institute.

Roald Maliangkay (Australian National University) is a Senior Lecturer in Korean Studies at ANU, where he specializes in East Asian music and popular culture. Recent publications include "Koreans Performing for Foreign Troops: The Occidentalism of the C.M.C. and K.P.K.," *East Asian History* 37 (2011) and "There Is No Amen in Shaman: Traditional Music Preservation and Christianity in South Korea," *Asian Music* 45 (1) (2014). He is coeditor of *K-Pop: The International Rise of the Korean Pop Music Industry* (Routledge, 2014,), and is currently finalizing a monograph on Korean folk songs, entitled *Broken Voices: Preserving Korean Folksongs from Seoul's Periphery.*

Abé Markus Nornes (University of Michigan) is Professor of Asian Cinema in both the Department of Screen Arts and Cultures and the Department of Asian Languages and Cultures.

Youjeong Oh (The University of Texas at Austin) received her Ph.D. from the Department of Geography at University of California, Berkeley, in 2013, and is now an Assistant Professor in Asian Studies. She is currently working on a book examining the relationship between Korean television dramas and the promotion of East Asian cities.

Index

40143318R00162